School Personnel Administration

A California Perspective

Fourth Edition

Arthur J. Townley
Professor Emeritus
California State University
San Bernardino, CA

June H. Schmieder-Ramirez
Professor
Pepperdine University
Malibu, CA

Lillian B. Wehmeyer
Professor
Azusa Pacific University
Azusa, CA

KENDALL/HUNT PUBLISHING COMPANY
4050 Westmark Drive   Dubuque, Iowa 52002

Table of Contents

List of Tables

Preface & Invitation

Public education is big business. In most states the cost of education exceeds that of all other endeavors. In California, for example, the legislature has guaranteed to public schools a minimum of 40% of state expenditures. In many communities the school district is the major employer. Not only does the school district budget exceed that of all other enterprises, but personnel costs typically comprise 80% to 90% of that budget. As a result, effective management of personnel is of primary importance in a school district.

This text recognizes the importance of public education in the United States. If this country is to exemplify democracy and provide leadership in the world, the nation's public schools must nurture wisdom and vitality in young people. This task is formidable. California's public school enrollment is projected to increase by 200,000 students each year for the next several years. In addition, the changing demographics of these students and their families are unprecedented in American history. In spite of natural disasters, including fires and earthquakes, California continues to attract citizens from other parts of the United States as well as large numbers of immigrants from Asia, Mexico, and Latin America.

In this arena the authors planned and wrote *School Personnel Administration: A California Perspective*. We believe that teachers and administrators must be bold and innovative as never before. Drawing on our collective experience of more than 70 years as teachers and administrators in California public education, this text offers a realistic perspective to students and practitioners. We believe they will find it useful in carrying out this most vital responsibility of personnel administration.

This text emphasizes the principles and practices of personnel management. These principles and practices apply to classified as well as certificated staff. Since students and teachers are the focus of education, the illustrations and discussions highlight instructional staff. However, we wish to acknowledge the importance of the classified service. A chapter has been devoted to these employees and their contributions to the education of young people.

We are committed to continued development and refinement of this textbook. To that end, we invite participation of instructors of courses in personnel administration. We encourage you to use the book in your classroom and to give us the benefit of your feedback and that of your students. We encourage proposals, not only for revisions or additions to existing chapters, but also for new or supplemental material or for entire chapters to be added. If you are interested in improving or contributing to the next edition, please contact one of the authors.

THE LAW ON THE NET!

All California codes, including the Education Code and the Government Code,
are available and searchable on the Internet at

http://www.leginfo.ca.gov/calaw.html

**SPECIAL OFFER TO
INSTRUCTORS & PROFESSORS**
who teach school personnel or human resources

Class notes for overheads may be obtained at Dr. Townley's Website
http://soe.csusb.cdu.atownley

If you would like a copy of Dr. Townley's school personnel examination,
please contact him by e-mail at atownle2@juno.com

Chapter 1

History of Personnel Administration

Just as education functions as a "mirror of society," so the personnel aspects of education mirror the country's economic, social, and political history. This chapter describes the historical development of personnel administration from the 1800s to present time.

PERSONNEL ADMINISTRATION IN THE 19TH CENTURY

In the 1800s employers in the private sector assumed a patriarchal role as they supervised personnel functions. In the education sector, select lay committees assumed these same tasks and attitudes. Usually, selectmen exercised very strict control as to which teachers were hired and how teachers behaved.

At the local level, the transfer of duties from selectmen to professionals evolved slowly. Typically, a member of a city council was given the title of "business executive" and was paid a stipend to handle the fiscal tasks of a school district. At the state level, the first Superintendent of Common Schools was appointed in New York in 1812. The duties of state superintendent were assumed by state government when that position was abolished, but it was soon reestablished.

As the demands of school district management increased, the need for fulltime administrators was recognized. By the late 1800s superintendents had become a staple of the educational community. By 1870 there were 29 superintendents in charge of school districts across the country (Lucio and McNeil, 1969).

IMPACT OF THE COUNTY SUPERINTENDENT

The county superintendency had a major influence on school personnel activities in the late 1800s and in the early part of the 20th century—an influence that derived from the type of school district that predominated at the time. Most districts were rural. They lacked resources to handle the fiscal and personnel tasks necessary to their operation. The county superintendency handled many of these tasks—among them teacher training, because those who wished to became teachers could not find competent training elsewhere. As urban populations increased toward the end of the 19th century, school districts also enrolled more students. As a result of this growth, local school districts gradually assumed more and more of the fiscal and personnel functions associated with education.

CENTRALIZATION OF PERSONNEL DEPARTMENTS

Toward the latter part of the 19th century, personnel functions in industry became more centralized. In school districts, too, tasks that had once been performed by the business office—tasks such as designing salary schedules, defining job classifications, and maintaining personnel records—were transferred to a separate department. Increasingly, this separate department was assigned a supervisor. The major tasks of this department centered on hiring and dismissing personnel.

After the turn of the century the true personnel director gradually emerged in school systems. At this time the title "assistant superintendent" was created for managers of both business and personnel functions. World War I increased the significance of personnel functions as the federal government recruited, trained, and compensated massive numbers of soldiers—and sought efficient procedures to do so. During the early 1900s other developments also shaped personnel practice in both industry and education. These developments included human relations, scientific management, and the behavioral sciences. These movements are explored in the following sections.

THE SCIENTIFIC MANAGEMENT MOVEMENT

At the turn of the century the major researcher who impacted personnel practice was Frederick Taylor (1856-1915). As his methods were adopted—first by industry, then by education—he earned the title "Father of Scientific Management." During this period, Taylor was chief engineer of a Pennsylvania steel company. His writings and his management style emphasized the following tenets:

- Each major task should be divided into a series of small tasks. These small tasks should then be studied to determine the most cost-efficient way to accomplish them.

- An incentive system is needed to reward high production and "punish" poor efficiency or production.

Taylor's system required that managers plan the daily schedule for their workers and monitor their production. Taylor's ideas were readily adopted by education professionals, who seized upon industrial and military models to bring efficiency into the school system. Terms such as "accountability," "personnel evaluation," and "merit pay" became popular during this time. Taylor's ideas (1911) are regarded as overly harsh by today's standards, but they provided a foundation for many personnel systems in industry and education.

Other writers at this period were Lyndall Urwick, Luther Gulick, and Henri Fayol. Fayol (1841-1925) set forth several elements for organizational management, among them controlling, coordinating, commanding, and organizing.

Gulick (1892-1992) added budgeting and reporting to this list as essential for cost-effective management. He also proposed the concept of "specialization," in the sense of an auto worker limited to a narrow task on an assembly line.

Urwick (1891-1983) set forth several principles of task assignment, all built on the basic notion that each person in an organization should be given one major task to perform. An organization was considered efficient if these tasks did not overlap.

In summary, the principles of scientific management movement call for specialization, individualization of assignments, division of labor, and studies of tasks to make them more cost-efficient. The tenets of this movement profoundly affected both private and public organizations.

THE HUMAN RELATIONS MOVEMENT

As the scientific management movement was implemented and sustained in the early 1900s, another school of thought came to the fore. This philosophy was known as the "human relations movement."

Mary Follett (1868-1933) was among the first to argue that organizations cannot survive without attention to the "human" side of the system. She felt that direct contact with employees, coordination, and horizontal relationships were keys to smooth operation.

Another individual who believed in the importance of the human relations movement was Elton Mayo (1880-1949). A faculty member at Harvard University, he studied such issues as employee motivation, work incentives, and working conditions. In the early 1930s Professor Mayo also conducted the classic Hawthorne studies at the Hawthorne plant of the Western Electric Company in Chicago. He intended to determine the effect of illumination upon workers and their production. However, the study found that illumina-

staff morale is very important!

tion was of little importance—rather, paying attention to the workers yielded higher production. As summarized by Hoy and Miskel (1991), other findings that emerged from the Hawthorne studies included the following:

- Employees sometimes judge their production level by the social norms of the organization, rather than by the dictates of management.

- Employee organizations often include informal leaders who, despite their lack of formal status, may be more influential than appointed supervisors.

- Salary is not the only incentive significant to employees.

Mayo's findings, especially those dealing with employee morale and the limited effect of compensation, supported the human relations point of view.

Other authors who endorsed the human relations theory include Ronald Lippitt, Kurt Lewin, Ralph White, and William Dickson. Many of these authors investigated leadership types, categorizing them as authoritarian, laissez-faire, and democratic. Authoritarian leaders establish strong rules for employees and monitor them closely. These leaders may gain high productivity, but at the cost of low employee morale. Laissez-faire styles yield low productivity and low morale. Democratic leadership, on the other hand, by recognizing the importance of the employee, fosters high morale.

As a result of the promised benefits of a human relations emphasis, many industries adopted aspects of this approach. This movement intensified the need for personnel services in both business and school districts. Consequently, after its beginnings early in the 1900s, centralization of personnel services in education spread rapidly in the 1930s and 1940s.

THE BEHAVIORAL SCIENCE MOVEMENT

Drawing from both scientific management and human relations approaches, the behavioral science movement saw an organization as comprising an administrative structure and a human structure that are always in tandem with one another. The behavioral scientist studies how each of these paradigms interacts with human behavior and how that interaction, in turn, becomes an incentive or disincentive toward goal achievement.

The first individual to use behavioral sciences in the study of organizations was Chester Barnard (1866-1961). Barnard wrote *The Functions of the Executive* (1938), a work highly regarded in the field of business administration. Barnard, President of the Bell

Telephone Company, felt there were certain essential functions of the executive. These functions include:

- maintaining communication throughout the organization so that each individual is aware of the purpose of the structure and of the activities directed toward that purpose

- maintaining a high level of performance among all members of the organization

- instilling a sense of purpose (today we would say "vision") so that employees seek common goals.

The sociologist whose work provided a basis for the later work of the behavioral scientists was Max Weber (1864-1920), who set forth his perceptions of the "ideal" organization. He declared the following elements essential:

- rules for employee behavior that prevent individual unpredictability

- defined competencies for work performance

- a hierarchical structure with well-defined spheres of authority

- a division of labor such that employees are assigned tasks they are able to perform.

Weber felt that the well-run bureaucracy is desirable to ensure that workers perform their tasks.

Weber also advanced a model of authority built on the concepts "traditional," "legal," and "charismatic." Traditional power, rooted in the history of a group, accords power to the person or position that has held power in the past. Legal power, by contrast, is invested in the leader's position by recognized authority. The third form of authority, charismatic, is based in the magnetic attraction of the individual person.

The behavioral science movement has been supported by others such as Talcott Parsons, James March, Frederick Herzberg, Chris Argyris, Herbert Simon, Douglas McGregor, Rensis Likert, and Kurt Lewin. Gradually, the behavioral science approach supplanted human relations as the dominant theory of personnel management.

ORGANIZATIONAL DEVELOPMENT

In the late '40s and early '50s the organizational development movement took hold in the United States. Organizational theory focuses on interpersonal interaction and the dynamics of an evolving group. Many studies in organizational development were completed under the supervision of Kurt Lewin, a prolific theorist who worked with McGregor at the Massachusetts Institute of Technology.

From these studies emerged techniques to train working teams in the organization. Flip charts were used to record the ideas of the group. The T-group, or sensitivity training group, although but one of the group training techniques devised, is frequently associated with the organizational development movement. In the late '60s and early '70s, California schools used T-group techniques to train employees in building interpersonal relationships.

JOB SATISFACTION AND MOTIVATION

As the 1960s began, topics dominating the personnel field were motivation and work satisfaction. Herzberg (1959) and McGregor (1960) set forth new theories with significant implications for personnel management. By interviewing accountants and engineers, Herzberg identified factors correlated with job satisfaction and dissatisfaction. He maintained that the first five satisfiers (Table 1) were the most important in job satisfaction; these were called "motivators." Herzberg also identified factors related to job dissatisfaction, which he called "hygiene factors" (Table 2).

Some researchers have examined the relationship of the educational system to Herzberg's findings. Sergiovanni (1967) concluded, after interviewing teachers, that the work itself and possibility for advancement were not important motivators. On the other hand, researchers such as Wickstrom (1971) found that responsibility, personal relations with subordinates, a sense of achievement, and the work itself were top-ranked satisfiers among teachers. Typically, administrative actions and policies were the major negative factors for teachers.

As discussed earlier, Taylor's scientific management approach viewed the worker as possessing little ambition and, therefore, in need of a strong authority. McGregor (1906-1964) called Taylor's view "Theory X." In contrast, he introduced "Theory Y," which emphasized:

- Employees will exercise autonomy in reaching management objectives without threat of punishment.

- Most human beings tend to seek out responsibility.

- The individual within the organization should be allowed as much self-direction as possible.

Table 1
Herzberg's Factors
Associated with Job Satisfaction

"Motivators)"

Factor
Achievement
Recognition
Work Itself → *challenging is good (tedious & repetitive is the worst!)*
Responsibility
Advancement
Salary
Possibility of Growth
Interpersonal Relations (Subordinates)
Status
Interpersonal Relations (Superiors)
Interpersonal Relations (Peers)
Supervision (Technical)
Company Policy
Working Conditions
Personal Life
Job Security

Source: *The Motivation to Work* (1959)

Table 2
**Herzberg's Factors
Associated with Job Dissatisfaction**

"Hygiene factors"

Factor
Company Policy and Administration
Supervision (Technical)
Salary
Interpersonal Relations (Superior)
Working Conditions

Source: *The Motivation to Work* (1959)

Personnel administrators absorbed McGregor's Theory Y into their thinking by recognizing the weaknesses in a totally centralized personnel function, placing new emphasis on human relations in organizations, and assuming a more positive approach to employee job performance.

TOTAL QUALITY MANAGEMENT (TQM)

In the 1980s and 1990s personnel administration in both the private and public sectors was influenced by the work of W. Edward Deming, to whom is attributed the concept of "Total Quality Management" (TQM). Deming's theories were first utilized in Japan, where his work is credited with rebuilding the Japanese economy after World War II. It was some years after his success in Japan that his work was rediscovered in the United States.

Total Quality Management is an integrated, strategic system designed to achieve client satisfaction. In a school district, it involves all administrators, teachers, and other staff members in improving the district's services and products. "Quality" means providing clients with services that meet their expectations and needs—the first time and every time. Basic to the concept of TQM is a clear sense of purpose that is well understood at all levels of the organization. The primary purpose of TQM is to develop teamwork and to empower all workers to serve the customer. "Customer" is anyone inside or outside the organization to whom members of the organization provide services and products. For example, the customers of a first-grade teacher are students, parents, community members, and the second-grade teacher who will receive the students.

Deming's concept of institutional goals has been expanded in such works as *The One Minute Manager, Megatrends,* and *In Search of Excellence.* Barker (1992) believes that Deming's ideas about TQM will dominate all work, including education, in the future. A key element of TQM is constantly asking people to do a better job tomorrow than they did today. This concept is based on the idea that everyone can be inventive and innovative.

Deming's "Fourteen Points" are consistent with much of the research about the characteristics of effective schools. His fourteen essentials, as applied to school organizations, are shown in Table 3.

Table 3

Deming's Fourteen Essentials
Applied to School Organizations

Point	Principle	Application
1	Create a constancy of purpose for improvement of products and services	Schools must focus on helping students reach their maximum potential by providing a basis for students and teachers to work together to improve.
2	Adopt a new philosophy	Continuous improvement will occur through greater empowerment of teacher-student teams. Decisions about scope and sequence of learning and about instruction are to be reached jointly with involvement of all stakeholders.
3	Cease dependence on mass inspection to achieve quality	Using test scores as the primary way to assess student achievement and progress is wasteful and frequently unreliable. The end of a unit or semester is too late to assess student progress. Tests should be diagnostic, helping teachers prescribe new learning, rather than summative evidence of the achievement. Students must be taught to assess their own work and progress.
4	Stop awarding business on the basis of price tag alone	Teachers must use high quality instructional materials. Too often, free or cheap materials come that way because they do not serve learners well.
5	Constantly improve the system of production and service	School districts should continually ask: "Why are we doing this? Can we do it a better way?" Everyone in the organization should be empowered to ask and to answer this pair of questions.

Table 3

Deming's Fourteen Essentials (cont'd)

Point	Principle	Application
6	Institute training on the job	Inservice programs for both new and longtime staff members should be an integral part of the work environment.
7	Institute leadership	Leading is helping others achieve worthwhile goals. A leader should be a coach and a mentor. Leadership should be encouraged, irrespective of title or position in the district.
8	Drive out fear	Fear is counterproductive. In a free society and in a productive school no one should be motivated by fear. Positive changes result from shared responsibilities, shared power, and shared rewards.
9	Break down barriers between departments	Competition among grade levels or departments dissipates energy that should be directed toward common ends. Establish a climate of cooperation with an emphasis on quality.
10	Eliminate imposed slogans, exhortations, and targets	Externally imposed slogans and exhortations show few results. However, by working together, administrators, teachers, students, parents, and community members may develop slogans and symbols that focus energy and cause them to pursue common goals and celebrate success.
11	Eliminate numerical quotas	When a grade or a score becomes the basic symbol of success, short-term gains replace long-term learning and development.
12	Remove barriers to pride of workmanship	Most people desire to do good work, and when they do, feel pride in it. They should be helped to achieve this goal. Self-fulfillment is a strong motivator. Realistic goals, cooperatively established, result in satisfaction and pride.
13	Institute a vigorous program of education and self-improvement	Educators and students require continuous learning programs. Self-renewal must be goal-oriented, systematic and regular. The effective organization provides an environment in which self-renewal may take place.
14	Put everybody in the organization to work to accomplish the transformation	Teachers, administrators, staff, students, parents, and the community are stakeholders and should contribute to realization of the new philosophy. Top-level commitment and community involvement are required. Teachers and students cannot do it alone (Hughes, 1994).

SIGNIFICANT EVENTS IN CALIFORNIA EDUCATION

Many events in California during the last 25 years have held significant implications for personnel management. Those with major impact include the following.

1975   The California Legislature passed the Rodda Act, which replaced the Winton Act and set the scope of collective bargaining. The act defined representation and established the Educational Employment Relations Board (EERB), later reorganized to include all public employees under the name Public Employee Relations Board (PERB). Other issues addressed in this act include unit determination, employee rights, confidential employee rights, and exclusive representatives.

1978   Voters approved Proposition 13, which created massive changes in school finance in California. A 1% limit was imposed on general purpose property tax rates.

1983   Senate Bill 813 (Hughes-Hart Educational Reform Act, 1983), a sweeping education package spanning kindergarten through postsecondary levels, became law in California. Some elements of this bill included new categorical funding, building and lease-purchase funds, deferred maintenance funds, incentives for year-round schools, and professional growth requirements.

1984   Proposition 37, the California State Lottery Initiative, was approved by California voters with great promises of additional funds for education.

1988   Voters passed Proposition 98, which sets aside a certain percentage of state revenue for K-12 purposes.

1992   Senate Bill 1448 allowed up to 100 schools to apply for charter school status, under which they could be freed of most legal restrictions.

1992   The Beginning Teacher Support and Assessment Program (BTSA) legislation was designed to provide a teacher mentor to offer assistance and support to beginning teachers. Additional discussion of the BTSA program is contained in Chapter 6.

1993   The Schools of Choice Initiative, which would have provided a scholarship, or voucher, for students to attend any school of their choice was defeated by nearly 70% of California voters.

1996   Senate Bill 1777, the class size reduction legislation, profoundly affected California schools by providing funds to reduce kindergarten through third-grade classes to 20 students.

1997   Senate Bill 376, the Standardized Testing and Reporting (STAR) program, requires all California school districts to assess each student in grades two through eight. California was ahead of the federal government, which instituted this requirement in the 2002-2003 budget.

1998   California voters approved Proposition 227, referred to by several names, including "English for the Children." This proposition has dramatically changed education for students whose primary language is not English.

1998   On May 7, 1998, Governor Wilson signed Assembly Bill 544, which permits expansion of charter schools. This legislation authorizes an increase from 100 to 250 such schools in 1998 and an additional 100 in each subsequent year.

1999   Governor Davis signed Assembly Bill IX, which established the California Peer Assistance and Review (PAR) program. Replacing the Mentor Teacher program, PAR was designed to assist veteran teachers in improving their teaching. Additional discussion of the PAR program appears in Chapter 6.

2000   The Voucher Initiative, Proposition 36, was another attempt by supporters of the voucher movement to provide public funds for private school education. The education community breathed a sigh of relief when the measure failed with a 71% "no" vote.

SUMMARY

This chapter has traced the influence of scientific management, human relations, and behavioral science approaches to personnel management. Power in the early 1800s rested with local selectmen, who recruited, hired, trained, and supervised personnel. As the population increased and these tasks became more complex, county superintendents and local administrative personnel emerged on the educational scene.

In the early 1900s the scientific management movement encouraged direct control of employees by management. Soon, with the human relations approach, employees became the center of attention. Finally, the emerging behavioral sciences dominated the field—especially through the writings of Chester Barnard, who emphasized the importance of communication and of creating a common vision for employees. By the early 1950s the personnel function was firmly entrenched in both education and private industry.

From 1960 forward, concerns for legal guidelines, the rise of collective bargaining groups, and demands for teacher accountability have focused interest in the personnel departments of school districts. Personnel administration, typically headed by an assistant superintendent, has come into its own in the educational system. Given society's emphasis upon its human resources in the world of work, this function will certainly continue to be vitally important in educational organizations.

In the 1980s and 1990s personnel administration was influenced by the work of W. Edward Deming, who is generally credited with fathering the concept of Total Quality Management (TQM). This system has been a major influence in business and industry, and the authors predict TQM will have strong impact on school districts in the next several years.

Other issues that will remain at the forefront in the future of personnel management in education include collective bargaining, accountability for personnel, employee compensation, personnel demands in face of declining resources, legal mandates, and application of technological advancements to efficient and effective operation. All these issues affect education, which inevitably mirrors the political, social, and legal occurrences in society.

KEY TERMS

1. behavioral science movement
2. Chester Barnard
3. Frederick Taylor
4. Henri Fayol
5. Herzberg's factors
6. human relations movement
7. industrial model
8. Luther Gulick
9. Lyndall Urwick
10. motivation
11. scientific management
12. W. Edward Deming

QUESTIONS AND ACTIVITIES

1. In the decades after the 1940s school personnel functions became more centralized. During the 1990s this trend was reversed, and several personnel functions were moved to school sites. What are the advantages and disadvantages of this trend?

2. During the first half of this century scientific management dominated personnel management. This movement was largely replaced by the human relations movement. Discuss the major differences between the two movements.

3. The work of Herzberg and McGregor had a significant impact on personnel management. Discuss the major contributions of these two authors.

4. Deming's work played a significant role in the development of the Japanese economy after World War II and, it is predicted, will have major impact on personnel administration in the U. S. Which of his fourteen points do you believe will lead to the greatest changes in school personnel administration? What will be their nature? Why will they occur?

5. In this chapter, several important events were listed that have had an effect on school personnel management. Which of these events do you consider to have had the greatest impact? For what reasons?

6. In a small group, discuss Herzberg's motivators for work. Do you agree or disagree with the priorities on this list? Would you add any additional motivators not on the list?

7. Write a one-page paper indicating your view of the movements identified in this chapter as antecedents of current patterns in organizational management. Do you see any such connections? Explain.

8. What role did female teachers play in the educational scene of the 1800s and early 1900s? Is this role identified in the literature of the time? Who were the authors of this history? Why might they have "left out" the woman teacher?

Chapter 2

The Chief Personnel Officer

INTRODUCTION

All school districts, from the largest with hundreds of thousands of students to the smallest one-room entity, must carry out three major management functions: instruction, business, and personnel. In a small district the same individual usually handles all three, while in a large district a multitude of staff members complete the necessary tasks. For example, personnel functions include recruitment, selection, orientation, staff development, and dismissal. Business managers must project the cost of salaries and benefits and ensure that expenditures in these areas stay within budget. Superintendents and boards of education face their knottiest problems in resolving personnel problems.

Of the three management functions, personnel duties were the last to be recognized by employment of a specialist. Nevertheless, emergence of directors of school personnel was not a surprise. The position had been predicted by academics and practitioners who identified and analyzed changes in demography, technology, and the economy. Directors of personnel were expected to lighten the burden of other administrators. Changing values in the workforce and unionization of teachers also contributed to creation of this position.

Personnel management encompasses perhaps the broadest spectrum of all administrative positions except that of superintendent, with the result that universities have developed degree programs for individuals who seek a position as school personnel director. Literally thousands of school systems have recognized their need for the special expertise of an individual trained in personnel management. This chapter presents the historical development of the position of personnel officer and discusses training and other qualifications. The major duties and responsibilities of the position are outlined.

· Functions → instruction, business, & personnel
· Developed by business

HISTORY OF PERSONNEL SERVICES

Prior to 1900, in the business and industrial sectors, employers assumed responsibility for personnel matters. In large organizations some personnel functions were delegated to front-line supervisors or foremen. A foreman generally took charge of hiring, training, and dismissal of employees, but rarely set policy or established wages. By the late

1800s, however, personnel departments began to appear in private industry. The first personnel departments were primarily responsible for keeping records, developing and implementing salary schedules, maintaining evaluation reports, and other clerical functions (McCoy, Gips, & Evans, 1983).

It is generally agreed that the position of personnel administrator was developed in business, industry, and other governmental agencies prior to its adoption by schools. School districts were latecomers in adding the position of personnel director. Nevertheless, the fact that personnel departments developed in the private sector prior to their introduction into school systems does not mean that personnel duties were not required. Personnel responsibilities have always been present in public schools. In the nation's early history lay committees usually employed, supervised, and dismissed teachers. Because parents and religious groups were reluctant to delegate the education of their children to teachers and principals, the members of these special lay committees were local citizens and religious leaders (Lucio & McNeil, 1969).

Moore (1966) states that personnel administration, as the term is commonly understood, began with World War I. Recruitment, training, and payment of masses of workers in war production forced assignment of such responsibilities to specialized personnel. At the same time, the country experienced rapid growth in federal and state civil service. In addition, consumer business and industry were also expanding, again creating demand for expertise in recruiting, training, and setting compensation for employees.

The first recorded public school personnel administrator was an assistant superintendent in Dallas, Texas, appointed in 1919 (National Education Research Division, 1962). Typically, however, in the years following World War I, even though districts grew in size and complexity, personnel functions were performed by superintendents and principals. As late as the 1950s, Green (1971) estimates, there were probably less than 50 fulltime school personnel administrators in the United States. Gradually, separate personnel departments were established in medium or larger districts, headed by a director or assistant superintendent. Green attributes the establishment of such a position to several factors:

Personnel's job to project enrollment... Can be big money~salaries

- growth of school districts, including consolidation or unification into larger units

- a shortage of teachers in the years following World War II, precipitating special efforts to recruit and train the teaching work force

- population mobility, which made it necessary for growing districts to recruit more aggressively and reach beyond their immediate geographic area

- the example of industry, where the position of personnel director had become more common.

Campbell (1984) noted that the role of the personnel administrator in schools was subject to radical changes in the 1960s as a consequence of unionization of public sector employees, a nationwide demand for accountability, and increased public interest in school curriculum and instruction. In 1968 Moore and Hodge projected the following trends:

Collective Bargaining
—1964 Winton Act
meet & confer
1975 Rodda Act
collective bargaining—
exclusive bargaining

- Medium and small schools would add fulltime personnel specialists.

- Personnel administrators would be assigned more and more responsibility, with higher status indicated by title and rank.

- The position would encompass certified and non-certified employees.

- Collective bargaining and negotiations would necessitate an active role in personnel policy development and contract management.

During the 1970s and 1980s the latter factor contributed to the increased number of positions for a personnel director. This factor was collective bargaining. The negotiations process, new to public education, called for special knowledge of the law, budgets, and finance, and for the human relations skills required to work in confrontive settings.

PERSONNEL SERVICES IN CALIFORNIA

From the end of World War II in 1945 to the mid-'60s, California experienced a serious shortage of qualified teachers. This change in demographics stimulated California districts to create separate personnel departments and to add the position of personnel director. During this period the primary task of the California school personnel administrator was teacher recruitment. It was not unusual for the personnel director to seek teachers all over the country. Many personnel directors, particularly those employed in large districts in southern California, spent a good portion of the year on university campuses in and out of state, interviewing and offering teaching jobs to prospective candidates. Some directors carried and offered contracts to teachers immediately upon concluding an interview. Out-of-state teachers actually accepted positions without ever visiting California, much less the school district where they would be employed.

The baby boom in California had ended by the mid-'60s. McCurdy (1974) reported a nationwide surplus of teachers that amounted to some 123,000 more newly trained teachers than teaching positions. It was estimated that teacher training programs were producing twice as many new teachers as there were openings.

This decline in student enrollment had not been anticipated by California colleges and universities, which continued to train teachers at an accelerated rate. Therefore, during this period, the teacher shortage turned into an oversupply of qualified teachers, and many competent candidates were unable to find employment. From the mid-'60s to the mid-'70s the role of the personnel administrator changed dramatically from active teacher recruitment to careful screening of multitudes of applicants. The personnel director also faced the unpleasant task of dismissing teachers and classified employees as services and programs were eliminated in the wake of declining student enrollment (Waters, 1976).

The passage of Assembly Bill 145, authored by Jesse Unruh in 1964, contributed to an increase in personnel directors in California schools. This bill encouraged California school districts to consolidate into larger districts. Prior to the passage of AB 145, California had approximately 1,500 districts. By 1984 this number had been reduced to 1,040. The consolidation of districts resulted in larger and more complex organizations that required the services of highly skilled personnel directors (Campbell, 1984). This number of California school districts has again declined slightly in the past decade, with the Educational Demographics Unit of the California Department of Education (2000) reporting 997 K-12 public school districts and 58 county offices in 2000-2001.

An additional factor that necessitated personnel administrators was increased militancy on the part of California teachers. This militancy led to passage of the Winton Act (Senate Bill 60) in 1964 and subsequently the Rodda Act (Senate Bill 160) in 1975. The Winton Act required school boards and unions to meet and confer on salaries, benefits, and teachers' working conditions. The Rodda Act eliminated the meet-and-confer process and replaced it with collective bargaining in California public schools. With the introduction of collective bargaining came increased demand for more accurate, up-to-date personnel information that, in turn, further solidified the need for a fulltime personnel administrator (Taylor, 1981).

California school finance underwent significant changes in the '70s. The most dramatic change was passage of the Jarvis-Gann initiative (Proposition 13) in 1978. This change to the California Constitution resulted in a shift of financial support for education from local property taxes to direct funding by the state. The outcome of this radical change was less control of schools by local boards of education and greater control by the state legislature.

The role, responsibilities, and scope of the personnel director continued to expand as the procedures of collective bargaining became increasingly complex. Laws were passed to ensure equal opportunity in employment practices, again demanding additional knowledge. Insistent demands for teacher and administrator accountability and heightened awareness of urgent needs in curriculum and instruction also require specialized skills and leadership.

With an estimated increase of 200,000 students each year, along with teachers leaving the profession for other careers, personal reasons, and retirement, the state will need some 30,000 new teachers annually throughout the next decade. This renewed shortage of teachers, coupled with particular need for teachers in special education, adds another dimension to the personnel director's already burgeoning duties. Finally, there is need for staff development programs for teachers and classified employees to keep attuned to the changing needs of students and society. These are but a few of the demands placed upon the personnel director that lead to increased responsibility and status for the position.

TITLES OF THE PERSONNEL OFFICER

Titles of school personnel administrators vary considerably. The three most common titles for the position are "Director of Personnel," "Assistant Superintendent of Personnel," and "Administrative Assistant for Personnel." Regardless of title, incumbents in these positions are usually responsible to the superintendent of schools or, in very large systems, to a deputy or associate superintendent.

EXPERIENCE AND EDUCATION REQUIREMENTS

Experience requirements vary somewhat from district to district, but both teaching and administrative experience are generally required, and a variety of assignments desirable. In unified school districts experience at both elementary and secondary levels is sought. In many settings, experience as a principal is listed either as a requirement or as highly desirable. Metzger (1988) found that 90.6 % of California personnel directors had between 16 and 31 years of experience. The group representing 21 to 25 years of experience fell at the median point and accounted for 29.7 % of directors included in his study.

In California all administrators responsible for the personnel program for certificated staff must themselves hold a California administrative credential. Obviously, the candidate would also have a teaching or services credential, which is a prerequisite for the administrative credential. Most job announcements also stipulate a master's degree with advanced coursework in personnel administration. In larger districts a doctorate is also desirable. These requirements do not apply to directors who are solely responsible for managing the classified program.

California personnel directors suggested the following elements should be included in graduate programs designed to train personnel administrators (Metzger, 1988):

● thorough preparation in personnel law and its practical application

● training in the use and benefits of a career assessment center

- training in preparation of inservice programs for classified and certificated personnel

- personnel counseling techniques and successful approaches in applied psychology

- collective bargaining processes and procedures designed to attain maturation in collective bargaining

- the overall effect of due process in the workplace and the maintenance of complete records

- recruitment of personnel utilizing public and private personnel recruitment services

- successful grievance resolution processes for classified and certificated personnel

- development of meaningful community relations and information programs

- development, adoption, and evaluation of affirmative action plans

- means of ascertaining the correct data necessary to sustain a staff transfer

- strategies for locating and retaining services of substitute teachers

- determination of statistics relative to personnel division interests and needs in the collective bargaining process

- best strategies for negotiating the classified and certificated labor contracts without "giving away the store"

- instruments to appraise personnel needs and their interpretation

- ability to write a complete and thorough job description

- techniques for accurately projecting future district enrollment figures

- the budgeting process and its application to personnel administration.

These needs for training pose a serious challenge to colleges and universities responsible for training school personnel administrators. Success requires that institutions of higher education cooperate with school districts and professional organizations such as the American Association of School Personnel Administrators and the Association of California School Administrators.

CONFLICT MANAGEMENT

A leadership skill that is essential for an effective personnel manager is conflict management. One can rest assured that a personnel manager, during the first day on the job, will either face a personal conflict or will be asked to assist in resolving a conflict involving others. Inevitably, conflict and stress are natural outcomes of everyday working relationships and are present in every facet of one's personal life and professional career.

The negative side of conflict can lead to stress, loss of productivity, poor employee morale, and personal and professional animosity. However, the positive outcomes of managed conflict include strength, energy, growth, and change for the better. Therefore, it is imperative that a personnel director possess outstanding conflict management skills.

The first step in managing conflict is to identify the types of individual behavior of conflict participants. What are the words and actions of the people involved in the conflict? This information is vital for planning successful conflict interventions. Administrators must also identify their own typical responses to particular conflict situations. For example, when a principal is questioned at a faculty meeting, does he or she become defensive or aggressive—or react in an open, positive fashion? As these behaviors and responses are identified, individual approaches and patterns become evident.

Particular response patterns may be functional in some conflict situations, but dysfunctional in others. No single style of conflict management works in all circumstances. A personnel manager needs an array of conflict management skills and strategies to ensure successful conflict resolution (Sweeney & Lindsey, 1992).

Conflict management skills are particularly important for the personnel director in the collective bargaining process. Fisher and Ury (1981), in *Getting to Yes...Negotiating Agreement without Giving In*, present a step-by-step method for negotiating personal and professional conflicts. They point out that many conflicts remain unresolved because individuals fall into the trap of arguing over positions, rather than examining their needs and interests. When arguments are limited to positions, basic needs and interests are obscured and often remain unaddressed. Consequently, arguing over positions often produces unwise agreements.

Positional bargaining is often perceived as a linear process. As a result, any change in a participant's position is viewed as either a "win" or a "loss." Those participating in conflict often identify with the positions they assume, and a "contest of wills" ensues. Positional bargaining endangers ongoing relationships, as hard and soft positional negotiators engage in a form of tug-of-war.

Fisher and Ury suggest that every negotiator has two kinds of interests:

- an interest in the substance of the agreement

- an interest in his or her relationship with the other participants in the conflict.

Successful negotiations result when the participants separate their relationships from the substance and deal directly with the people problem. Successful negotiations result when participants are able to affirm and understand other participants' points of view, perceptions of the problem, interests, and needs. The authors propose that successful negotiators are "hard" on issues and "soft" on people.

COMMUNICATION SKILLS

The personnel director interacts every day with teachers and classified employees, parents, principals, the superintendent, and members of the school board. These interactions require effective communication skills. Bennis and Nanus (1985) write, "Leaders communicate at all times, and the more effective the communication, the more effective the leadership." To overcome communication barriers and to arrive at mutual understandings, school administrators and employees must invest sustained effort. Although effective communication should be the responsibility of both employees and supervisors, responsibility for successful communication seems to lie primarily with school administrators because the latter set the tone for communication.

Just as the principal sets the style for communications at a school site, the personnel director has a major role in establishing effective communication at the district level. The number of grievances filed in a district depends in part on the communication skills of the personnel director. For example, if the personnel director is able to give a clear and sympathetic rationale for a section of the board-employee contract, a grievance may be resolved without additional conflict. Similarly, in recruiting employees, the personnel director's interaction with the candidate may be the deciding factor in whether the candidate accepts or rejects a position in the district.

In addition to managing employee grievances, a personnel director is asked frequently to resolve disputes between employees and supervisors or between administrators and parents before they reach the stage of a formal complaint. The impression made by the personnel director is often the deciding factor in resolving an employee grievance or avoiding a lawsuit by an angry community member.

Effective communication skills are particularly required for successful conflict resolution. Many adults have had little training in listening and responding skills. As a result, they listen to evaluate, probe, advise, or interpret. Successful conflict resolution requires listening of a different nature. Empathetic listening skills and strategies, which "echo" or "rephrase" the content of the communication and "reflect" the feelings of the speaker, are demanded. Such abilities establish a climate that facilitates critical thinking, problem-solving, growth, and change (Covey, 1989).

JOB DESCRIPTION

In 1988 the American Association of School Personnel Administrators (AASPA) saw the personnel director as meeting two important obligations. First, the director must respond to the needs and requirements of public education, with welfare of students the basic concern. Second, the personnel director must create and maintain a positive employment climate in which school district employees can make the greatest contribution to students while attaining their own highest personal satisfaction.

This same association also developed a general guide for school districts desiring to identify the job responsibilities of the personnel director (AASPA, 1988). Responsibilities were listed in four broad areas:

Employee relations	To maintain records and plan and implement a staff development program
Staff employment and assignment	To coordinate recruitment, selection, evaluation, and termination of employees
External compliance requirements	To ensure that the district meets requirements posed by equal employment opportunity programs, categorically funded programs, wage and hour laws, and other external demands
Labor relations administration	To be an active participant in the actual negotiation of the labor contract through collective bargaining, to be active in developing personnel polices and regulations, and to be the primary director in implementing contract, policies, and regulations.

To gather input from practitioners, Metzger (1988) completed a study of the role of 150 California public school administrators. Personnel managers identified the following tasks as most important.

Preparation	Being as well prepared as possible in personnel law, due process, affirmative action plans, collective bargaining (contract negotiations), and grievance resolution
Counseling	Having the ability to counsel teachers, administrators, and staff in relation to individual and collective needs, both personal and professional
Needs appraisal	Conducting accurate personnel needs appraisals and then developing meaningful, professional inservice programs for both certificated and classified personnel
Recruitment and selection	Recruiting certificated and classified personnel and substitute teachers, selecting personnel for specific jobs, and assigning these people
Community Relations	Developing effective community relations programs.

DEVELOPING BOARD POLICIES

One of the most difficult and challenging responsibilities of the personnel director is to develop board policies. Such policies provide structure and set direction for the district as a whole and the personnel department in particular. The personnel director must possess a keen awareness of Education Code requirements so as to develop policies that conform to the law. In 1994 there were approximately 270 laws in the Education Code affecting credentialed staff, and about half that number relating to classified staff. In addition, countless rules and regulations developed by the California Department of Education must be considered. As if this were not enough, federal laws, rules, and regulations set parameters for district policies. Federal and state court decisions must also be taken into account. Although involvement adds to the complexity of the process, successful personnel directors are nevertheless strongly committed to involving staff in policy development.

The importance and benefits of well-conceived, carefully written policies are thoroughly documented in personnel and management literature. These policies establish a foundation on which organization practices and procedures are constructed. Well-developed policies guide decisions and actions of management and staff. Polices provide a road map for avoiding conflict and, when conflict does occur, a method for its resolution. Incidentally, they also create an historical record of decisions that reflect changes in the state and district.

The chief personnel officer is in a unique position to provide leadership in the development of policies. The place of this position on the organization chart of most districts gives the personnel administrator direct access to both the superintendent and middle management. He or she is uniquely placed to strike a balance between the needs and desires of the board of education and those of employee organizations.

STRATEGIC PLANNING

Planning for the future is undoubtedly one of the more difficult assignments of the personnel director. To cope with constant change in social and economic conditions affecting school districts, it is imperative to have a strategic plan that looks ahead several years. Uncertainty as to local and state budgets and the shifting political climate that exists in every school district make this task a formidable pursuit (Peters, 1988).

Strategic planning is the process by which an organization envisions the future and develops the necessary procedures and operations to achieve that future. This vision not only sets direction, but also provides a blueprint for the move to that future (Pfeiffer, Goodstein & Nolan, 1986). Strategic planning does not make future decisions; rather, it focuses upon current decisions and their future implications. In other words, strategic planning yields decisions about actions to be taken today to realize desired outcomes tomorrow.

Many authors do not discriminate between long-range planning and strategic planning. Shirley McCune (1986), on the other hand, differentiates between them by noting that long-range planning begins with an assumption of comparative organizational stability, whereas strategic planning does not necessarily assume that the organization will remain stable.

Business has devoted much attention to strategic planning (Dyson, 1990). The concept evolved from business planning as practiced in the early 1970s. Effective business managers discovered that strategic planning helped relate management decisions to organizational objectives. Specifically, the process brought about improved allocation of financial and other material resources to maximize planned organizational outcomes. At the same time, strategic planning became an instrument for measuring the success of a company and the effectiveness of its leadership. The CEO's of America's corporations came to recognize that a firm's future, and its profits, often rest on their leadership in strategic planning. Consequently, compensation for corporate CEO's is often based on achieving the objectives of the strategic plan.

In business, a strategic plan typically focuses on emerging markets, production, customer satisfaction, sales, and accounting structures. Financial and other material resources and transactions, unlike human resources, are typically measured in dollars and cents.

Only recently has strategic planning been emphasized in school settings. Developing a strategic plan in a school district is far more difficult than planning the acquisition and allocation of material resources. Systems for assessing and administering human resources are not as well developed as are systems related to markets and finance. People, who typically absorb the lion's share of a district budget, cannot be transferred, changed, or modified in response to an organization's needs as expeditiously as the elements in a financial or market plan (Baird, Meshoulam, & DeGive, 1983).

A school district strategic plan usually opens with the district's mission statement. Then it asks (and answers): What does the district hope to accomplish within the next five years? What resources will be required to achieve those goals? That education is a personnel-intensive industry is a factor of major consideration in developing the district's strategic plan. Accurate student enrollment projections and the required staff to teach and service those students go to the heart of the strategic plan.

Many school districts have used a team approach in developing a strategic plan. The team is usually composed of teachers, administrators, and support staff. Parents and community representatives are also an integral part of the team. After the team and school board reach agreement on the district's mission statement, that statement becomes the base for goals, objectives, and action plans. The strategic plan also specifies management responsibilities for monitoring the timeline of action plans and achievement of established objectives.

NEGOTIATIONS AND COLLECTIVE BARGAINING

Scope expanded by PERB

During the 1960s and 1970s the responsibilities of a school personnel director took on a new dimension in most states with the passage of collective bargaining laws governing public education. In California this process came into being with the Rodda Act in 1975. This legislation mandated that school districts and employee organizations bargain in good faith. In most districts this new responsibility was assumed by the personnel director, often with assistance of legal counsel.

The original interpretation of the Rodda Act was that negotiations were limited to three topics: salaries, benefits, and working conditions. However, judicial interpretations of the act have broadened the scope of negotiations to include virtually everything relative to certificated and classified personnel employment, provided that the items are logically and reasonably related to the three topics stated in the law. The impact of these decisions has been extremely broad, extending to policy planning, budget preparation, personnel needs, and instructional programs, as well as teacher recruitment, selection, evaluation, retention, and dismissal.

In the last two decades teachers' unions have become very powerful. This fact is particularly exemplified in California with the increasing power of the California Teachers Association (CTA). This association, or union, often outspends all other organizations on lobbying efforts.

Most California classified employees are represented by the California School Employees Association (CSEA). This organization, too, has considerable clout in most school districts.

Collective bargaining added to the stress of personnel directors as they attempted to maintain a balance between organizational goals and those of individuals as represented by the union. For example, setting wages and benefits often gives rise to adversarial roles and divides management and staff. Redfern (1968) offered several principles for personnel directors to keep in mind if they wish to succeed as the district's negotiator.

- Negotiations are here to stay.

- Teachers' importance in decision-making will continue to increase.

- Well-defined and properly functioning negotiation procedures affect the attractiveness of a system as a place to work.

- Good negotiations procedures are an asset to recruiting; poor ones, a liability.

- The personnel administrator has a stake in stable, dispassionate negotiations.

- Leadership in developing policies and standards for interpersonal dealing is the personnel director's responsibility and duty.

Negotiations will continue to be a critical responsibility for the personnel administrator. Effective collective bargaining can yield improved employee morale and productivity. Conversely, instructional innovations are doomed to failure without support from an enlightened and satisfied staff. As a reflection of the importance of this topic, three chapters in this book are devoted to aspects of negotiations.

RECRUITMENT

Effective recruitment of an outstanding teaching and classified staff is a major responsibility of the personnel director. Although the current trend toward decentralized decision-making in selection of personnel will probably continue, the organization and management of this duty will remain with the personnel officer. This need is particularly acute in most California districts, where a flood of new students each year requires a proactive recruitment effort.

Personnel directors are also faced with employing minority staff members and balancing the number of men and women in their respective school districts so as to achieve the goals of affirmative action plans. Recent court decisions have introduced uncertainties into this arena, yet with or without legal mandates, thoughtful personnel administrators feel responsible for seeking diversity in employment. At times when a district experiences decline in student enrollment, this task is particularly difficult.

Personnel directors must have a complete understanding of laws and regulations governing recruitment. Creative policies and practices are necessary to ensure that outstanding candidates are attracted to a district and accept a position when it is offered. Recruitment is so important that a separate chapter in this book takes up the topic.

SELECTION

After recruitment comes selection. The selection process includes collecting and checking references and scheduling candidates for a personal interview. Careful attention must be devoted to interview questions that assist in identifying the best candidate for the position. As in so many arenas of personnel management, federal and state laws and regulations must be considered to avoid any problems or justifiable complaints during the selection process. Like recruitment, selection is dealt with in a later chapter of this book.

STAFF DEVELOPMENT

A district's staff development program actually starts with recruitment, because candidates form an opinion about the district's priorities during the recruitment and selection process. Then, after selection, a planned program of orientation to the district and school is important. In addition, the personnel director, in concert with the assistant super-intendent for educational services and site principals, is often responsible for districtwide staff development programs. Research underscores the importance of including faculty in designing activities that keep them abreast of new curriculum developments, teaching strategies, and instructional materials. Classified staff also need programs to update and improve their skills; responsibility for this training, too, is typically assumed by the personnel director in cooperation with supervisors and principals. This topic is explored in greater depth in a separate chapter.

DISCIPLINE AND DISMISSAL

A responsibility that threatens to keep personnel administrators awake at night is that of disciplining and, when necessary, dismissing unsatisfactory employees. These decisions involve complex legal issues and procedures, serious human considerations, and many hours of work.

CREDENTIALS

California's credential program is administered by the Commission on Teacher Credentialing. Expertise in the California credential program for teachers and administrators is a must for the personnel director. This area is constantly changing as new credentials and new requirements for existing credentials are set in place. Moreover, legislation in recent years has placed ever more stringent requirements on districts and county offices of education to ensure a match between the credentials held by an employee and that individual's job assignment.

PERSONNEL RECORDS

Good personnel practice includes establishment and maintenance of complete, accurate personnel files for each probationary and permanent employee. Proper records must document dates, actions, and status (including appointment, assignments, and separation), as this information may become critical in promotions, dismissals, grievances, or other actions affecting each employee. Details recorded in personnel files may include date of hire, job title, address, and other pertinent biographical data. In addition, the file should record salary placement, vacation and sick leave data, and supervisor evaluations.

Several Education Code sections give specific direction regarding maintenance of personnel files. The following are examples from Education Code section #44031:

- All materials in the personnel file that may serve as a basis for affecting the status of employment shall be made available for inspection by the person involved.

- Every employee shall have the right to inspect these materials upon request.

- An employee shall have the right to enter, and have attached to any derogatory statement, his own comments thereon.

To ensure that personnel records are properly maintained, very specific procedures must be written to govern information that may and may not be placed in the file. The security of personnel files is also of utmost importance; it is recommended that they be stored in a locked, fireproof cabinet. Access to the files should be carefully delineated in board policy and limited to authorized personnel. Although the day-to-day maintenance of personnel records may be assigned to a secretary or clerk, ultimate responsibility rests with the director, who must be sure to monitor their maintenance and confidentiality.

PUBLIC RECORDS

Another duty that often becomes the responsibility of the personnel director is the maintenance and release of public records. Department of Education Legal Counsel Joseph Symkowick observed, as reported in *EdCal* ("Just How Public," 1997), "Most administrators are familiar with student privacy laws, but they don't know the Public Records Act, and due to that lack of knowledge often inappropriate information about the district, employees, or students is released to the public."

The Public Records Act requires a district to honor or deny within ten days a request for documents from the public. Most administrators are aware that a majority of district and school information is public information, and that the public has a right to obtain copies of such documents.

California Senator Bill Leonard found that this right was not always honored. In 2001 he sent an intern to 11 Southern California school districts. The intern asked for a copy of the superintendent's contract, which is a public record. Only two of the 11 districts complied with the request (Luna, 2001).

However, a number of documents may legitimately be denied to the public. One of the best examples of information that may be withheld from public scrutiny is material about an individual student. Personal information about public employees that does not pertain to their employment is also exempt from release to the public. The Public Records

Act and Education Code sections #49073-#49076.5 provide examples of documents that are exempt. Some of these documents include:

- preliminary drafts, notes, interagency or intra-agency memoranda

- records pertaining to pending litigation to which the school or district is a party

- personnel, medical or other files, the disclosure of which would constitute an unwarranted invasion of privacy (For example, the roster of teachers at a school site might be public information, but addresses and phone numbers of school personnel are not.)

- records contained in or related to: *Employee criminal background vs*
  • Substitute employees
  • Legal requirements

  applications filed with any state agency responsible for the regulation or supervision of the issuance of securities or financial institutions

  preliminary drafts, notes, or inter/intra-agency communications prepared by, or on behalf of, any state agency

  information received in confidence by a state agency ("Just How Public," 1997).

A well-written board policy based on the Public Records Act can provide the public with proper information and at the same time protect the district, employees, and students from release to the public of inappropriate information.

EMPLOYEE CRIMINAL BACKGROUND CHECKS

Personnel offices acquired a new task in 1997 when legislation was passed to require a more extensive background check of new district employees. This legislation, formulated in Assembly Bills 1610 and 1612, was a swift reaction to the violent murder of a California student. Her alleged attacker had been a substitute janitor, a felon with a history of violent behavior. The legislative response was to require all public and private California schools to conduct a thorough background check on prospective employees prior to their hiring and to prohibit the hiring of any person convicted of a violent or serious felony. The district completes a background check by submitting the prospective employee's fingerprints to the Department of Justice (DOJ) for clearance. The DOJ is required to notify school districts by telephone if an applicant has been convicted of a serious or violent felony and to follow with written confirmation.

Background Checks on Certificated Employees

Districts are required to complete background checks on all current probationary, temporary, and substitute teachers. Prior to this legislation all individuals applying for a California credential were required to submit fingerprints with the credential application. Now, however, prior clearance by the California Commission on Teaching Credentials no longer satisfies the law, which requires that a new set of fingerprints be submitted to the DOJ when employment is contemplated.

All parttime certificated employees must also be fingerprinted. If the district is notified by the DOJ that a certificated employee has been convicted of a violent or serious felony, the employee must be automatically terminated. The district must immediately place a certificated temporary, substitute, or probationary employee on leave without pay when notified by the DOJ of the conviction for such an offense.

All tenured, permanent employees are exempt from the law. When a credentialed person moves from one district to another, however, new fingerprints must be taken and submitted to the DOJ. Clearance from another district does not satisfy the law.

Classified Employees

Local districts have always had responsibility for fingerprinting new classified employees. The major change in the new legislation is that a classified employee may no longer be employed prior to district receipt of results of the background check. In addition, the new legislation adds a new group that must be fingerprinted—contracted employees. Such employees might work in transportation, food services, maintenance, gardening, or the like. The law does not apply to a contractor if a district determines that the employees of the contractor will have limited contact with pupils. In these cases, however, a school district must take appropriate steps to protect the safety of students.

When a school district is notified by the DOJ that a current classified substitute, temporary, or probationary employee has been convicted of a violent or serious felony, the district must immediately place that employee on leave without pay and terminate the person automatically when the conviction is confirmed in writing.

SUBSTITUTE EMPLOYEES

An adequate pool of substitute and classified employees is necessary for a smoothly running district. This responsibility is usually assigned to the personnel director. Recruiting and assigning substitute teachers is complex because they are required to possess a California teaching credential. It is particularly difficult to maintain an adequate number of substitute teachers with the necessary training and experience to teach specialized classes such as chemistry or foreign language. Such difficulties may be ameliorated with procedures that facilitate timely notice from teachers and classified staff that a substitute will be needed. For example, a clerk is often assigned an early morning start time to transcribe substitute requests from an answering machine and call prospective substitutes for that day.

The nature of the classroom also makes the work of the substitute difficult. Many adults who work in schools can share "horror stories" of a day in the life of a sub when students changed names and seats and generally made life miserable for the substitute. Knowing this, a wise personnel director develops orientation sessions to help substitutes make their day as worthwhile and useful as possible for themselves and their students.

LEGAL REQUIREMENTS

The nation's public schools, like all other institutions, operate within a framework of laws. Legislation that affects schools is approved by both federal and state governments. School operations are also controlled by ordinances, rules, and regulations approved and adopted by numerous federal, state, and local entities. Court decisions also direct operations of schools and districts.

Duffy (1975) asserted that personnel directors need a thorough knowledge of broad legal concepts and the specific laws pertinent to school personnel operation. This is true even though the school district's attorney should be consulted whenever a legal problem might arise. Thus, if a district is to operate smoothly, a personnel officer must have an astute understanding of legislation and court rulings, yet not place undue restrictions on policies and procedures. Greater attention is devoted to this subject in a later chapter.

SUMMARY

The personnel director is a key person in a school district. Education is a labor-intensive enterprise, and the utmost skill is essential to securing topflight teachers and classified staff. Consequently, the personnel director's duties are perhaps the most encompassing of district staff with the exception of the superintendent.

The major responsibilities of this position include all aspects of personnel management, from the recruitment of staff to their dismissal or resignation. Technical expertise is required to administer the credential program and to comply with national and state laws and regulations. In the past two decades, two new duties have been typically assigned to this position. These responsibilities—managing an effective affirmative action program and representing the board of education in collective bargaining—require technical knowledge as well as superb human relations skills. The role of the personnel director in effective school management is projected to expand in scope and importance.

KEY TERMS

1. board policies
2. California School Employees Association
3. California Teachers Association
4. collective bargaining
5. credentials

6. job description
7. negotiations
8. personnel records
9. Rodda Act
10. substitute employees

QUESTIONS AND ACTIVITIES

1. School districts manage three major functions: instruction, business, and personnel. Of these three, personnel was the last added by most districts. Discuss why this was the case.

2. Collective bargaining significantly changed the role of the school personnel director. What new responsibilities were added to this job classification to create such a change?

3. Three major responsibilities of the personnel director are recruitment, selection, and staff development. Which of the three responsibilities do you consider most important for the success of a school district? Support your answer with specific examples.

4. It has been argued that the personnel director needs greater awareness, knowledge, and understanding of school law than the director of instruction or business. Do you agree or disagree? Why?

5. Maintenance of personnel records is a major responsibility of the personnel director. List and discuss three California Education Code requirements regarding employee personnel records.

6. Obtain the job descriptions of the chief personnel officer in three school districts. Analyze the duties assigned to each. Point out similarities and differences in the three descriptions.

7. Review board policies for personnel in your district, noting particularly whether policies have been adopted for recruitment of staff, affirmative action, and initial placement on the salary schedule. Examine the negotiated agreements in these same districts to see whether any of these issues have moved into the arena of collective bargaining.

Chapter 3

Recruitment of Personnel

INTRODUCTION

All school districts need to recruit classified personnel (staff who do not require certification) and credentialed personnel (teachers, administrators, librarians, counselors), at least occasionally. The demand for a constant supply of new teachers in California is particularly daunting. The continued growths of the student population, class size reduction, and an increasing number of teachers reaching retirement age have created a critical teacher shortage.

Recruitment is the process of generating a pool of competent and qualified applicants to fill vacancies in the district. The goal of personnel recruitment should be to attract the best people available, both beginners and experienced. Therefore, all districts need to place a premium on obtaining an outstanding staff for the school and the district. Desirable candidates cannot be expected unless school districts actively and continuously engage in recruitment.

One quick avenue to an improved instructional program at a school is effective recruitment followed by selection of an outstanding staff. Every vacancy gives a principal an opportunity to improve instruction at his or her site. A well-planned recruitment and selection process has the potential to identify a teacher, administrator, or classified staff member who will bring new life into a school.

Consequently, most superintendents and personnel directors agree that the process of recruiting and selecting competent staff is the single most important job of the Personnel Department. If this task is performed without a flaw, the time invested in all other aspects of school district management is reduced. For a moment, consider that all new teaching personnel are excellent teachers, with all that the term "excellent" implies. Just imagine the reduction of time for staff development programs and administrative observation and supervision. Add reduction of time to deal with student discipline problems, which now take a major portion of the day of most site administrators. Principals would willingly give more time to calls from satisfied parents, rather than complaints about poor teaching. Student achievement would significantly improve, which would lead to higher morale among the staff and rising satisfaction with the school among parents and citizens of the community.

If one supposes that the quality of teaching is actually distributed along the normal curve, with a small percentage of truly outstanding teachers, a few rated poor or inadequate, and the largest percentage average, the above fantasy is exactly that—a fantasy. Unfortunately, personnel directors achieve a good batting average if 80% of new staff are rated good to excellent. Nevertheless, a conscientious personnel administrator sets the goal of employing a highly competent and effective staff, even if that ideal is not always possible.

TEACHER SHORTAGE

A shortage of teachers to fill America's classrooms is not a new phenomenon. A strong demand for teachers was created by the baby boom in the wake of World War II and continued until the 1970s, when many of the nation's schools experienced a rather dramatic decline in student enrollment. As a result, many college students changed their career objective from teaching to another field. In the 1960s as many as 20% of college freshman planned a teaching career, but by the 1990s, this percentage was less than 10% (AFT, 2000).

The challenge of educating and training an adequate supply of teachers was then exacerbated by the large number of teachers who retired in the 1980s combined with a rise in student enrollment. Another factor that contributed to the teacher shortage was that many states, in an attempt to improve student achievement, reduced class size, thus creating openings for more teachers. The economic prosperity of the 1990s also resulted in greater salary increases in professions that compete for teachers, as compared with salaries in school districts. One example is that of computer program analyst, a position not even heard of prior to the 1980s.

The recruitment and training of a quality teaching force have received strong national attention since the 1988 election of George Bush, who campaigned on a platform promising to serve as "The Education President." That attention gained sharper focus with the elections of William Clinton and, subsequently, George W. Bush. A reflection of this priority was included in the national 2001-2002 budget, which requires that, to receive federal funds, states must provide a qualified teacher in each classroom by 2005.

This provision will be difficult to achieve, as the U. S. National Center for Education Statistics projects that 2.4 million teachers will be needed over the next decade to meet increased student enrollment and to replace teachers who retire (National Center, 2000). The shortage of qualified teachers is further exacerbated by the reality that 30% of new teachers leave the classroom within the first three years of teaching, and 50% within the first seven years (Wong, 1988).

California joins other states in attempting to meet the demands of recruiting and training qualified teachers, but the problem is far from solved. The state has more than 326,168 full-and part-time public school teachers. In 1999 California school districts hired

26,000 new teachers. Of these, 17,000 had completed their teacher-training programs at California colleges or universities.

The problem is most severe in schools that serve poor and minority students. Urban schools are more than twice as likely as suburban campuses to have teachers without full credentials. California's poorest children are nearly four times as likely as the most affluent to have uncredentialed teachers. The number of uncredentialed teachers is concentrated in Los Angeles County, where nearly half of the state's uncredentialed teachers work. By contrast, a more affluent county, Ventura, has only about 1% of the state's uncredentialed teachers (Helfand, 2000a).

TEACHER PREPARATION

A significant number of California's teachers are underprepared. During the 1998-1999 school year more than 10% of the California teaching force, approximately 28,500 teachers, held only an emergency credential, as reported by the Center for the Future of Teaching and Learning (2000). This center completed a comprehensive study of the California teaching profession in 2000. The findings of that study highlight the challenges faced by the state in trying to place a qualified teacher in every classroom.

- There will be a continued demand for teachers. From 1900 to 2000, the number of California teachers increased by 50%. There were approximately 220,000 California teachers in 1992-1993; this number increased to 326,168 by 1999-2000. Since 1/3 of California teachers are over age 50, large numbers of retirements are expected during the next decade. It is projected that the state will need to employ approximately 26,000 teachers per year. The number of teachers educated in California is insufficient to meet the demand, since all California public and private universities combined train only 17,000 per year.

- Emergency permits and waivers allow a district to employ a teacher to teach a grade or subject without completing the courses required for the appropriate credential. Of California teachers in 1999-2000, there were 35,425 with an emergency permit and another 5,812 under a credential waiver. These 41,237 school employees represented 13% of the workforce.

- Barely more than half of California secondary teachers hold a degree in the subject they teach. Only Louisiana has a greater number in this category. The largest number of waivers was issued for teachers of mathematics, with 43% requiring a waiver to teach that subject, followed by 16% of science teachers (Center, 2000).

The problem is not limited to that of having a fully certified teacher in each classroom; another difficulty is that many newly credentialed teachers feel unprepared for their teaching responsibilities. The California State University (CSU) system is the nation's largest public university system, educating 60% of California's kindergarten through 12th-grade teachers. A 2001 study found that more than 25% of students who completed CSU teacher preparation programs said they were inadequately prepared to teach English and math in grades K-8. More than 40% said they were not sufficiently prepared to teach science, history, or social science. (Carter, 2001).

NEEDS ASSESSMENT

The first step toward employing new staff members should be an assessment of the district's needs. Needs assessment is a systematic way of determining the requirements of the school or district by asking whether established objectives are being satisfactorily accomplished. Needs assessment compares "what is" with "what should be." If results do not match desired outcomes, priorities must be established and action plans developed.

Occasionally, an effective needs assessment may consist simply of a review of the district's mission statement. More often, however, it requires a detailed review of the district's educational philosophy and objectives. A needs assessment should always include financial considerations. Among other factors to be reviewed during the needs assessment process may be changes in the educational program and increased or decreased enrollment, as well as staff retirements, resignations, and transfers.

Often, formulas for determining the needed number of district certificated employees are clearly defined, calculated on such factors as the number of students enrolled, the district's student-teacher ratio, and class size. These figures must be computed with care to meet requirements in law and the negotiated contract. If errors are made, penalties may result; for example, overloading of primary-grade classes eventuates in reduction in district income. Penalties are also incurred for administrative positions in excess of state limits.

A needs assessment is not an isolated event; rather, the process should be ongoing, always with reference to the district's goals and objectives. For example, should an elementary music teacher resign, a careful examination should be made of the district's curriculum. This review may determine that replacing the music teacher is still the number one priority, or it may reveal a greater need in another program.

THE JOB DESCRIPTION

After the needs assessment has been completed, explicit qualifications should be established as a basis for recruitment and selection. A written job description is the end-product of a detailed analysis of job requirements, expectations, and qualifications for the position. This analysis is based on information about the position and describes what an employee does and the skills, education, or training necessary for initial employment in the position. Along with minimum educational requirements, any necessary certification is listed. The title of the supervisor of the position is noted. Specific duties of the assignment are described. Since job requirements change from time to time, job descriptions should be reviewed on a regular basis to ensure that they reflect current needs.

A well-developed job description accomplishes three purposes:

- It provides specific information for the supervisor of the position.

- It clearly delineates the job requirements for an employee who holds the position.

- It guides the recruitment process.

Thus, it is extremely important that a job description be developed for each position or classification in the district.

For the teaching staff, job descriptions are usually written for secondary teachers, elementary teachers, and teaching specialties such as special education teacher, reading resource teacher, elementary or secondary music teacher, and so on. Arthur E. Wise (1988), Director of the Center for the Study of the Teaching Profession, strongly recommends that senior teachers be involved in developing job descriptions, as they are aware of current job requirements. He also suggests that senior teachers participate in the screening process by reviewing the paperwork of applicants.

Districts usually have more job titles for classified than for certificated staff. Larger districts typically chart a hierarchy of positions. For instance, custodial positions may progress from Custodian 1 to Custodian 2, Senior Custodian, and finally Custodian Supervisor. A similar hierarchy may be applied to clerks and secretaries, food service workers, maintenance and gardening staff, and other classified positions.

While job descriptions must be detailed enough to ensure that a candidate who meets the requirements is also appropriately qualified, they should not unnecessarily limit the field of recruitment. Qualifications that are too restrictive may reduce the number of available candidates. Many states, including California, require that management and labor negotiate changes in job descriptions because they have implications for compensation, hours of work, and conditions of employment.

VACANCY ANNOUNCEMENT

After developing the job description, writing a vacancy announcement becomes an easy task. The announcement should contain the job title of the vacant position, major responsibilities, and minimum qualifications. It also should describe hours of work and compensation. An announcement must explain how one applies for the position and state a closing date. Common practice is to allow at least two weeks for classified applicants and somewhat longer for teaching or administrative candidates to submit paperwork, although this period varies greatly from district to district and even from position to position, depending on the situation. The local job market and pool of candidates have a major bearing on the length of time needed to recruit a competent employee.

The job announcement should be widely distributed within the district. It may be disseminated via bulletin boards at each site and included in district correspondence, newsletters, or announcements. Telephone hotlines and Internet postings have become routine in personnel offices. The union contract may give direction as to posting of job vacancies.

In addition to internal posting of vacancy announcements, ads in local newspapers are a common method of recruiting employees, especially in the classified service. The local newspaper can be an effective means of reaching clerical and secretarial candidates, bus drivers, custodians, and food service workers. Bilingual candidates may read notices placed in newspapers written in their language. Because college placement offices and professional associations are good resources for teaching and other professional staff positions, they should be notified of certificated vacancies.

AFFIRMATIVE ACTION

Affirmative action programs are designed to increase employment opportunities for ethnic groups, women, and other minorities, including veterans, the aged, and the disabled. Often, the stated intent of affirmative action programs is that minorities are represented in the school district in proportion to the percentage they comprise of the school district community. For example, if 50% of the students enrolled in a school are Hispanic, then approximately 50% of the school's staff should be Hispanic. Obviously, this balance is not possible at every site.

Affirmative action requirements apply to public and private employers and educational institutions that either have contracts with or receive monies from the federal government. Almost all public schools receive some federal funds; therefore, an affirmative action program is required. Note that special education, food services, American Indian education, Head Start programs, and funds for the educationally disadvantaged are but a few among many federal funding sources.

Every school district should be aware of federal and state legislation and court decisions requiring equal employment opportunities. This legislation and related court cases prohibit discrimination in employment because of race, age, disability, color, religion, sex, pregnancy, national origin, or military service. California Education Code section #44100(d) sets forth the philosophy of the legislature regarding affirmative action:

> It is the intent of the Legislature to establish and maintain a policy of equal opportunity in employment for all persons, and to prohibit discrimination based on race, sex, color, religion, age, disability, ancestry, or national origin in every aspect of personnel policy and practice in employment, development, advancement, and treatment of persons employed in the public school system, and to promote the total realization of equal employment opportunity through a continuing affirmative action employment program.

In addition, the legislature requires school districts to adopt and implement plans designed to increase the proportion of women and minority persons at higher levels of responsibility. Section #44101(a) defines an affirmative action employment program as "one that has planned activities designed to seek, hire, and promote persons who are underrepresented in the work force compared to their number in the population, including disabled persons, women, and persons of minority racial and ethnic backgrounds."

With this mandate from the state and the consequent necessity for representation of all groups in a district, a personnel office is compelled to adopt policies and practices to recruit, employ, and promote a diverse and protected group of employees. Districts demonstrate equal opportunity employment by placing vacancy announcements where they may be seen by all segments of the community, by providing promotional opportunities to minority persons, by establishing criteria that ensure equal access to positions, and by fostering career advancement. Affirmative action provides another reason—in addition to union contracts and the search for the best candidates—for posting notice of all vacancy announcements throughout the district, thus informing all eligible candidates of their opportunity to apply for the position.

Affirmative action does not require employment or promotion of unqualified candidates, but it does require that all qualified candidates be given equal opportunity. An effective affirmative action program ultimately changes patterns of employment and promotion, largely unconscious patterns of human behavior, and thus requires imaginative, energetic, and sustained action by the personnel administrator.

RECRUITMENT BROCHURE OR MEDIA PRESENTATION

In addition to the job vacancy announcement, many districts produce a recruitment brochure, Website, or media presentation highlighting advantages of employment in the district. The brochure or presentation provides potential candidates with information about the school or district and is designed to interest the reader in applying for the position. The best way to attract highly qualified individuals is to have a district with an excellent reputation—and to publicize that reputation.

To attract candidates, a recruitment brochure or Website announcement must be attractive in design, emphasizing the positive elements of living and working in the community. Such brochures often feature photographs of students in such aspects of school life as reading, science experiments, athletic or music programs, or other curricular or co-curricular activities in which the district takes pride. The community portion of the brochure or presentation may feature enticing geographic features such as a ski resort, clear skies, rivers, or mountains. Information about community colleges and universities, churches, shopping centers, and recreational and cultural activities or programs is highlighted. The brochure also may address employment opportunities for spouses, proximity to other cities, and data such as the cost of living in the community, rental rates, and the average purchase price of a home.

Statements from the current staff, indicating their satisfaction with salary and other working conditions, are powerful attractors. Strong staff support for the board and administration is taken to indicate that the district is a good place to work. Other comments from the staff might be selected to make the prospective candidate sense that the district is a warm and welcoming place.

The design of the brochure, Website, or media presentation may range from a simple, but attractive, folder prepared in-house by the personnel staff to a professionally designed work of superior quality that may cost several thousand dollars. Each district executes this step of the recruitment process in accordance with its needs and resources.

SOURCES OF QUALIFIED CANDIDATES

Once the needs assessment has been completed, the job description reviewed or updated, the vacancy announcement prepared, and affirmative action needs addressed, recruitment of potential candidates is the next step in the process. Even in the most attractive districts, it is a major mistake for the principal or personnel director to adopt a wait-and-see attitude. Effective recruitment of talented and dedicated employees requires a planned and vigorous strategy on the part of personnel staff, who turn to many sources, including those described in the following paragraphs, for qualified candidates.

Colleges and Universities

The greatest number of potential teacher candidates are students at colleges and universities. If a district is fortunate enough to have a teacher training institution within or near its geographic boundaries, recruitment of competent instructors is a much easier task. For one thing, universities place student and intern teachers in school districts that are in close proximity to the university. This placement gives the personnel director and principals an opportunity to observe potential candidates during training. Outstanding candidates can be recruited and offered employment during this phase of their education.

Unfortunately, many districts do not have the benefit of student teachers placed in their classrooms. Even if they do, the specialties of those teachers may not match the district's vacancies. Therefore, all personnel directors need to develop a close relationship with teacher placement officers at several colleges and universities. Given such a relationship, university placement staff provide recommendations to the district while also encouraging competent candidates to seek employment there.

Colleges and universities in California have been unable to meet the demand for new teachers. Consequently, many districts, particularly those with a growing student population, must seek teachers in other states—even other countries. This need arises most often in teaching fields that consistently experience a shortage of candidates—among them special education, English as a second language, mathematics, and science.

Internal District Search

A second major source of recruits is the district's own community. For example, in recent years districts have employed many paraprofessionals, including instructional aides. Many such individuals, encouraged to complete coursework for a credential, become excellent teachers. The instructional aide is usually a resident of the community, able to avoid the expense of relocation that occurs when out-of-district staff are employed. This approach to career development has several advantages, among them a first-hand assessment of the person's skills and a boost in morale for the staff.

Substitute List

An additional source of teacher candidates is the district's substitute list. As vacancies occur, good substitutes may have reached a stage in their personal lives and professional careers consistent with interest in a full-time position. As is the case with an instructional aide, the principal or supervisor often has first-hand knowledge of the qualifications of such a candidate. Like paraprofessionals, substitute teachers are usually well known in the community and can avoid the expense of relocation.

The classified substitute list is an excellent source for filling vacancies in that service. Most districts regularly employ substitutes in the food services program, clerical and secretarial positions, transportation, maintenance, and custodial programs. The supervisor has opportunity to note the work ethic and job skills of these temporary employees. Usually, a substitute classified employee also lives in the community, making relocation a much simpler task for the employee and the district.

Referrals

Referrals by current employees are also an excellent source of applicants. The teacher who is new to the district is often aware of individuals who are just completing certification requirements. Other staff members may have acquaintances or friends who are genuinely interested in the community and school district. Because his or her own reputation is at stake, one would not usually recommend someone unless he or she believes that individual would do a good job; hence, a person who is recommended for a position by a current employee is often an outstanding candidate. Of course, this applicant should undergo the same rigorous screening as other candidates, since occasionally a current employee may, for personal reasons, recommend a mediocre applicant.

Certain practices encourage employees to recommend candidates for job vacancies. For instance, as job vacancies are posted at each school site, principals may encourage staff to nominate excellent candidates for the vacancy, typically by submitting the individual's name to the personnel office. An application is then mailed to the candidate indicating that he or she has been recommended for the opening and is invited to apply.

Professional Organizations or Conferences

Conferences and meetings of professional organizations are another source of applicants for district vacancies. Teachers and principals who are active in professional organizations often become aware of a colleague who has an excellent reputation and would be interested in relocating. Such referrals may be more credible than those based on social contact or friendship.

Out-of-State Candidates

Although the teacher shortage is nationwide, there are always disparities in need from one region to another. For this reason, some California districts search out of state and in other countries, especially Mexico and Spain. District recruiters travel to university campuses and circulate advertisements in other states.

A major problem faced by California personnel directors as they attempt to recruit teachers from other states has been obtaining a California credential for them. During the late 1990s, Governor Davis and the California Legislature implemented a number of actions to make this process a bit easier.

To facilitate employment of out-of-state candidates, 1998 legislation required the Commission on Teacher Credentialing to establish credential reciprocity with states that meet California standards. This has been accomplished with eight states. In addition, teachers with three or more years' successful teaching experience in other states may complete their credential requirements by participating in a Beginning Teacher Support and Assessment (BTSA) program. Teachers with five years of experience automatically qualify for a full credential. Another avenue to a California teaching credential is to have obtained a certificate by meeting the rigorous requirements established by the National Board for Professional Teaching Standards.

Walk-in Applicants

In many districts unsolicited, or walk-in, applicants also may be hired to fill vacancies. The personnel office may develop a job interest form for such inquiries. Even though the district may not have a matching vacancy at the time, the interest form may be kept on file should an opening occur. A brief notice can be mailed to the applicant at that time. A word of caution—the personnel staff must be extremely careful not to seem to promise a job. In addition, a time limit should be placed on the length of time an interest form is to be kept. For example, renewal of the job interest card could be required after six months. Otherwise, not only do the files become voluminous, but applicants may misunderstand the process.

EMPLOYMENT APPLICATIONS

Application forms should gather basic information about the candidate. Spaces are provided for name, address, phone number, and previous employment. If the position requires a credential, specific authorizations must be requested. The application form should contain a statement requesting applicants to send to the personnel department relevant documents such as letters of reference or placement papers, transcripts, and a copy of each credential.

Until the 1970s school districts could ask prospective employees for almost any type of biographical information. However, the federal Equal Opportunity Act of 1972 drastically changed the types of information sought. It is no longer acceptable to ask a candidate's maiden name, name of spouse, age, date or place of birth, height, weight, or other personal characteristics. Ethnic or racial background is commonly requested on a form separate from the employment application itself. This information assists districts in complying with affirmative action regulations, but the candidate must be informed that the response is given voluntarily and is handled apart from the selection procedure.

In most school districts a personnel clerk receives all job applications. The clerk should be directed to date-stamp all applications and place them in a folder for the position. The clerk usually has responsibility to check that each application is complete. For example, if candidates are requested to include transcripts, letters of recommendation, or verification of a recent chest x-ray, these items should be checked and placed with the application. In some instances, the personnel clerk also notifies the candidate of an incomplete file. To keep candidates informed of their status, the clerk may mail a postcard to the candidate stating that the application has been received and is complete. If the interview timeline is available, candidates may be notified when interviews will be scheduled.

Many personnel offices now have data processing equipment into which the clerk enters information for each candidate, thus allowing a principal or personnel officer to monitor progress toward filling each vacancy. Computer-generated letters can be sent to the candidates at each step in the employment process.

After the deadline for applications has been reached, the personnel clerk prepares a master list of all applicants for the vacancy. The master list records the title of the vacant position and the names, addresses, and telephone numbers of all candidates. Each person's application and all supporting documents are placed with the master list, which is now ready for the principal, supervisor, or personnel director to use in initial screening.

INTERNET TOOLS

Perhaps the most revolutionary communication tool since the printing press is the Internet. As usual, private business pioneered the use of the Internet prior to its adaption by public agencies. Almost every large business now hosts a Website. School districts are learning the advantages of this communication device and are establishing their own Web pages. Typically, these Web pages contain information about the district and its schools, including enrollment data, student test scores, college information, and parent handbooks.

In the last few years personnel departments have discovered the advantages of the Internet as a tool for recruitment of certificated and classified employees. There are three levels a district may utilize for this purpose.

- The first level consists simply of listing the personnel department on the district Website. The site includes the names of staff in the personnel department and their telephone numbers.

- A second level may also provide a listing of job opportunities, descriptions of the positions, salary schedules, and closing dates.

- A third level extends the information offered in the earlier levels by giving an applicant greater access to information and the application process. Applicants can download the district's application packet and print the forms on their own printer. In addition, an applicant may submit the entire application packet electronically. Some districts have added an FAQ (frequently-asked questions) page on which to post information about housing, cost of living, college or university availability, and cultural opportunities in the area. Still a further feature may be e-mail, by means of which the applicant may ask other questions.

What's next? Much of the selection process, too, may be automated. Suppose, for example, that a district prepares a vacancy announcement for an English teacher—not just any English teacher, but one with a minor in Spanish who can teach one or two periods of the latter. It would be desirable if the applicant could also coach one or more sports. Thus, the required qualifications for the position include a California secondary teaching credential with a major in English and a major or minor in Spanish. Desired qualifications are given as a master's degree in English, a minimum of three years' teaching experience including experience in an urban setting, a record of strong classroom management skills, and background or interest in coaching.

Candidates' applications, résumés, and letters of recommendation are received via the Internet and automatically recorded by the district's computer. The computer scans this material for the required and desired qualifications and makes a list of the most qualified candidates. After the personnel director reviews the list, the computer generates an interview schedule and completes a list of questions for the interview. Following this task, the computer, by e-mail or fax machine, generates a letter inviting candidates for an interview with the date and time established. A computer-generated map is also included, giving directions from the candidate's home to the district office where the interview is to be held.

Obviously, use of the Internet to post vacancies, to provide applicants with information about positions, and to receive and submit completed applications to the district electronically will have a profound effect on the personnel department. Just visualize the reduction in time and expense of mailing brochures, receiving applicants, and contacting applicants by phone or by mail. Think of the happiness of the personnel director who will no longer spend days, if not weeks, on the road recruiting teachers. For potential candidates, consider the reduction in time and frustration when vacancy information is instantly available, phone calls are unnecessary, and applications are readily completed and returned.

RECRUITMENT TRENDS

In 1989 the American Association of School Administrators completed a survey of trends in school personnel recruitment (Steuteville-Brodinsky, 1989). The following items were reported.

- As site-based management has emerged, principals and teachers are assuming more responsibility for staff recruitment.

- Most school districts are desperately seeking to employ teachers from minority populations.

- School districts in high-growth areas are adopting innovative and aggressive strategies for recruiting teachers.

- School districts are forming partnerships with colleges and universities to provide teacher training programs.

- Districts are forming consortia and other cooperative relationships to improve recruiting efforts.

CALIFORNIA INITIATIVES

During the late 1990s the California Legislature and Governors Wilson and Davis enacted a number of laws to make teaching more financially attractive and to assist prospective teachers in finding information about the teaching profession.

In 1997 the legislature appropriated money for new state-funded centers called CalTeach. The centers are located in six California areas. CalTeach has the goal of making it much easier for teachers, both inside and outside California, to find jobs and other information about teaching in the state. The web site is at http://www.calteach.com.

Governor Davis, with concurrence of the state legislature, provided several incentives in the 2000-2001 state budget to recruit and train California teachers. The primary incentives include the following.

Beginning teacher salaries	The minimum salary was increased from $32,000 to $34,000 per year.

Tax credit	Teachers were granted a credit on their state income tax ranging from $250 to $1,500, depending on their years of experience.
Governor's teaching fellowships	Fellowships were provided in the amount of $20,000 per candidate toward living and educational expenses while completing teacher training. The successful candidates must commit to teach for four years in a hard-to-staff school. The authorization for this program was $20 million.
Teacher hiring incentives	Each district will receive $2,000 for every credentialed teacher hired to replace an emergency permit teacher. An additional $2,000 will be awarded to each new fully credentialed teacher employed.
National Board for Professional Teaching Standards	Teachers who are nationally board certified were already eligible for a $10,000 bonus. If the teacher agrees to teach in a low-performing school for a minimum of four years, he or she will be eligible for an additional $20,000 bonus.
Teacher housing incentives	Up to $10,000 in loans for the down payment on a home will be granted to 5,000 fully credentialed teachers. These loans are forgivable if the teacher agrees to serve for five years in a hard-to-staff school.
Additional bonuses	Teachers in low-performing schools where students' scores improve significantly on the Stanford 9 test were made eligible for bonuses between $5,000 and $25,000.

The hope is that these incentives will attract more candidates to join the teaching profession. However, they may not be enough to achieve the objective of a credentialed teacher in every classroom, as California is not the only state with a teacher shortage and an aggressive recruitment program. For example, in 1999 educators from Massachusetts were in San Diego offering a $20,000 signing bonus for new teachers. In addition to the bonus, teachers were to receive an intensive summer training program and help in finding housing (Magee, 1999).

SUMMARY

An extensive, aggressive program of recruitment, directed toward placing and holding qualified individuals in every position in the school system, is essential to organizational effectiveness. The major steps in an effective recruitment program proceed as follows:

Needs assessment	The first step in deciding to employ a new staff member should be an assessment of the district's employment needs. The assessment should be ongoing and related to the district's goals and objectives. The assessment should always include financial considerations, as every organization has some unmet needs and must establish priorities to accomplish its mission most effectively.
Job description	The second step in the recruitment process is to review the job description for the vacant position. Detailed suggestions for developing effective job descriptions have been included in this chapter.
Vacancy announcement	After the job description has been developed, the vacancy announcement should be a relatively easy task, as the latter should flow from the former. The vacancy announcement should contain both complete information about the position and application procedures.
Affirmative action	As reviewed in this chapter, legislation calls for equal employment opportunities for minorities, including women, veterans, the aged, and the disabled. Suggestions have been provided as to ways a district can demonstrate equal opportunity employment. A personnel administrator needs to mount an imaginative, energetic, and sustained effort to accomplish this goal.
Recruitment brochure	Many districts develop a recruitment brochure or media presentation highlighting advantages of working in the district. Each district completes this part of the personnel recruitment function in response to its own needs and resources.

Sources of
qualified
candidates

Colleges and universities, district staff and their contacts in the community, substitutes, involvement with professional organizations, and walk-in applicants have been described as potential sources for qualified candidates.

Employment
applications

Finally, the chapter closed by discussing elements in an employment application form that will make it useful to screening committees and conform to legal limitations. Lest the entire series of steps break down at this point, applications must be processed in timely and organized fashion.

One of the quick means to an improved instructional program is effective recruitment and selection of staff. Every vacancy gives a principal opportunity to improve instruction at his or her school. A well-planned recruitment process holds potential to identify a teacher, administrator, or classified staff member who will engender new life in a school or district.

KEY TERMS

1. affirmative action
2. CalTeach
3. certificated employee
4. classified employee
5. employment applications
6. hierarchy of positions
7. internal search

8. job description
9. needs assessment
10. recruitment
11. recruitment brochure
12. skill and knowledge requirements
13. vacancy announcement

QUESTIONS AND ACTIVITIES

1. One of the first tasks in establishing an effective employee recruitment program is to develop a "needs assessment." Why is a needs assessment so important? What should be included?

2. Discuss three key elements to be included in an employee job description.

3. Affirmative action is currently the subject of debate at the state and national levels. What is affirmative action? What are the pros and cons of an affirmative action program?

4. Discuss three major sources in recruiting certificated employees.

5. Employment applications are an important component of an effective employee recruitment program. What information should be included in the application? What information must *not* be included?

6. Obtain three district personnel policies regarding recruitment and selection of staff. Compare the policies, noting similarities and differences.

7. Review the job descriptions in your district. Observe when they were last revised and check to see whether they are complete.

8. Obtain copies of the district's last few vacancy announcements. Discuss how they could be improved.

9. Review the recruitment brochure or media presentation for your district. Obtain copies from other districts. Develop suggestions for improving the brochure from your district and/or the others. If your district does not have a recruitment brochure or media presentation, volunteer to develop one.

10. Obtain employment applications from three school districts. Design a new application using the best elements and design features from each of the forms.

11. Locate CalTeach on the Internet. Note the subject areas and grade levels that have the most vacancy announcements.

Chapter 4

Selection of Personnel

INTRODUCTION

With the recruitment process completed, a school district's next task is to select the most qualified candidate for the vacancy. Recruitment and selection of personnel create a major expense. If the district makes an error in the process, the cost is often incalculable, both because the individual performs poorly on the job, with all the errors and problems that implies, and because hiring and training a replacement are expensive. Therefore, the goal of the selection process is to employ an individual who will be successful on the job.

Arthur Wise and associates (1988) completed a comprehensive study of teacher selection and found that most school districts commit few resources to the process. Districts depend on low-cost techniques, such as letters of recommendation and transcripts, rather than high-cost techniques, such as on-the-job assessments. These researchers also found that the common practice in private industry of compensating prospective technical or management employees for travel and moving expenses is rare in teacher recruitment.

Ronald Rebore (1998) wrote that school districts spend a minimum of $1,000 to recruit and employ a new employee, but as much as $25,000 to hire a new superintendent. These amounts are truly minimal relative to the cost of dismissing an unsuccessful employee. Ralph Villani, a senior California personnel director, estimates that termination of a certificated employee can cost as much as $300,000 dollars in legal fees alone (1998, personal communication). This amount does not include the hours of administrative time required for classroom observation and documentation of poor performance. The process may require several months—even years—to complete. Therefore, a district must exercise utmost care to ensure that the selection process is of the highest quality.

Selecting individuals who will be successful and will remain with the school district for a reasonable amount of time is an extremely important personnel function. Proper selection of staff is necessary to offer a quality instructional program for students. If the selection task is poorly accomplished, the results can have a major negative impact on district finances, morale, and effectiveness.

INITIAL SCREENING

The first step in the selection process is initial screening of applicants. Assuming that several candidates have applied for a vacancy, weaker candidates are usually eliminated at this stage of the selection process. Personnel directors admit that viable candidates may be eliminated during the initial screening, but reducing the list to a manageable number early in the process releases more time and resources for the final selection.

Ordinarily, the personnel officer has responsibility for the initial screening process. It is good practice for the supervisor of the vacant position to screen the applicants independently a second time. This practice reduces the risk of eliminating a viable candidate at the outset. If either the personnel officer or the supervisor includes a candidate for additional screening, then that applicant should be included in the next step in the selection process.

Personnel officers use the term "red flag" at this stage of the selection process. This term refers to any item on the application that disqualifies the applicant from further consideration. For example, preliminary screening can eliminate applicants who do not meet the announced job requirements. If the vacancy announcement seeks a teacher of elementary music and calls for a music credential, all candidates who do not hold that credential are eliminated from further consideration. If the vacancy announcement for an electrician requires rating as a master electrician and the candidate is only a journeyman, he or she should be eliminated from the screening process.

The personnel officer or supervisor also may eliminate candidates who have not completed all the information on the application—or completed it in an unsatisfactory manner. For example, mistakes in grammar or spelling for a teaching position usually result in elimination of that individual from competition. Applicants who do not follow directions on the form also may be eliminated. Applications in handwriting that are difficult to read may be eliminated at this stage. If the job announcement requires recent experience or training, candidates who do not meet this criterion should be removed from the list.

Personnel directors also review the application for a characteristic referred to as "holes in experience." This term refers to years unaccounted for on the application. For instance, a teacher candidate may list experience from 1992 to 1995 in the Paradise School District followed by employment in Beach Falls District from 1997 to date, but does not account for the years 1995-96 and 1996-97. Perhaps the applicant has a satisfactory reason for this break in experience, but the personnel officer at least notes the omission for inquiry, should the candidate remain on the list for further consideration.

LETTERS OF RECOMMENDATION

Although letters of recommendation are rarely required for classified vacancies, they are widely used for certificated positions. At best, these letters are of minimal value in the screening process. Several factors account for this situation.

First, as a result of the Privacy Act of 1974, individuals have the right to examine letters of reference unless they waive that right. Writers of reference letters are reluctant to point out an applicant's perceived weaknesses when they know the letter may be read by the individual. Writers may also fear a lawsuit if negative comments are made (Clear, 1978). Defamation of character is a very serious charge against a personnel director or principal. Defamation occurs when false information is communicated, either by word of mouth (slander) or in writing (libel). The communication must have produced some harm to the person. For example, the harm produced by defamation might be loss of a job opportunity or a promotion.

Second, job applicants usually request references from persons who are likely to write a complimentary letter that is biased in the applicant's behalf. As personnel directors review letters of recommendation, it is not uncommon to hear the phrase, "Here is another one who can walk on water." A third shortcoming of letters of recommendation is that supervisors have been known to write a favorable letter for an incompetent employee to facilitate that person's leaving the present employer.

However, in spite of these realities, reference letters do serve several useful purposes. For one thing, an applicant's file does occasionally contain a candid letter that points out a candidate's shortcomings. In addition, reference letters are an important source of information about first-year teachers. These beginners do not have a track record of employment in the profession, and the references from the master teacher and university supervisor include information about the candidate's experience and strengths. Such letters usually add comments pointing out areas for additional growth. For the more experienced candidate, moreover, among the letters of reference one or more usually contain the name of a colleague known to the personnel officer. A personal telephone call to this educator may yield a more balanced view of the candidate's qualifications.

TRANSCRIPTS AND CREDENTIALS

Evaluation of credentials has become a highly technical field in most states. With the proliferation of teaching credentials and restrictions on subjects or grades authorized by each, personnel officers must continually update their knowledge of the subject.

Some states, including California, may penalize a district or superintendent if individuals are assigned to teach outside the subjects or levels authorized on their credentials. Employment of out-of-state teachers creates another nightmare for the candidate and the personnel department as the teacher attempts to obtain a credential in the new location.

Along with review of references and credentials by the supervisor and the personnel officer, a transcript review by two individuals is also a good practice. Of course, transcripts should be evaluated cautiously, with consideration for differences among students, professors, and universities. However, the personnel director and supervisor need some assurance that the applicant is sufficiently educated to be instructing others. No school principal would accept grades as the best indicator of teaching performance, but mastery of fundamental skills and knowledge at college level is a minimum. A word of caution: take particular care in checking a candidate's statement of his or her grade-point average (GPA). Seidler (1990) estimates that 25% of all applicants have inflated their GPA.

The transcript review should be carried out in light of the grade level and subject that the applicant is expected to teach. For example, a "D" in calculus may be relatively unimportant in evaluating an applicant to teach the first grade, but that same low mark may be a major consideration if the candidate is to teach trigonometry and calculus at the high school. As with most selection tools, transcripts are more useful for screening out the clearly inferior candidate than for selecting the superior applicant.

TELEPHONE REFERENCE CHECK

Personnel officers debate among themselves the issue of checking references by telephone. Although the value of telephone reference checks has not been subject to much study, it is reasonable to assume that personal communication is more informative than other reference checks. There is little disagreement about the importance of the telephone call; indeed, personnel officers consider this step of primary importance in final selection of a candidate. The controversy, then, centers on timing. Should the telephone check be made prior to inviting the final candidates for an interview, or after interviews have been completed and a recommendation for employment has been made by the interview team? Each district must make its own decision on this issue.

Successful personnel officers form a strong network of professional and personal communications. One means of extending this network is to join and attend meetings of professional organizations. Picking up the telephone to call a colleague in another district often yields more candid information about an applicant than can be obtained by any other means. Of course, an effective personnel officer is astute in posing questions to his or her colleague in another district. Some typical questions are: "How effective was the employee in the classroom or on the job?" " What were relationships with other staff members and parents?" "What was the employee's attendance record?" "How did he or she contribute to staff morale?" When inquiring about a teacher candidate, a favorite question is: "Would you place your child in this teacher's class?" Obviously, telephone reference checks must be kept in the strictest confidence.

PRE-EMPLOYMENT TESTS

Although employment tests are common in private industry, they rarely appear as a screening device in the employment of certificated school employees. However, Madaus and Pullin (1987) found that examinations are extensively used earlier in one's career, as part of the teacher credential process. They found that 34 of the 50 states require prospective teachers to pass an examination assessing their knowledge of basic skills and professional practice. Some states require prospective teachers to take the National Teacher Examination core battery or specialty exams, and about the same number require state-developed examinations. Three states require practicing teachers to pass a test.

California and Oregon require all prospective teachers to pass an examination: the California Basic Educational Skills Test (CBEST). CBEST was designed as a general measure of basic proficiency in reading, writing, and mathematics. The test is not a measure of teaching skills or abilities.

A more recent California test—one that *is* intended to measure teaching skill—is the Reading Instruction Competence Assessment (RICA), required of multiple subject credential candidates since fall, 1998. The examination involves not only a written test, but assessment of a videotaped teaching activity.

Not required, but encouraged by a state merit allocation of $10,000 per teacher, is certification by the National Board for Professional Teaching Standards. This incentive was funded in 1998-99. Those working toward the certification may be required to serve as a mentor teacher in exchange for support and release time from the district.

Given the requirements for a college or university degree and the examinations built into the process, another test at the selection stage for teacher applicants seems redundant. Apparently, this belief is widely accepted, as Kahl (1980) found that only 13% of 320 large school districts gave examinations to prospective teachers. By contrast, according to a survey of 2,500 U. S. corporations by Alexander (1990), 64.5% of employers in private industry use test results in hiring and promotion decisions. Most firms administer an hour-long test to entry-level blue-collar workers. Applicants for top management positions may take personality tests that last a full day.

Although school districts avoid tests of teaching candidates, they strongly resemble private industry in testing classified applicants. A skill-related test can help determine whether bus drivers, secretaries, food service workers, maintenance staff, and other classified applicants are likely to serve as competent employees. Prior to administering a skills test, the district must establish the skill level necessary for the position and translate that level into a minimum score for further consideration in the selection process. Intelligence, ability, aptitude, and interest tests also provide valuable data.

Two words of caution when using tests as a personnel screening device: First of all, testing programs have come under strong criticism by minority groups in recent years on the ground that they discriminate against the minority candidate. Testing has been challenged in the courts for this reason, and the courts have consistently ruled that pre-employment tests must be clearly job-related to justify their administration. The second word of caution is that other factors than a test should be considered in selecting an employee. Previous work history, references, and the interview—rather than simply a test score—should be the final determinants of the individual to whom employment is offered.

ASSESSMENT CENTERS

Although assessment centers are not widely used in the employment of teachers or classified staff, they are gaining in popularity for selection of principals (Hersey & Beers, 1989). Many universities have established assessment centers in conjunction with their administrative training programs. For example, an administrative assessment center is located on the campuses of California State University at Fullerton and San Diego State University. Some universities use the assessment center to determine areas of strength and weakness in graduate students who are enrolled in their administrative training program. Faculty and students can then focus on needs identified in the assessment profile. Also, some county superintendents of schools have formed consortia with local school districts to provide an assessment program for potential administrators.

On the national level, the National Association of Secondary School Principals (NASSP) manages several assessment centers for potential administrators. A typical NASSP Assessment Center lasts two days, with groups of six to twelve assessees participating in a variety of administrative exercises. These assessment activities include two in-basket tests, two leaderless-group exercises, a fact-finding exercise, and a personal interview. A panel of NASSP-trained assessors evaluates candidates individually on a number of dimensions, using a standardized scale. After the assessment exercises are completed, a profile of each candidate is developed.

Hersey and Beers (1989) state that assessment centers are valid predictors of administrative success, and some business firms now use them for hiring technical workers. Assessment centers are also used to help design training and development with the objective of improving the leadership skills of principals.

THE INTERVIEW

In most school districts the face-to-face interview is the last step in the selection process. An interview is defined as a meeting between two or more people to elicit information from the person being interviewed. Joe M. Smith (1980) from Trenton State College states, "The most feasible system at the present time is to grill the most likely candidates on knowledge of their teaching performance. It is not very scientific; that is, you cannot be sure of its validity or reliability, but it is probable that it will be better than not directing questions in this area."

Nicholson and McInerney (1988), professors of educational administration and former school administrators, strongly recommend a team approach in the final interview. They wrote, "A team is less likely to miss key aspects of a candidate's personality or potential than a single interviewer. The team approach also erases the problem of the dominant personality of a single interviewer."

Auren Uris (1978) outlines four characteristics that distinguish an interview from normal conversation. First, an interview is a structured conversation with direction and format; it has a beginning, middle, and conclusion. Second, the interview is conducted by an individual who is prepared to move it in a direction dictated by the occasion. Third, both parties to the interview understand its purpose, which can be accomplished only through cooperation. Finally, the nature of the interview is clearly defined and specified.

Interviewing is a useful practice only if the interviewer is cautious about the information collected and the inferences drawn (Muller, 1978). If the interview format is carefully constructed and the interviewers are carefully trained, significant information can be obtained from the process. Inexperienced interviewers tend to ask too many questions that allow a "yes" or "no" answer. The skillful interviewer, however, obtains information and impressions about the applicant's opinions, beliefs, and attitudes by asking questions that stimulate the candidate to reply in narrative fashion. Questions should be restricted to obtaining information not already provided in the application.

The importance of well-constructed interview questions designed to assess the applicant's skills and competencies for the position cannot be stressed too strongly. For example, asking "How would you establish your reading program?" of an applicant for a third-grade teaching position permits assessment of the teacher's knowledge of this area. In addition to assisting the interviewer in assessing an applicant's knowledge and skills, responses also provide insight regarding the applicant's philosophy of teaching.

All members of the interviewing team should be cautioned about asking any questions that may give the perception of bias on the part of the panel. A safe guideline for the panel is: "If it is not job-related, don't ask it."

Panel members must be aware of acceptable and unacceptable questions. For example, it was once common practice to ask a candidate if he or she had ever been arrested or spent time in jail. As a result of a court case, *Gregory v. Litton Systems*, personnel directors may ask only about a candidate's record of criminal conviction ("New Rules," 1977). Table 4 lists areas that are legally sensitive and indicates topics that may and may not be raised in each.

Table 4

Interview Questions with Legal Implications

Legal Issue	Inappropriate Questions
Age	For a minor, requiring proof of age in the form of a work permit or certificate of age is lawful. It is unlawful to require adults to present a birth certificate or baptismal record or to ask their age.
Place of Residence	To request an applicant's place of residence and how long one has been a resident of the city or state is lawful.
Race	To request information about distinguishing physical characteristics is legal. However, to ask the color of the applicant's skin, eyes, etc., is illegal if, directly or indirectly, this question indicates ethnicity.
Religion	In public schools, all inquiries about religion are illegal. For example, one cannot ask whether a candidate attends or belongs to a church.
Sex	Questions about sexual preference are prohibited under anti-discrimination laws.
Birthplace	Questions about the birthplace of an applicant or the applicant's parents, spouse, or other relations are illegal.
Ethnic Background	Inquiries about applicants' national origin are illegal. However, it is legal to ask which languages an applicant speaks, reads, or writes.
Marital and Family Status	Questions to determine whether a man or woman is married, single, divorced, etc., are unlawful (Nemesh, 1979).
Credit Rating	All questions about charge accounts or credit rating are unlawful.
Lifestyle	Asking about future career plans is lawful. Asking an applicant if he or she plays cards, drinks alcoholic beverages, or takes drugs is illegal.
Photographs	A statement may be made that a photograph is required after employment, but a photo may not be required prior to hiring.

Finally, the interview must be brought smoothly to an end. Commonly, the leader of the interview panel closes with a statement similar to the following: "That concludes our questions, but we would like to give you [the applicant] an opportunity to ask any questions of the interview team or to make any closing statement, if you so desire." The leader also expresses appreciation for the candidate's application and participation in the interview. To conclude, one should give the applicant as much information as possible about the timeline for reaching a final decision.

LEGAL REQUIREMENTS FOR EMPLOYMENT

All employees who serve on interview panels should receive training in legal standards for the selection process. They should know about equal employment laws and regulations that guarantee a person's rights to fair consideration for employment. This information includes knowledge of questions that may and may not be posed in an interview, as just discussed. However, legislation has created additional considerations.

During the past two decades, Congress has enacted several statutes that protect prospective and current employees from employment discrimination. The statutes address a wide range of conduct that would differentiate job applicants on the basis of race, age, sex, ethnic or national origin, religion, and handicap or disability. These laws were written to ensure equal opportunity for employment and nondiscrimination in compensation, promotion, and benefits for each position. All personnel involved in the selection and employment of staff should be familiar with the federal statutes enumerated in Table 5.

NOTIFYING THE CANDIDATES

The final step in the selection process is to notify all candidates that the position has been filled. It is good personnel practice to make a personal telephone call to the successful candidate with the offer of employment. Depending on the position, the call might be placed by the personnel officer or the immediate supervisor of the position. In some classified positions of a technical nature, the candidate may have questions that only the supervisor can answer. Teacher candidates also may have specific questions about the school and grade level or subjects to which they will be assigned, money available for supplies, conference attendance, and textbooks. The new employee may also need information of a more personal nature—availability of housing, employment for a spouse, or other factors that may influence their decision to accept the position.

Except in rare cases, final approval of employment is required by the board of education. Unfortunately, this step in the process is rarely accomplished in expeditious fashion, since school boards ordinarily meet only twice or, in some cases, once a month. If the board has a track record of nearly always accepting the personnel recommendations of the superintendent, the candidate can be informed of this fact and given assurance that employment will be approved. If the board might not accept the superintendent's

Table 5

Federal Legislation affecting Personnel Selection

Legislation	Implications
Equal Pay Act of 1963	This act was amended by the Fair Labor Standards Act of 1963. The act makes it unlawful to discriminate on the basis of sex in the level of wages for equal work and responsibility under similar working conditions.
Title VII, Civil Rights Act of 1964	Title VII prohibits discrimination on the basis of race, color, religion, sex, or national origin. Title VII, as originally enacted, did not apply to public employers such as school districts. However, in 1972 the statute was amended by Congress to include public employers. As a result of Title VII and other employment statutes, school districts are required not to discriminate in employment practices.
Age Discrimination and Employment Act of 1967	This act prohibits private and public employers from discrimination in hiring or firing workers who are 40 years of age or older. The purpose of the act is to promote employment of older persons based on ability rather than age, and to prohibit arbitrary age discrimination in employment.
Civil Rights Act of 1968	The Civil Rights Act sets criminal penalties for interfering with an individual's employment rights on the basis of race, religion, color, or national origin. Although not widely invoked, the act provides remedies for discrimination by employers.
Title IX, Education Amendments of 1972	These amendments provide that no person will be subject to sex discrimination under any educational program or activity receiving federal financial assistance. In 1982 the Supreme Court, in *North Haven Board of Education v. Bell*, ruled that Title IX coverage was limited to specific programs within an institution receiving federal funds. In 1987 Congress approved the Civil Rights Restoration Act, which superseded the *North Haven* decision and the decision of the U. S. Supreme Court in *Grove City College v. Bell*. In other words, the Civil Rights Restoration Act expanded the scope of Title IX so that an entire institution receiving federal funds is subject to civil rights requirements in Title IX and other civil rights laws, including the subsequent Vocational Rehabilitation Act of 1978.

Legislation	Implications
Vietnam Era Veterans Readjustment Act of 1974	This act in support of Vietnam veterans applies to employers who hold contracts or subcontracts with the federal government in the amount of $10,000 or more. These employers are required to take affirmative action to hire and advance in employment disabled veterans and veterans of the Vietnam era. The act applies only to contracts, not to federal grants and aids.
Vocational Rehabilitation Act of 1978	The Vocational Rehabilitation Act was passed in 1973 and amended in 1978. It requires employers who have a contract with the federal government worth $2,500 or more to take affirmative action to hire and promote qualified disabled persons. The definition of "handicapped" is a physical or mental disability that interferes with such activities as walking, seeing, speaking, or learning. The law stipulates that the handicapped individual must be capable of performing the particular job for which he or she is being considered.
Pregnancy Discrimination Act of 1978	This act was approved by Congress and signed by President Carter in 1978. The Pregnancy Disability Act was a separate piece of legislation, but became an integral part of Title VII. Congress enacted the amendment to specify pregnancy as a disability that should be treated in the same manner as any other employee disability. Thus, the sex discrimination prohibitions contained in Title VII were expanded to cover a medical condition unique to women.
Immigration Reform and Control Act of 1986	This act makes it unlawful to knowingly hire an unauthorized alien, to continue employment of one who becomes an unauthorized alien, or to hire any individual without first verifying his or her identity and employability.
Americans with Disabilities Act of 1990	This act, which took effect in 1992 for employers with 25 or more employees and in 1994 for employers with 15 or more, prohibits employment discrimination against qualified employees with disabilities. The law, similar to the Rehabilitation Act of 1973, does not require that unqualified persons be hired. Rather, the act makes it more difficult for employers to discriminate against disabled persons by inquiring about disabilities before a job is offered. Employers are also required to make reasonable accommodations for known mental or physical disabilities.
Omnibus Transportation Employee Testing Act of 1991	This act, signed by President Bush in 1991, required the Secretary of Transportation to develop regulations for testing for alcohol and controlled substances for persons in safety-sensitive positions, including motor carriers. School bus drivers are required to submit to controlled-substance testing.
Family and Medical Leave Act of 1993	President Clinton signed this legislation in 1993. The primary purpose of the act is to provide eligible employees with a right to 12 weeks of unpaid leave per year for the birth and initial care of a child. An employee may also be eligible for leave for illness or to care for an ill spouse, child, or parent.

recommendation, great care should be taken to inform the candidate that final approval is required by the board.

Strong human relations skills are required to notify unsuccessful candidates that a position has been filled. Notice should be as timely as possible and appreciation expressed to the candidate for the time, money, and energy expended in the interview process. Often the applicant requests feedback regarding his or her paperwork, interview techniques, and the like. Most personnel officers regard such requests as mentoring opportunities and, although respecting the confidentiality of the selection process, offer information that might be helpful to the candidate at another time.

SUMMARY

Once the recruitment process has been completed, the school district faces the task of selecting the most qualified candidates for the vacancy. Even though recruitment and selection of personnel are of vital importance to a school or district, and even though errors are costly in time and money, most districts commit few resources to the process.

This chapter contained a review of the steps in the selection process:

Initial screening	Ordinarily, the personnel officer has responsibility for the initial screening process, although good practice suggests that the supervisor of the vacant position independently screen the applicants. This step reduces risk of prematurely eliminating a viable candidate.
Letters of recommendation	Although letters of recommendation have several limitations, they are widely used in the screening process and are, in the hands of a trained supervisor or personnel director, a valuable tool. Letters of recommendation are particularly useful in reviewing the training and ability of first-year teachers.
Transcripts and credentials	Evaluation of credentials is a highly technical field in most states. Personnel staff need to keep current on state credential requirements. Few errors are more devastating than to employ a teacher who does not meet state requirements for a credential. Transcripts should be reviewed in light of the grade level and subject that the applicant will be teaching. As with most selection tools, transcripts are more useful for screening out the clearly inferior candidate than for selecting the superior applicant.

Telephone reference checks	Most personnel officers find the telephone reference check an invaluable part of the screening process. This step is particularly effective for the personnel director who has a strong network of professionals whom he or she knows personally. The telephone conversation often produces greater candor than written references.
Tests	Although employment tests are customary in private industry and in the initial screening of classified applicants, they are not widely used in the employment of teachers. This fact is due, in part, to the requirement by most states that a teacher applicant complete a battery of examinations to qualify for a teaching credential.
The interview	Safeguards ensure that interviews are as objective as possible and elicit information that truly measures the potential success of the candidate.
Notifying the candidates	Both successful and unsuccessful candidates should be notified properly; expediency in notifying the finalist is especially important. Unsuccessful candidates must also be treated with proper respect and courtesy.

Selecting individuals who will be successful and will remain with the school district for a reasonable amount of time is an extremely important personnel function. Careful selection of staff is necessary to offer a quality instructional program for students. If the selection task is poorly accomplished, its results inevitably lead to major negative impact on a district.

KEY TERMS

1. assessment center
2. CBEST
3. cut-off score
4. face-to-face interview
5. holes in experience
6. initial screening
7. letters of recommendation

8. NTE
9. Privacy Act of 1974
10. red flag
11. team approach
12. telephone reference check
13. transcript

QUESTIONS AND ACTIVITIES

1. School districts spend less money for the selection of employees than does private industry. Why is this the case? Would spending additional funds on selection of personnel enable a district to employ better employees? Support your answer with specific examples.

2. Initial screening of employee candidates is an important function of the personnel officer. Discuss three items that, at the initial screening, may eliminate candidates from further consideration for employment.

3. Face-to-face interviewing is widely used in the employment of teachers. What are the advantages and disadvantages of this process?

4. Federal law has established several requirements for selection of personnel. Discuss three of these requirements and the reason for the federal law in each case.

5. Schedule an appointment with the personnel director in your school district and ask him or her to review the initial application process in the district.

6. Review several letters of recommendation for a certificated position and a classified position. Note how the letters could have been improved.

7. With permission of the personnel director, review the transcripts of several candidates for a teaching position. Do you see a correlation between the candidates' qualifications as noted in the letters of recommendation and their grades on the transcript?

8. In your interview with the personnel director, ask him or her whether telephone reference checks are used. What value does he or she place on this technique?

9. In a small group, debate the merit of giving a test to prospective classified and credentialed employees.

10. Discuss the major components of a successful interview and pitfalls to be avoided.

Chapter 5

Evaluation of Personnel

INTRODUCTION

However critical to ensuring an effective staff, recruitment and selection are only brief processes at the beginning of an employee's career in a district. Supervision and evaluation of that employee, on the other hand, continue for years, perhaps decades. If staff evaluation has potential to recognize excellence, support professional development, and enhance student learning throughout all those years, then surely it ranks among the most important administrative responsibilities—and its management among the most important roles of the chief personnel officer. Nevertheless, perhaps because it does continue year after year, personnel evaluation is frequently shunted aside in favor of more urgent demands (Natriello, Ellett, & Garland, as cited in Glickman, 1990).

Is evaluation of classified and certificated staff unavoidably routine, unworthy of high priority on the list of administrative duties? Or is it, contrariwise, critical to retention, motivation, and professional growth of a district's employees? We believe the latter and hope, through the contents of this chapter, to convince you that supervision and evaluation can yield these positive results.

PURPOSES OF EVALUATION

The supposed purpose of employee evaluation is surely to improve, or at least maintain, job performance. Within this overall purpose, the following items represent a standard list of the functions of teacher evaluation:

- to improve teaching

- to reward superior performance

- to guide professional development

- to protect students from incompetence and teachers from unprofessional administrators

- to validate the district's selection procedures

- to supply a permanent record for placement, promotion, or termination (Bolton, as cited in McGreal, 1983).

Perhaps these purposes seem self-evident. However, such a list fits an authoritarian approach to evaluation. It gives little, if any, attention to the employee as problem-solver, as independent thinker, as (to borrow Maslow's term) self-actualized person. Should those qualities play into supervision and evaluation?

To focus on teachers for the moment, Glickman (1990) quotes research showing that most teachers exhibit moderate to low stages of ego, conceptual, and moral development; that they are concrete and conformist, rather than abstract and autonomous. Yet high-stage teachers have been shown to ask better questions, to plan better for student needs, to use a wider variety of instructional strategies, and so on.

How, then, might the standard purposes listed above, and the processes of supervision and evaluation, be modified or expanded to support teachers in reaching those higher stages? To bring more teachers—and other staff members—to the level of reflection-in-action described by Donald Schön (1989) as characteristic of the best practitioners in every profession? To empower staff to participate in important decisions about the school?

This dilemma, how to harmonize evaluation and empowerment, should remain in the reader's mind throughout this chapter. It will not be resolved here, for as a profession we still seek the solution—or solu*tions*. Yet each administrator must work out a provisional framework for joining these two issues, for they reflect two powerful emphases in education. That is to say, personnel evaluation is an important component of accountability; and empowerment, an important component of achievement.

SUPERVISION VS. EVALUATION

Before proceeding to survey criteria and procedures for staff evaluation, let us consider the relationship between supervision and evaluation. Supervision may be equated to formative evaluation, an ongoing process intended to keep a program or an employee on track. Evaluation, on the other hand, is summative evaluation, a final, formalized judgement to guide decisions on continuing, modifying, or abandoning a course of action. Some writers, McGreal (1983) among them, argue that if supervision is to be a positive experience, it must be sharply divided from evaluation. The usual premise is that evaluation is perceived so negatively and causes so much anxiety that supervision must be seen as a wholly separate process, lest it fail to support or improve employee performance.

Another approach, typified by Daresh (1989), views supervision as a continuous process in which evaluation—whether diagnostic, formative, or summative—is but one step. In other words, if the supervisory relationship is an ongoing dialogue between employee and supervisor, then the formal evaluation simply dips into that dynamic relationship at a moment in time to note progress and identify future directions. Thus, instead of separating supervision to protect it from the tension associated with evaluation, an administrator might create a positive ambience for supervision and extend that feeling tone to evaluation. While admittedly difficult, this approach is realistic in recognizing that the people who supervise most of the staff in a district, the site administrators, are the same people who write formal evaluations. This identity of supervisor and evaluator makes it virtually impossible to split the two processes. Whether to divide them, however, is a decision each district, or at least each supervisor, must make.

Before leaving this topic, we draw attention to a recent approach to personnel development and integration that integrates feedback with summative evaluation. Called "dynamic assessment," this process is currently discussed on the Internet in business settings. The same phrase, however, is currently being introduced in special education, again to join formative with summative evaluation (Jensen, Robinson-Zañartu, & Jensen; 1992-2000; Swanson & Lussier, 2001). The Asian Development Bank Institute has posted on the Internet a document entitled *Actionable Learning* (Morrison, 2001), in which a chapter is devoted to dynamic assessment. In comparing dynamic with static assessment, Morrison describes assessment as a learning process involving particular individuals in a specific context or community. He calls for an emphasis on process rather than product in a dynamic and unpredictable approach that encourages the evaluatee to "invent new knowledge." Perhaps this approach could be useful in expanding human capital in school systems.

LEGAL REQUIREMENTS: THE EVALUATION

Personnel evaluation in California is directed in part by law. As stipulated in the Rodda Act, procedures for evaluation are subject to collective bargaining (Govt. Code #3543.2), but not the standards or criteria by which employee effectiveness is judged. The Education Code adds no guidance with respect to classified employees, other than to underscore due process rights in case of disciplinary action or dismissal (Ed. Code #45113-#45116). With respect to teachers, however, California law sets requirements for both procedures and standards (Ed. Code #44660-44665).

The Education Code requires that each school district establish a system of evaluation and assessment (Ed. Code #44660). Probationary certificated employees must be evaluated at least once each year; permanent teachers, at least every other year. Results of Peer Assistance and Review are to be made available to the certificated employee. Noninstructional certificated employees are also to be evaluated.

All evaluations, positive or negative, must be provided to teachers at least 30 days prior to the last day of the school year and reviewed in a meeting between the employee and the evaluator before school dismisses for the summer. For 12-month employees, the written evaluation is to be delivered by June 30 and the meeting held before July 30. A certificated employee must be permitted to prepare a written response to be attached to his or her evaluation in the personnel file (Ed. Code #44663).

Should a permanent teacher need to improve, the evaluation must contain recommendations. Should the teacher be rated as unsatisfactory, not only must written notice and recommendations be provided, but the teacher must be rated at least once each year until satisfactory performance is achieved. (Of course, if an administrator anticipates building a file to support dismissal, evaluative documents are written even more often.) The teacher may be required to participate in particular activities designed to remediate problem areas (Ed. Code #44664).

The law is also specific as to bases for assessing teacher competence. Although a governing board may develop additional guidelines or criteria, certificated employees are to be evaluated with respect at least to:

- progress of students toward established standards of pupil achievement

- instructional techniques and strategies

- adherence to curricular objectives

- establishment and maintenance of a suitable learning environment (Ed. Code #44662).

To support these requirements, district boards must establish standards of expected pupil achievement at each grade level in each area of study.

Note that despite the focus on student achievement, norm-referenced tests are specifically *excluded* as tools for teacher evaluation (Ed. Code #44662). Might this legislation be headed for amendment? Already, in connection with the Public Schools Accountability Act of 1999 (PSAA, Ed. Code #52050-52058), teachers have received cash bonuses up to $25,000 each as a result of rises in the Academic Performance Index (API), which initially was calculated only on the basis of the SAT-9 norm-referenced test. Surely this is a form of teacher evaluation, albeit in a positive direction. Jason Millman of Cornell

University has edited a book entitled *Grading Teachers, Grading Schools* (1997), suggesting that teacher effectiveness can and perhaps should be evaluated through student learning. The book examines the pros and cons of programs in Oregon, Dallas, Tennessee, and Kentucky—programs that supplied precedents for California's high-stakes testing program.

The stakes are indeed high! Site principals and possibly other certificated employees of an "underperforming school" are to be reassigned if performance targets on the API are not met within 24 months. A principal would not be reassigned by the district board, but by the State Superintendent of Public Instruction. Such action would be subsequent to a public hearing in the school district to ascertain whether or not the principal had "authority to take specific enumerated actions that would have helped the school meet its performance goals" and failed to take those actions (Ed. Code #52055.5(c)).

EVALUATION PROCEDURES

Turning now to practice within the legal constraints, let us consider another knotty issue: treating everyone alike versus responding to the differences in employees and their performance. The primary purpose of personnel evaluation is to support successful employees with encouragement, recognition, and perhaps ideas for enhanced performance that are viewed by the employee as evidence of a shared role in seeking constant improvement. However, the most distressing supervisory situations involve an employee whose performance is unsatisfactory.

Consider first, then, the example of a permanent employee whose performance is clearly unsatisfactory and—despite well-defined expectations, assistance, and, finally, repeated warnings—continues to perform poorly. Bridges (1992) points out "the inclination of administrators to tolerate and protect, rather than confront" such an employee, and cites reasons why supervisors often settle for such a situation. He also reviews the strategies for "induced exits" that lead to employee resignation. However, since toleration means living with unacceptable performance and inducing an exit does not always work, eventually an administrator faces the task of, first, trying to "salvage" the employee, and failing that, preparing a case for dismissal on grounds of incompetence. Procedures will be much alike for all employees in that situation (Bridges & Groves, 1984; Ruud & Woodford, 1984). The supervisor builds a file of notes, memos, and other evidence to document the employee's unsatisfactory performance. The chief personnel officer (or in some districts, another central office administrator) serves as consultant, guide, and perhaps a second observer as the employee's immediate supervisor moves through the process. In this situation, procedures are determined by the administration, although constrained by law and the negotiated employee agreement.

Critical to success in dismissing an incompetent employee is that the individual be judged against a set of relevant, unambiguous criteria that are applied fairly to all persons holding that position. Dismissal for incompetence is, however, the exception rather than the rule. Job performance of most employees reaches a minimal level such that dismissal is not an issue. Moreover,

> the protections provided by judicial precedent, legislative mandate, statutory requirements, and contractual language—when combined with the political implications of dismissal, the strength of unions, and the expensive and time-consuming nature of termination proceedings—make the actual application of sanctions . . . very rare (McGreal, 1983).

What, then, about that vast majority of staff members whose competence ranges from marginal to superb? While fairness demands consistent evaluation criteria for all workers in the same classification, must procedures also be uniform?

As already mentioned, procedures—as opposed to standards—for evaluating California school employees, certificated and classified alike, are subject to collective bargaining. At the negotiations table employee representatives have sought uniformity in treatment of employees, a preference from which evaluation procedures are not excepted. Thus, in most districts any variations in the process of evaluation, whatever their basis, require discussion with the union.

Nevertheless, some writers argue that differentiated approaches hold far greater promise for improvement than uniform, lockstep procedures. Moreover, they believe that matching evaluation procedures to employee characteristics promises to evoke that high-stage, self-actualized individual who will reflect on his or her professional performance and independently seek means of betterment. To exemplify the principle of adapting evaluation to employees, we now describe briefly three approaches to teacher evaluation: clinical supervision, developmental supervision, and differentiated supervision.

First, clinical supervision. Let us begin by pointing out that, as most often used in California, the phrase "clinical supervision" actually combines two models: "clinical teaching" as formulated by Madeline Hunter in her work at the University of California at Los Angeles (Hunter, 1967-71) and "clinical supervision" as first developed at Harvard University (Goldhammer, 1969; Cogan, 1973). Since Hunter's model originally dealt only with teaching, and specifically, practices to be assessed, we now focus on the Cogan-Goldhammer definition. In this latter formulation, clinical supervision describes the manner in which supervisors would best observe classroom interaction and counsel a teacher.

As described by Goldhammer (1969) and Cogan (1973), the administrator first meets with the teacher to inquire about the objectives of the lesson to be observed and the areas, if any, in which the teacher particularly desires feedback, the first point of adaptation to the teacher. During the observation, the administrator writes an extensive "anecdotal record," jotting down what the teacher and the students say and do. After analyzing the anecdotal record, the supervisor sets one or two objectives for the follow-up conference. A clinical conference typically begins with an opportunity for the teacher to comment about the lesson. Another adaptation to the teacher, this discussion may give the supervisor new insights into the lesson, even altering the judgements reached from the observation. Next, the supervisor attempts to lead the teacher through the same analysis to the same conclusions the supervisor had already reached. Depending upon the supervisor's assessment of the lesson and its relationship to previous observations and plans, the supervisor may be either minimally or strongly directive and followup agreements either more or less specific. Thus, the administrator controls the clinical supervision process, even though strategies for the conference —actually, strategies for teaching the teacher—are selected with consideration to the teacher's needs and preferences.

Glickman (1990) believes that clinical supervision, although a sound process, is but one mode of teacher supervision. He assumes that "supervision, to be effective, must be a function that responds to the developmental stage [and] adult life transitions of teachers." Thus, he argues for "developmental supervision." He proposes that supervision practices should move from directive through collaborative to nondirective. In Glickman's model an administrator selects a level between directive and nondirective that matches the teacher's development and life stage, then strives to support the teacher in growing toward greater independence and self-direction.

Glatthorn (1984) is unconvinced that teachers' developmental levels can be simply and appropriately assessed or that supervisors have time to adapt evaluation to each unique teacher. Therefore, he proposes "differentiated supervision." Like Glickman, Glatthorn describes models that range from directive to nondirective. He endorses a refinement of clinical supervision that he calls "learning-centered supervision." He calls for cooperative professional development and self-directed development and describes a drop-in style labeled "administrative monitoring." However, Glatthorn departs sharply from Glickman in proposing that teachers themselves choose the model under which they are to be supervised. Safeguards are two:

- that "no supervision" is not an option, and

- that the supervisor may veto the teacher's choice.

Glatthorn acknowledged that he had "no solid evidence that the differentiated approach will result in improved teaching." He recognized that his proposal might not work in all schools, and might not be appropriate year in and year out, yet he argues that differentiated supervision frees administrators and teachers of time demands and paperwork and offers professional choice to teachers.

In comparing these three procedural approaches to employee evaluation—for the same concepts are adaptable to all personnel, classified as well as certificated—note that they vary along two dimensions. One is consistency: the degree to which procedures vary from uniform (the same for all employees) to adapted (uniquely suited to each employee). The second is direction: the degree to which procedures are selected and implemented by administrators or by employees themselves. These dimensions may be symbolized on a coordinate plane, as shown in Figure 1.

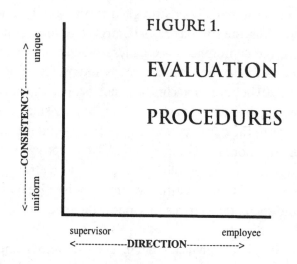

FIGURE 1.

EVALUATION

PROCEDURES

Evaluation procedures range from the most directive (those in the lower left quadrant of the above diagram), in which an emplo*yer* dictates uniform standards for all employees in the same job classification, to the least directive (those in the upper right quadrant of the diagram), in which an emplo*yee* sets his or her own goals unique to his or her own situation. Most evaluation procedures fall somewhere between these two extremes.

EVALUATION STANDARDS

Standards or criteria for employee evaluation, too, may be directed by the supervisor or employee or may be developed collaboratively, as just discussed for procedures. A second important dimension of standards is the focus of the goals, which may relate to process (for example, teaching strategies, greeting the public, or planning school lunch menus) or product (for example, student learning, parents' sense of community with the school, or nutritional value of cafeteria meals).

Like procedures, standards for personnel evaluation may be dictated by the organization or immediate supervisor, developed by the employee, or more likely, worked out cooperatively. Standards, however, may focus on process (how the task is done) or on product (what the outcome looks like). In most cases, however, at least some attention is given to both (see Figure 2).

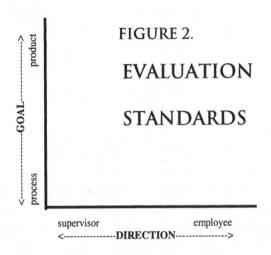

FIGURE 2.

EVALUATION

STANDARDS

Among teachers, the folklore of teacher evaluation bemoans the administrator who visits classrooms only occasionally and briefly—and always during a test or silent reading or writing period—and judges teachers primarily by the design of their bulletin boards. Although one can, in fact, draw valid inferences from student work and other material on display, teachers and all employees deserve recognition of the breadth and depth of their work that goes well beyond materials visible on the walls of a classroom. Thus, evaluation standards should touch on all significant aspects of the job. Moreover, simple justice demands that both employees and supervisors understand the criteria for employee evaluation and that this understanding precede the evaluation process.

Hunter's "clinical" or "targeted teaching," just noted as having been formulated before the "clinical supervision" procedures to which it became conjoined, provides one set of standards for the teaching act. These standards are drawn from educational psychology in the behaviorist school, broadly construed, and apply theories of motivation, reinforcement, retention, accelerated learning, and transfer (Hunter, 1967-71) to the classroom.

The "clinical teaching lesson plan," varying from five to eight steps in its several formulations, is sometimes viewed as synonymous with clinical teaching. As a consequence, Hunter's work has been widely criticized. However, the lesson plan is only a model to assist teachers in incorporating several basic principles into their teaching; like all models, it simplifies, even oversimplified, the material from which it is drawn. It is best examined after teachers or supervisors have worked through the more complex (and real-life) principles. For example, the principles that facilitate transfer of learning to new situations call upon a teacher to ensure mastery of the prior learning, emphasize similarities of the new learning to the old, promote associations between the two, and help students identify critical attributes that differentiate one learning or one situation from another.

Standards are also set by local school districts, sometimes in the form of a job description. Thus, the job description developed for recruitment (see Chapter 3), with its statement of job responsibilities, serves multiple purposes, including criteria for personnel evaluation. This function underscores the importance of reviewing job descriptions from time to time to ensure that they remain current. The job description is a managerial tool; therefore, its list of responsibilities is externally imposed on the employee. However, since they affect working conditions, revisions in job descriptions must, under California law, be reviewed with the union whose employees are affected.

Imposed evaluation criteria may also take the form of performance standards, that is, "levels of performance identified as corresponding to predesignated levels of effectiveness" (Bernardin & Beatty, 1984; Beatty, Baird, & Schneier, 1995). Measurement of performance standards calls for "assigning a numerical value to performance in terms of a criterion of effectiveness such as quantity, quality, timeliness, and so on." Although performance standards are dictated in the sense that, once developed, they are applied uniformly to all personnel within a job class, employee representatives may help write and field-test the standards before they are put into use.

At the other end of the "direction" spectrum, each individual employee may set standards. The original Stull Bill for teacher evaluation in California required, as a significant part of the process, that teachers set objectives for pupil learning. Teachers became responsible to show evidence that the objectives were achieved. Unfortunately, this process often becomes perfunctory, and the goals so certain of accomplishment as to be meaningless. The ultimate responsibility for this weakening of the evaluation process must rest with administrators, since they, after all, must agree to the objectives. For this reason, Stull Bill objectives are not a pure example of self-selected standards any more than job specifications are a pure example of administratively imposed criteria.

Ideally, the push for excellence in a school or district is so strong that all employees take pride in stretching themselves a bit by setting challenging, yet reachable, goals for each new evaluation cycle. The Ontario-Montclair School District [1999] has posted sample objectives as part of its handbook for new teachers. One of these reads as follows:

> During the 1999-00 school year, a positive learning environment will be established. This will be accomplished by (1) school and classroom discipline plans are posted and consistently followed, (2) room is neat and orderly, (3) students are on-task, (4) seatwork is meaningful and promotes independence, and (5) bulletin boards reflect students' work and are related to areas of the curriculum. This will be measured by evaluator observation and teacher self-evaluation.

Goals, as just observed, may deal either with outcomes, that is, employee products and services or student learning and development, or with processes intended to yield the desired outcomes. A classroom observation shows how a lesson is taught (process); the observer may even gather evidence of student attention and motivation (product for the teacher, process for the students), but actual student learning (product) is difficult to assess within a single observation. A maintenance person or groundskeeper may be observed leaving and returning to the central shop and may check off sites that have been visited (process), but a supervisor must invest additional time to visit schools or departments to check the condition of the equipment or facilities that have been serviced (product).

Products, or outcomes, seem more important than processes, so why not focus on the products and ignore the processes? In some circumstances that might be appropriate. However, certain products (such as student learning and properly repaired equipment) are so complex, inaccessible, or delayed that processes are measured in lieu of products. And sometimes processes are important in themselves. For example, a supervisor would not be pleased to discover that student writing improved (product) because an anxious teacher had allowed students to copy from library books (process) or that students learned their multiplication tables (product) only because a teacher had threatened them with a stool and dunce cap (process). Neither would a supervisor be satisfied with a custodian who cuts in half the time needed to clean bathrooms, but does so by failing to clean and disinfect the commodes. Good processes create—and poor processes destroy—positive school climate, high staff and pupil morale and motivation, and enthusiastic parent support. Thus, both processes and products deserve consideration in an evaluation scheme.

Before leaving evaluation standards, we must note that the attention typically given to teacher evaluation, and secondarily to administrator evaluation, far outweighs that given to evaluation of support and classified staff. Evaluation of these individuals is complicated by the reality that the supervisor may not have had experience or training in the employee's specialty. One recommended procedure for evaluating professional support personnel calls for collecting multifaceted data based on standards developed jointly by employer and employee (Helm, 1994). First, the needs of the system are defined from the perspective of the institution, then the duties of the position (as opposed to personal traits) are listed by the evaluator and evaluatee jointly, next performance indicators are agreed upon, and finally, performance standards are stated in the form of behavioral objectives. These objectives then become the basis for a continuous cycle of documenting performance, conferencing, and maintaining or improving the service. Each objective contains the measurement and criterion for success. This system, then, combines procedure (the conference cycle) and standards as expressed in behavioral objectives. A similar model, performance-based developmental evaluation (PBDE) has been described by Valentine (1992) and extended to special education teachers, instructional materials specialists, school counselors, coaches, sponsors of co-curricular activities, and paraprofessionals. We turn now to a closer examination of evaluation measures.

EVALUATION MEASURES

Like evaluation standards, evaluation measures may be applied to processes or products. And as already suggested, measures may gather and make judgements based on qualitative or quantitative information. This relationship is illustrated in Figure 3.

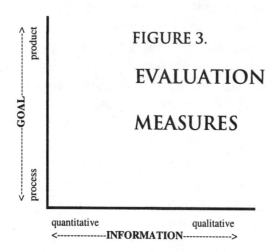

FIGURE 3.

EVALUATION

MEASURES

What instruments or procedures yield this information?

Consider first the anecdotal record, mentioned earlier. A supervisor observes an employee at work, perhaps a teacher giving a lesson or a kitchen worker serving lunch, notes down everything seen and heard, and subsequently analyzes the record against criteria that describe the activities and interactions of an effective teacher or kitchen worker. With the anecdotal record, information is gathered about a process and analyzed qualitatively. Such an instrument may also facilitate mutual analysis by employee and supervisor, thus encouraging the thought processes characteristic of Schön's reflective practitioner (1989).

If quantitative information is desired, a rating, perhaps on a Likert, scale can turn qualitative findings into numbers. For this purpose, a set of numbers from, say, 1 to 6 with one extreme labeled "high" and the other "low" is printed next to each criterion. The supervisor circles one number on each line, and *voilà!*—a quantitative measure. However, an important caution must be stated at this point, for however objective such numbers may appear, simply because they *are* numbers, rating scales capture judgements; they are subjective. Still, they may prove helpful because the words used to communicate an evaluative judgement sometimes suggest a more negative or positive meaning than was intended. For instance, a supervisor might use the word "satisfactory" in dealing with two different employees, yet circle "4" on a 6-point scale in one instance and "6" in another; the number clarifies the communication.

Numbers may also be gathered directly during an observation. Rather than to write an anecdotal record, an observer might tally the number of lunches served in a given period of time, or the number of servings of mashed potatoes dished up from each container. An observer might count the number of questions posed by a teacher in half an hour, the seconds of "wait time" before the next question is asked, or the number of times each student is called upon. Such quantitative measures of process might seem better suited to jobs like custodian or order clerk than to responsibilities like those of teachers, for whom qualitative standards seem more appropriate.

Nevertheless, numbers, although they seem mechanical and reductionist, are sometimes useful. For example, even an experienced master teacher may be astounded to discover that he calls on certain students far more frequently than others, and that the pattern of those called upon suggests that, after glancing down to consult the questions prepared in advance, the teacher's eyes trace a consistent path across the classroom, perhaps an arc from front left to back right. Thus, data can create cognitive dissonance, a conflict between a person's suppositions and his or her real-life experience. Reflection on these conflicts often leads to significant change.

Information may be gathered in many ways and from many sources. Some data are routinely available: attendance records, discipline referrals, grade-point averages, retention practices, and equipment inventories. Performance appraisal systems call for statistically valid and reliable instruments, among them the weighted checklist; summated scale; critical incident; behaviorally-anchored, mixed-standard, and forced-choice rating scales; distributional measurement model; personnel comparison system; and management-by-objectives appraisal instrument (Bernardin & Beatty, 1984; Beatty, Baird, & Schneier, 1995). At a less technical level, some documents easily collected include lesson plans, grade books, teacher-made materials and tests, and student work. A supervisor can inspect restrooms and classrooms, sample the cafeteria lunch, or trace selected purchase orders from the moment they are initiated to the time the items are received. Employees may be encouraged, even required, to gather feedback from peers, subordinates, students, parents, and community members—as appropriate to their responsibilities. Cangelosi (1991) provides a compendium of evaluation instruments.

How good are evaluation measures? After reviewing teacher competency tests, performance ratings, and measures of teaching outcomes, Medley (1994) concluded that "none of them is working satisfactorily at present." The primary limitation, he concluded, was that these approaches "measure academic knowledge rather than functional knowledge." Thus, a supervisor does well to remember that all the evaluation measures currently in use have their limitations. Above all, the wise supervisor encourages staff as they consider and analyze their own effectiveness and seek their own paths to improvement.

California New Teacher Project (CNTP) Instruments *Replaced by BTSA*

The California New Teacher Project, funded by the state from 1988 to 1992, undertook to develop both standards and evaluation measures that would be particularly helpful in developing and assessing new teachers. Twelve evaluation instruments were pilot-tested with beginning teachers. As reported by Long and Stansbury (1994) in an article in *Phi Delta Kappan*, these instruments were of seven types:

- high-inference classroom observations

- semi-structured interviews

- structured simulation tasks

- performance-based assessment center exercises

- videotaped teaching episodes

- an innovative multiple-choice examination

- portfolios.

The high-inference classroom observation begins with a script much like the anecdotal record mentioned earlier in this chapter. A comprehensive script requires that the observer focus entirely on events as they transpire in the classroom, setting aside judgement until the teaching sequence has been completed.

A semi-structured interview (structured questions with follow-up questions to be used at the interviewer's discretion) asks teachers to talk their way through such skills as unit and lesson planning and assessing student performance. These tasks are specific to a content area; thus, they inevitably call upon knowledge of that content.

The semi-structured tasks involve writing in response to simulated classroom problems. Like the interviews, they look for both content knowledge and pedagogical skills.

Similar types of questions and tasks are presented in assessment center exercises. An added dimension in this environment is opportunity for teachers to work cooperatively.

In another type of instrument, videotaped teaching episodes are presented to teachers. Afterwards teachers respond orally or, more often, in writing to questions that probe their insights into the lesson.

Finally, the innovative multiple-choice examination used in the CNTP had two characteristics. First, questions were always based on a description of a classroom situation, and second, some items involved reading of such materials as lesson plans, test reports, and student worksheets. A seventh format, the portfolio, is discussed in greater detail below.

In all these assessment types, valid and reliable modes of scoring were an important part of the investigation. Scoring systems were developed, sometimes holistic, but more often based on ratings of particular knowledge or skills or comparing teachers' responses against a preestablished list of acceptable responses. The investigators concluded that no single assessment measure is universally appropriate, but that different instruments, and adaptations of those instruments, suit different situations. After the California legislature received reports on the California New Teacher Project, it pursued similar outcomes in the Beginning Teacher Support and Assessment Program, first at the state level and then in each district.

Teacher Portfolios

To identify advantages and disadvantages of performance-based assessments, we now examine portfolios in greater depth. Portfolios have been designed to assess teacher performance across all levels, preschool to university, and in many content areas. Wheeler (1993) lists items that might be included in a portfolio. Her list is based on Scriven's five duties-based domains: knowledge of subject matter, instructional skills, assessment skills, professionalism, and other services to the school. Examples of items to be included range from unit plans to videos of the teacher giving a lesson, from a first aid training certificate to a log of times the teacher has assisted other teachers.

The portfolio in the California New Teacher Project was more limited in scope (Tierney, Long, Quellmalz, Stansbury, & Estes, 1992). Beginning high school English teachers submitted the following:

- an outline of a unit plan

- a weekly log of events, anecdotes, observations, and questions

- a compilation of materials and assignments given to students

- samples of student work with the teacher's responses

- written evaluations from students

- an essay in which the teacher reflected upon the unit taught.

Sixteen teachers participated in the study. Their portfolios were assembled over a three-month period, then mailed in for scoring. Participating teachers provided their perceptions of the portfolio process and of the value of the feedback they received.

This pilot illustrates some of the difficulties associated with performance-based assessment in general. First, **costs**. The contents, standards, and scoring rubric had to be developed. Development and field-testing cost more than $57,000. These costs, of course, would not be repeated for future administrations, except to the extent that modifications might prove necessary.

Then each teacher spent one to two hours weekly over a three-month period assembling the portfolio. No costs were assigned to this stage.

Next came the scoring process. The scorers spent a half day in training, but as a result of their experience, a two-day training was recommended. Training was estimated at $160 per day per scorer. This covers the scorer's reimbursement only, not the salary of the trainer, cost of materials, or transportation.

A portfolio was scored by two readers, each spending an hour to an hour and a half per portfolio. This cost, assuming a daily rate of $160 per scorer and $210 for a lead scorer, is estimated at $86.50 per portfolio.

Then, **reliability**. Six areas were rated on a four-point scale. Overall, there were 96 ratings (six categories for 16 portfolios). Of these, 49 were in exact agreement, 36 differed by one point, and 10 differed by two points. Five others were considered not able to be rated by one scorer, but were scored by the other. No single area exceeded 10 exact agreements on the 16 portfolios. Several recommendations were made to improve the convenience and reliability of the process.

Finally, **validity**. Gellman (1992) points out that portfolio assessment gathers a broader and more representative sample of teacher performance than, for example, a classroom observation. However, that fact alone is no guarantee of validity. So, one might establish concurrent validity by correlating portfolio scores with the results of simulation task assessments. Or one could establish predictive validity by comparing portfolios used in personnel selection with subsequent evaluations by principals or other supervisors. Such steps *can* be taken. The question is, are they? And are they feasible?

What, then, are the advantages and disadvantages of portfolio evaluation? Some advantages of a teacher portfolio lie outside the realm of teacher evaluation. For instance, it may be true that portfolios document a teacher's growth over time. Portfolios may encourage and facilitate reflective self-analysis. A portfolio may be useful to a teacher seeking employment or promotion. However, these advantages should be considered separately from the issue of portfolios as a tool for teacher assessment (Gellman, 1992).

With respect specifically to teacher evaluation, a portfolio has the advantages of greater breadth of material, greater depth in selected areas, relevance to the job, complexity that more closely matches the complexity of teaching itself, and support for reflective self-analysis and (one hopes) improvement. Its disadvantages include the demand on teacher time, complexity of scoring, difficulties in establishing validity and reliability, and cost. As Wheeler (1993) remarks, "simply collecting materials for a portfolio is of little value; the value lies in the use of the portfolio with other assessment, development, and evaluation processes." She further urges that schools and districts proceed with caution, first using portfolios for teacher development, then perhaps building to portfolios as an approach to performance evaluation.

THE WRITTEN EVALUATION

Eventually, the formal evaluation must be reduced to writing. Designing these forms is typically the responsibility of the chief personnel officer. However, since everything but the standards embodied in them constitute procedures, the forms are usually regarded as negotiable. Classified employees are most often evaluated on a simple form or checklist, rarely exceeding two pages in length. Forms for teachers are more complex, generally covering student objectives, classroom observations, and adjunct duties.

A few circles or numbers are not much to offer an employee as a reward for a year or two of work. Consequently, evaluation forms often include a narrative section. If they do not, supervisors might consider adding at least a paragraph or two of comment. Often, supervisors write narrative portions in the third person ("he/she"), as if they were reporting their evaluation to a third person. In fact, however, these forms are rarely read by a third party (unless it is the supervisor's own supervisor), so that the second person ("you") may be more effective, especially in the usual case of a document intended to support and encourage the staff member.

Already noted is the legal requirement for specificity in the case of employees, especially teachers, who are required to improve their job performance. However, specific examples of the behaviors one wants to reinforce also reduce likelihood of misunderstanding and increase probability of maintaining that behavior. Examples:

Less effective: You do a good job of motivating students.

More effective: You use sound strategies for motivating students toward improvement, among them your display of "This Week's Best Writing" coupled with the specific suggestions offered to help students achieve that honor (e.g., "Next time, try for adjectives that appeal to all five senses!").

Less effective: You are a positive force for good morale among staff, parents and students.

More effective: Your warm smile, the care you take to address every
                    person by name, and your patience with those whose
                    English is not fluent make you a positive force for good
                    morale among staff, parents, and students.

ABOUT THE SUPERVISOR

This chapter has described many choices in evaluation. The chief personnel officer is responsible for informing administrators of the choices available within constraints of law and the district's negotiated contract with each employee group. The chief personnel officer is also responsible for training supervisors in the procedures and standards to be used, the forms to be completed, and the skills to be developed.

As to skills and qualities, supervisors of certificated staff are expected to be masters of instructional strategies and classroom management as well as caring individuals—in other words, capable mentors. As to curriculum content, especially at the secondary level, and classified staff responsibilities, no one supervisor can possibly know them all; an administrator may need at times to call on other supervisory personnel for assistance. A joint publication of the National Education Association and three administrator associations lists these attributes of a person who observes and evaluates teachers: credibility, persuasiveness, patience, trustworthiness, a track record of successful suggestions, and ability and willingness to model the desired behavior or skill (Duke & Stiggins, 1986). The same list applies equally to supervisors of those in the classified service.

Yet, however capable the supervisors and however clear and consistent the evaluation system, human factors may still interfere with fair, humane evaluation. With the thought that to know the pitfalls is to have a tool for avoiding them, we draw the following obstacles to accuracy in personnel evaluation from Bernardin & Beatty (1984), who in turn synthesized them from several researchers. Although the authors focused on raters using performance appraisal systems, we believe that in any personnel evaluation:

- The evaluator may have too limited a sample of the employee's behavior.

- The evaluator may be unduly influenced either by a general impression of the employee or by a single characteristic or incident.

- The criteria may be so abstract or complex that the evaluator has difficulty relating them to on-the-job performance.

- The evaluator may have insufficient knowledge of, experience with, or motivation to use the system.

- The evaluator may selectively remember only the evidence that confirms an early impression.

- The evaluator may rely too heavily on a pre-existing prototype of a successful employee in the job classification.

- The evaluator may be influenced by a pre-existing stereotype related to the gender, ethnicity, age, attractiveness, or other personal characteristic of the employee.

- Evaluators may vary in the extent to which they attribute particular outcomes to the situation, environment, or institution—or to the employee. In particular, evaluators who have had experience in the particular position are more likely to attribute problems to external factors than to the employee.

- Evaluators may be influenced by their own emotional responses to the employee or the situation.

- Evaluators may be influenced by consequences they anticipate for themselves as a result of the evaluation.

- An evaluator may be influenced by the purpose of the evaluation, for example, assessment versus promotion.

To reduce inconsistencies due to these items, Bernardin and Beatty recommend training designed to enhance evaluators' observational and categorization skills. Such training would fall within the purview of the chief personnel officer of the district.

SUMMARY

This chapter has reviewed the purposes of personnel evaluation in schools and school districts, chief among which must certainly be the improvement of teaching and learning. Within the restrictions imposed by California law and negotiated agreements with employee organizations, choices are possible and, indeed, encouraged by many writers. Evaluation procedures may vary in consistency from total uniformity to unique adaptations matched to individual employees. The procedures may be directed by administration or the negotiated contract, or they may, usually within some constraints, be selected by the evaluatee. Evaluation standards, too, may be set by administration, chosen by employees, or developed collaboratively. And they may be applied to processes and/or products. Finally, evaluation measures, whether of process or product, may be quantitative or qualitative. This chapter has offered suggestions to enhance the effectiveness of written evaluations and to guide supervisors in preparing themselves for their responsibilities as evaluators of personnel.

KEY TERMS

1. consistency
2. developmental levels
3. diagnostic
4. evaluation
5. formative
6. performance appraisal
7. portfolio
8. procedures
9. process
10. product
11. qualitative
12. quantitative
13. standards
14. summative
15. supervision

QUESTIONS AND ACTIVITIES

1. The primary purpose of evaluation is to improve job performance. Discuss four objectives of teacher performance.

2. In many districts both supervisors and employees confuse supervision and evaluation. What are the differences between the two? Which should be used for formal recognition of superior teaching or poor performance?

3. The California Education Code requires four components in teacher evaluation. List each of the four components and discuss them briefly.

4. What are the major components of clinical supervision? What are the advantages and disadvantages of this type of supervision?

5. Even with very effective supervisors and a clear and consistent evaluation system, human factors may still interfere with fair, humane evaluation. Discuss three obstacles to accuracy in personnel evaluation and how they might be avoided.

6. Obtain from at least two districts the standards of expected pupil achievement intended to meet the requirements of Education Code section 44662. Compare and evaluate them as tools for teacher evaluation.

7. Select three or four standards of expected pupil achievement (as required by Education Code section 44662) that represent different subjects and grade levels and decide how, given a choice, you would assess each one.

8. Obtain from at least two districts their written procedures and forms for evaluating classified personnel. Ask particularly for the standards against which each employee is to be evaluated. Try to discover how the standards were developed, by whom, and how recently reviewed. What changes would you recommend?

9. Extend activity #8 to certificated staff.

10. From a school district or a private sector employer, obtain a performance appraisal instrument. With the help of the text by Bernardin and Beatty or another reference on performance appraisal, determine which type of instrument is being used. If possible, also find out how the instrument was checked for validity and reliability. Evaluate the instrument for practicality and for its potential to elicit improved job

performance. List every public school position for which you think this type of instrument might appropriately be used.

11. Read about clinical supervision (Cogan or Goldhammer), developmental supervision (Glickman), and/or differentiated supervision (Glatthorn) of teachers. Try out one or more of these models, decide what other knowledge or skills you need to use the system at optimal effectiveness, and write a development plan for yourself to gain that additional background.

12. With permission of your personnel officer, peruse the files of two teachers who have been with the same district for at least 12 years, preferably at different schools. Based on this limited sample, how have evaluation forms, procedures, and attitudes changed over time?

13. Again with appropriate permission, read the most recent evaluation of six faculty members who teach the same grade or subject in a single district, preferably in as many different schools. To what extent do supervisors differ in applying the same evaluation procedures and standards?

14. Obtain procedures and standards for a teacher portfolio currently being piloted or implemented in a California district. Evaluate the procedures and standards as to cost, practicality, reliability, and validity.

15. With permission of the teacher and supervisor, obtain three portfolios developed in the district selected for activity 14. If possible, also obtain the feedback given to each teacher. Evaluate these portfolios as a means of improving instruction.

Chapter 6

Certificated Personnel

INTRODUCTION

Not only is employment of certificated teachers and administrators the "lifeblood" of the personnel department, but administration of certificated personnel services falls among the most complex tasks of the personnel manager. For example, missing a deadline for employee notification of layoff may result in a loss to the school district of thousands, if not millions, of dollars.

It is important to note, with respect to citations of California Education Code sections dealing with classified and certificated personnel, that these are always changing. Thus, one must check to be sure that code sections have not been modified, added, or deleted since this book was printed. Moreover, court decisions that change any of the sections mentioned in this book may be handed down any day. Therefore, a personnel administrator must track modifications in personnel law on a regular basis.

The current text of California law is available on the World Wide Web at
http://www.leginfo.ca.gov/calaw.html
Most decisions of higher courts may be found at
http://www.findlaw.com
However, given that law is a dynamic force and that its interpretations are open to change, nothing can substitute for legal counsel on personnel issues.

COMMISSION ON TEACHER CREDENTIALING

The California Commission on Teacher Credentialing (CCTC) was created by the state legislature in 1970. It is the oldest of the state standards boards in the United States. The commission's staff prepares an annual report (Braegar, 2001), from the latest of which the following information is gleaned.

The primary tasks of the CCTC include licensing and credentialing professional educators, enforcing professional practices of educators, and disciplining credentialed educators. The commission consists of 19 voting members and four ex officio, non-voting members. Fourteen members are appointed by the Governor, while the State Superintendent of Public Instruction serves as the 15th voting member. The four non-voting members represent California private and public colleges and universities. Commissioners are appointed for four-year terms.

In addition to the credential responsibilities of CCTC, the commission also monitors the moral fitness and professional conduct of credentialed educators who are working in California schools. A subcommittee is established for this purpose. This committee reviews all allegations of misconduct and determines whether probable cause exists for disciplinary action against a teacher, counselor, or administrator.

Referrals may be as minor as petty theft or as serious as murder or child molestation. The subcommittee membership includes one elementary teacher, one secondary teacher, one school board member, one school administrator, and three public representatives. The subcommittee becomes aware of criminal infractions in a variety of ways:

- All credential applicants are fingerprinted. If the individual has a record of criminal conviction, the CCTC receives a "rap sheet" from the Department of Justice (DOJ) and/or the FBI.

- If an employee is arrested later or convicted, the DOJ sends an "arrest notice" to the CCTC, and a review is commenced.

- Local law enforcement agencies are required to inform CCTC whenever a credential holder is arrested for specified sex or drug offenses.

- Districts also notify the CCTC if a credential holder is dismissed, is suspended for more than 10 days, or resigns or retires while allegations of misconduct are pending.

Upon conclusion of a case, the final action taken by the CCTC becomes public information. The decision is placed on the "All-Points Bulletin," which is mailed monthly to all California public and private schools. Notice of adverse actions taken by the CCTC is also published nationally. Between 1995 and 2000, CCTC denied 322 credential applications, revoked 833 credentials, suspended 192, and issued 60 private admonitions.

CALIFORNIA CREDENTIALS

A challenge facing all California personnel directors is the complexity of the teacher credentialing process. Despite the myriad credentials that qualify teachers and other staff to perform specialized duties, one must monitor each specific assignment. Many district offices employ an individual fulltime for the responsibility of credential management.

The Bergeson Act, or Teaching Credentialing Law, of 1988 established the basic credentialing structure (Ed. Code #44200). The provisions of this act define basic requirements for a teaching credential: possession of a bachelor's degree, completion of a one-year program of teaching methodology, passing a test of basic skills, and a semester as a student teacher.

Credential requirements in California are subject to legislative concerns and mandates. For example, when California students scored below the national average in reading, the California legislature mandated that all candidates for a credential must complete a course in the methods of teaching reading. Therefore, requirements for any given credential are subject to change each year. Following is a list of basic teaching and service credentials, along with requirements as of press time. A reader should contact the CCTC at its Web site (http://www.ctc.ca.gov) for the most recent credential requirements. The following descriptions have been taken from that Website.

Elementary School Teaching

In California, elementary school teachers are required to have a Multiple-Subject Teaching Credential. This credential authorizes public school teaching in a self-contained classroom in preschool, kindergarten, grades one through twelve, and classes organized primarily for adults. A self-contained classroom is most often found at the elementary school level.

Secondary School Teaching

Secondary teachers must hold a Single-Subject Teaching Credential. This credential authorizes public school teaching in a departmentalized classroom in preschool, kindergarten, grades one through twelve, and classes organized primarily for adults. The holder may teach the specific subject(s) named on the credential in departmentalized classes, such as those found in most middle schools and high schools.

Special Education

The Education Specialist Instruction Credential in special education is offered for six groups of students: mild/moderate disabilities, moderate/severe disabilities, visual impairments, deaf and hard-of-hearing, physical and health impairments, and early childhood special education. Each applicant must complete a special education teacher preparation program, including student teaching, in the area of specialization.

Designated Subjects Credentials

Designated Subjects Credentials authorize teaching or service in technical, trade, or vocational courses or in courses organized primarily for adults. The requirements generally include experience in the subject. Some of the credentials include Adult Education, Vocational Education, Special Subjects, and Supervision and Coordination.

Other Specialist Credentials and Certificates

Many specialists in public schools must earn credentials or certificates authorizing service in their area of specialization. These credentials and certificates are dependent upon the applicant first obtaining a multiple- or single-subject teaching credential. Some of the specialist credentials include a Specialist Credential in Reading and Language Arts, Agriculture, Early Childhood Education, Gifted Education, and Mathematics. A student may also prepare to instruct limited-English-proficient students by obtaining a Crosscultural Language and Academic Development (CLAD) or Bilingual Crosscultural Language and Academic Development (BCLAD) certificate.

Services Credentials

Individuals providing school services such as administration or pupil counseling must hold a credential authorizing that service. Among the service credentials are School Nurse and Other Health Services, Library Media Teacher Services, Administrative Services, School Social Work, School Child Welfare and Attendance, Pupil Personnel Services (including counseling and school psychology) and Clinical or Rehabilitative Services (including speech clinician).

BASIC CREDENTIAL REQUIREMENTS

California teachers first receive a preliminary credential. Once granted a preliminary credential, certificated employees have five years in which to complete a fifth year of commission-approved study. After successful completion of the prescribed year of study beyond the bachelor's degree, teachers may apply for a professional clear credential. This credential must be renewed every five years, with renewal dependent upon a minimum of 150 hours of documented professional development.

The first step in the process of obtaining a credential is to complete an appropriate bachelor's degree. Secondly, the individual enrolls in a credential program at a college or university whose credential program has been approved by CCTC. Although the commission has set six common standards for all approved college and university programs, some differences are found from college to college.

Education	Completion of a baccalaureate degree
Professional teacher preparation	Completion of an approved college or university professional teacher preparation program, including successful student teaching and formal recommendation for the credential by the college or university
California Basic Skills Test (CBEST)	Passage of the CBEST test with a minimum scaled score of 41 in each of the three sections (reading, mathematics, and writing) or a total scaled score of at last 123 and no section score below 37
Provisions and principles of the U. S. Constitution	Completion of a course in the provisions and principles of the United States Constitution or passage of an examination in the subject
Methods of teaching reading	Completion of a course in the methods of teaching reading or passage of the Praxis Series Subject Assessment entitled "Introduction to Teaching of Reading"; for the Multiple-Subject Credential, passage of the Reading Instruction Competence Assessment (RICA)
Subject-matter competence	Verification of subject-matter competence by either of two methods: (a) a passing score on the Praxis Series Subject Assessment or (b) completion of a commission-approved liberal arts subject-matter program or its equivalent combined with verification of completion from the authorized person in the education department of the college or university

At first glance, the requirements for a California Teaching Credential appear to be straightforward: complete a bachelor's degree plus a year of graduate work, pass a basic skills test, complete student teaching, apply for the credential, and receive certification. However, this apparently clear path to the credential and employment in a California school district has numerous additional complications too numerous to cite here. Some of these special circumstances include emergency credentials, intern programs, and certification of out-of-state teachers. Emergency and intern credentials as well as credentials for out-of-state teachers were discussed in Chapter 3, where we pointed out that California faces a serious problem in meeting the federal requirement to staff each classroom with a fully certificated teacher.

EMPLOYEE DUTIES AND RIGHTS

Education Code sections on teacher rights and duties and similar sections for classified staff are organized, for the most part, in parallel. The functions performed by a credentialed employee, as listed in Education Code #44065, may include:

- the work of instructors and the instructional program for pupils

- educational or vocational counseling, guidance, and placement services

- school extracurricular activities related to and an outgrowth of the instructional and guidance programs of the school

- planning of courses of study to be used in the public schools of the state

- selection, collection, preparation, classification, or demonstration of instructional materials for any course of study or for use in the development of the instructional program in the schools of the state

- research connected with the evaluation and efficiency of the instructional program

- the school health program

- activities connected with enforcing the laws relating to compulsory education, coordination of child welfare activities involving school and home, and the school adjustment of pupils

- school library services

- preparation and distribution of instructional materials

- inservice training of certificated personnel

- interpretation and evaluation of the school instructional program using authorized textbooks

Other code sections call for teachers to

- use authorized textbooks (Ed. Code #44805)

- enforce the course of study (Ed. Code #44805)

- teach morality, truth, justice, patriotism, citizenship, equality, and human dignity (Ed. Code #233.5(a))

- create an environment that encourages pupils to realize their full potential, is free of discrimination, and prevents acts of hate violence (Ed. Code #233.5(b))

- hold pupils accountable for their behavior (Ed. Code #44807)

- record attendance of pupils (Ed. Code #44809)

- make reports required by law (Ed. Code #44816).

It is interesting to note that one of the teacher rights in the Education Code is to a "duty-free" lunch. This right evolved from resistance to a past pattern in which many school districts required teachers to use their lunch periods for student supervision.

THE TEACHER ASSESSMENT CENTER— A CALIFORNIA MODEL

Because many thousands of teachers will be employed in California within the next few years, districts need a predictable and standardized way to hire competent instructors (Bond, 1985). Some districts have developed a teacher assessment center to conduct a standardized assessment of teaching behaviors by observing an individual's performance in simulations of classroom tasks.

One teacher assessment center, for example, focuses on six skills considered critical to the competency of a teacher. These skills include ability to

- manage the classroom   *most important!*

- motivate and create a learning environment

- instruct students

- plan and organize the classroom

- evaluate students

- communicate effectively.

The skills are tested in simulated exercises. For example, the ability to evaluate student skill is presented in four parts. In one simulation the teacher listens to a tape of a student reading a selection three paragraphs long. The teacher's job is to make an informal evaluation of the student's ability by following along and recording errors on a written copy of the material being read.

Teacher assessment centers offer a valuable tool to districts that must employ a great number of teachers. The simulation model allows candidates to carry out actual tasks that a teacher must perform daily. However, in addition to information gathered in assessment centers, the personal interview continues to be recommended as a vital part of the selection process.

CLASS SIZE

The number of students assigned to each teacher is a critical issue for the education, business, and personnel divisions of each school district. The instruction division needs to answer questions regarding class size and student achievement, while the personnel department is responsible for the recruitment of teachers to staff each classroom. The business department has responsibility for finding the money to pay salaries and benefits.

Although not definitive regarding student achievement and class size, teacher and student testimonials and empirical research clearly indicate that there is an improved learning environment in smaller classes. There is little argument that an elementary school teacher can establish a closer relationship with 20 students than with 40. It is the exceptional secondary teacher with a class load of 150 to 180 who can find time to get to know his or her students well. Obviously, a teacher's workload greatly increases as the class load increases. Class size becomes a major factor as states compete for the services of teachers. The student-teacher ratio may influence a teacher's decision to accept employment in one state rather than another.

The number of students assigned to each teacher varies greatly from state to state. In 1999-2000 the National Center for Educational Statistics developed a table of median student-teacher ratios, state by state (National Center, 2001). The median ratio for elementary classes was 16.2; middle school, 15.5; and high schools, 14.8. California had the highest middle school ratio in the nation with 22.8 and also the highest at the high school level with 21.8. California's class size reduction in K-3 grades saved the state from being the highest ratio at this grade level with 19.9 students per teacher. Kentucky with 21.6 and Utah with 20.8 shared the honor of the largest number of students per teacher in the primary grades.

California has often been compared to Texas on several educational issues regarding student achievement. It is interesting to note the comparisons in student-teacher ratios between the two states.

Median Pupil:Teacher Ratio

	Elementary Grades	Middle Grades	High School Grades
National	16.2	15.5	14.8
California	19.9	22.8	21.8
Texas	15.2	14.2	12.4

As the nation's schools move to greater accountability with President George W. Bush's education plan of testing of all American students, perhaps more definitive answers will be found regarding optimum class size. Until that day, districts will struggle with finding adequate resources to staff each classroom with a qualified teacher.

COMPENSATION *Salary Schedule*

"Nothing is possible—not building a democratic society, not creating a market economy—nothing is possible without educated people" (Daniszewski, 2001). If you were given a multiple choice test and had to choose who made that statement, whom would you select?

A. Thomas Jefferson B. John F. Kennedy C. George W. Bush
D. Gray Davis E. Vladimir Putin

If you selected all five, you probably would be correct. However, you may not have selected Vladimir Putin, president of Russia, who made the statement in his annual back-to-school observance in September 2001. He also promised to double the size of the average teacher's salary, equivalent in American dollars, from $35 a month to $70 (Daniszewski, 2001).

Historically, school finance has been the deciding factor in determining the compensation of teachers. Education is labor-intensive, and labor costs money. The largest expenditures in a district budget go to salaries and benefits. Obviously, there is a direct relationship in a district budget between smaller classes and compensation. If a larger slice of the budget pie is allocated for more teachers to reduce class size, less money remains for salary increases, and vice versa.

As indicated by the previous discussion of class size, California has allocated more money for salaries at the expense of greater class size. The American Federation of Teachers calculates the average teacher salary each year, state by state. The following information is from that survey (Nelson, Draws, & Gould, 2000).

Teacher salaries in 1999-2000 accounted for a smaller portion of total education spending than in 1960-61. Forty years ago states earmarked, on average, 51% of their budget for teacher salaries. In 1999-2000 the figure had dropped to 36.7%.

In the 1999-2000 school year, the average U. S. teacher made $41,820. The highest state average was Connecticut with $52,410. Connecticut teachers were followed by New York at $51,020. The first seven jurisdictions were Connecticut, New York, New Jersey, Michigan, Pennsylvania, District of Columbia, and Rhode Island. California teachers were in 8th place with an average salary of $47,680, 14% above the national average of $41,820. Texas, a state similar to California in many ways, was 27th with an average teacher salary of $37,567.

California teachers actually lost ground in the 1990s; the state had ranked sixth at the start of the 1990s with an average salary of $37,795. The lowest average teacher salary at that time was in South Dakota with a salary of $29,072. Other states near the bottom of the list were Oklahoma, North Dakota, Mississippi, and Montana.

As discussed earlier, potential teachers compare starting salaries in the teaching profession with other professions requiring a college degree. The comparisons show that average salaries in other professions are higher than in teaching. For example, in 1999-2000 the average full college professor was making $82,535. Attorneys made $77,150, and engineers, $72,427. A study by Lindquist (1991) found that several occupations that did not require a college degree also averaged a higher salary than teachers. Some of these occupations included city bus driver, sanitation worker, and construction worker.

SALARY SCHEDULES

Denver, Colorado, in 1921, was the first U. S. school district to introduce the single salary schedule (Kelley, 2000). By 1950 almost every school district in the country had adopted the single salary schedule. California's Education Code section 45028 requires each teacher to be placed on a salary schedule that gives credit for training and years of experience. However, other criteria are allowed if the board and union negotiate and mutually agree on a different standard for the schedule.

The governing board may arrange to pay certificated employees in either 10, 11, or 12 equal payments (Ed. Code #45038). However, the time of payment for fulltime teachers is stipulated by the Education Code as between the last working day of the month and the fifth day of the succeeding calendar month, inclusive (Ed. Code #45048).

Deductions and fringe benefits are similar for certificated and classified employees. Usually, a district contributes an amount toward the employee's retirement and group insurance. Deductions from a credentialed employee's gross pay typically cover income taxes, group insurance contribution, State Teachers Retirement System, workers' compensation insurance, workers' disability, and dues for a certificated union, such as California Teachers Association.

CAREER LADDERS AND MERIT PLANS— WORKABLE ANSWERS TO TEACHER REWARD?

Given the single salary schedule, which allows no recognition for quality of work, two problems that have always baffled educators are enticing college graduates to the teaching profession and rewarding teachers for excellence in their professional practice. Currently, advancement in salary and status is accomplished only by moving into an administrative role, but some states have turned to the career ladder as a means of recognizing teachers without drawing them away from working directly with children. A career ladder is intended to reward those who exhibit increased competence and take on additional instructional roles. Most career ladders begin with the first year-teacher and advance to master teacher status, usually a three- to six-step process. At each level the teacher assumes more responsibilities or is rated for superlative performance. Examples of additional duties are:

- consulting with parents

- developing innovative projects

- assisting other teachers to improve

- working with individual students.

A merit plan is another approach to rewarding highly competent teachers. There are major differences between the merit plan and the career ladder. A career ladder rewards teachers for non-teaching duties and additional tasks, as well as superior teaching. Merit pay, however, is granted in response to a teacher's evaluation as related to improved student learning and performance on standardized measures.

Many states are either looking closely at the career ladder or have enacted legislation detailing the elements of the plan. The National Council on Teacher Quality (NCTQ) has extensively documented states and districts that are implementing career ladder programs. For more information, visit their Website at www.nctg.org.

On the other hand, some states have already reconsidered the career ladder because of problems with its implementation. In Tennessee, for instance, teachers complained about the excessive amount of paperwork required to participate in the program.

Career ladders are still in their infancy, so that predicting their impact is not possible. However, many states are looking to such a program to create incentives that will keep good teachers in the profession.

MERIT PAY *Very controversial!*

As just noted, merit pay is based on student learning and performance. Merit pay has garnered little support from classroom teachers. The National Education Association (NEA) has taken a formal stand in opposition to merit pay (NEA, 1991). However, in recent years NEA leaders have slightly modified their opposition by allowing "bonus pay." It was made clear that bonus pay should not replace pay based on seniority or be based on student performance on tests (McQueen, 2000.)

The American Federation of Teachers reports that the first merit plan was implemented in Britain in 1710 ("AFT," 2001). They note that when British teachers received a pay raise for improved student test scores, teachers had students memorize reading passages for the tests.

Teachers have watched merit pay plans come and go since the first United States experiment in Texarkana, Arkansas. The Texarkana plan was implemented in 1969 and received nationwide attention when it was supported by President Richard Nixon. Texarkana teachers were eligible for financial incentives if test scores improved. Students who improved their test scores would also receive rewards of free transistor radios, sweaters, green stamps, and music albums. Private companies were hired to test the students and evaluate the performance of teachers. The program soon became mired in scandals when the test company was caught cheating on tests.

NEA's opposition to merit pay is based primarily on the argument that without agreement on the definition of teaching, merit pay is impossible to implement fairly (Bishop, 1987). A second argument is that many variables, not just the teacher, contribute to a student's success. In particular, continuous and consistent instruction of high caliber by a number of well-qualified teachers, the argument continues, really makes the difference in children's test scores. Why provide rewards to one "deserving" person? Instead, many teachers and administrators believe, rewarding an entire school is more appropriate than awarding additional income to individual educators.

A final reason that merit pay has not achieved widespread acceptance is that most teachers feel that differential pay will divide the staff and discourage participation in cooperative planning and other shared activities. Merit pay recipients might not choose to share the successful behaviors that resulted in their selection for additional compensation. Thus, instead of fostering widespread communication about effective practices, merit pay may actually counter collegial efforts toward excellence throughout the school. Indeed, this may be the most important argument against such a policy.

MENTOR TEACHERS

SB813 considered passée has been replaced

The Mentor Teacher Program was approved in 1983 as part of the Hughes-Hart Educational Reform Act. Districts were provided funds to employ mentors, each of whom received a stipend of $4,000 per year. The mentor's primary duties consisted of assisting teachers, conducting staff development programs, and developing curriculum.

After almost 10 years of existence the mentor program was supplemented by the Beginning Teacher Support and Assessment Program in 1992 (BTSA). Almost 20 years later, with the development of the Peer Assistance and Review (PAR) program in 2000-2001, state funds for the mentor program were eliminated.

BEGINNING TEACHER SUPPORT AND ASSESSMENT (BTSA)

California personnel directors have been aware for many years of the major loss of beginning teachers. Almost half of all new teachers move to other professions within five to seven years, with as many as 80% leaving the profession after 10 years (Fischer & Shipley, 1995; Mathison, 1996).

Reacting to this loss of teachers, the California Commission on Teacher Credentialing (CCTC) conducted a study to test alternative models designed to support first- and second-year teachers. The study found that beginning teachers have the education and certification to teach, but not the experience necessary to be successful teachers (Nash, 1999). University teacher education programs provide teachers with pedagogical and theoretical knowledge. However, many programs do not adequately prepare teachers for the realities of the classroom. These findings resulted in passage of the Beginning Teacher Support and Assessment Program (BTSA), which was implemented in 1992.

Few aspects of school administration are more important than nurturing and mentoring new teachers, and few endeavors have greater payoffs (Rodda, 2000). The BTSA program matches support providers with beginning teachers, thus providing opportunities for teachers to increase and expand their teaching knowledge and skill.

The skill providers are assigned a specific number of beginning teachers to mentor during the first two years of their career. The BTSA teacher facilitates the beginning teacher's journey through a cycle of planning, teaching, reflecting, and applying. BTSA facilitators do not serve as evaluators of a new teacher, but rather as mentor; they help the new teacher with lesson planning, content standards, goal setting, and assessment.

A study completed by the California Teaching Commission found that the BTSA program, which served more than 20,000 teachers annually, improved the teacher retention rate from 68% to 92% during the first three years of teaching (Birdsall, 1998). Another study found that 90% of BTSA participants were still teaching after five years, compared with only 40% to 50% of teachers who did not receive such support (Bradley, 1998).

PEER ASSESSMENT AND REVIEW (PAR)

Employee evaluation is a major problem in every profession. Yet, employers definitely have need to inform employees of their strong points and areas for improvement. In addition, when areas for improvement are identified, a plan must be developed to provide assistance designed to improve performance.

In addition to administrative supervision and evaluation of a teacher's performance, a strong case can be made for assistance from other teachers through peer review. The Oxford English Dictionary defines "peer review" as an examination or review of professional or academic efficiency by others in the same occupation. Toledo, Ohio started such a program in 1981. The Poway District in San Diego County, California, has been using peer review for more than 10 years. Since that time, peer review has been implemented in several other districts and states.

In 1999 Governor Gray Davis addressed this issue by creating the California Peer Assistance and Review Program (PAR), now in Education Code sections 44500-44508. The governor said, "The best person to improve a teacher's performance is another teacher" (Colvin, 1999). Assembly Bill 1X established the PAR program, which replaced the Mentor Teacher Program. Districts were not required to establish a PAR program. However, if they did not do so by July 1, 2001, they could not receive funds for this purpose.

The bill was touted as the school accountability and education reform measure of the decade ("Latino," 1999). Those who urged establishment of the PAR program argued that teachers were in the best position to assist teachers in improving instruction and that many administrators did not have the time or expertise to evaluate teachers effectively.

Those who opposed the PAR program claimed that evaluation is a supervisory role that should be completed by management. A second argument was that peer evaluation could destroy collegiality among teachers and pit one against another.

PAR requires teachers, administrators, districts, and unions to work together to assist veteran teachers in improving their instructional program. In addition, districts must establish a joint teacher-administrator peer review panel to select the consulting teachers and to evaluate annually the impact of the district program.

Experienced teachers are selected to observe and assist probationary teachers. The qualifications for serving as a PAR teacher, or "consulting teacher," are very similar to those formerly required in the Mentor Teacher Program. A PAR teacher must be a permanently credentialed teacher with substantial recent experience in the classroom and demonstrated exemplary teaching ability (Ed. Code #44504).

For school districts to receive state funds to implement the PAR program, the district must comply with requirements outlined in Education Code 44500(b). These requirements include multiple classroom observations, establishment of performance goals based on the California Standards for the Teaching Profession, and staff development opportunities. Although peer review focuses on formative feedback, rather than the summative evaluation provided by administrators, the PAR teacher does prepare a final evaluation that may be placed in the teacher's personnel file.

Teacher participation may be voluntary or by referral as a result of a performance review or referral based on the terms of the district's collective bargaining agreement. PAR holds great potential: the promise of improving teacher effectiveness and subsequently student achievement, the promise of retaining a greater number of teachers in the profession, and the promise of terminating ineffective teachers.

ADMINISTRATOR CERTIFICATION

Certification of administrators is delineated in Section #44270 of the Education Code. Obtaining an administrative credential is a two-step process known as "Tier One" and "Tier Two." Tier One, the Preliminary Administrative Services Certificate, authorizes the holder to accept a position as a school administrator in California. Upon gaining an appointment, the new administrator exchanges the certificate for a Preliminary Administrative Services Credential. Tier Two, the Professional Administrative Services Credential, is required within five years of beginning service as an administrator. The objective of the Tier Two credential is to ensure continued education for neophyte California administrators.

The minimum requirements for the preliminary certificate with a specialization in administrative services are as follows:

- possession of a valid teaching credential requiring the seeker to have earned an accredited baccalaureate degree

- a minimum of three years' successful full-time classroom teaching experience in the public schools

- either an entry-level program of professional preparation approved by the commission or a one-year internship in a program of supervised training in administrative services.

A professional level credential requires:

- a valid Preliminary Administrative Services Credential

- a minimum of two years' successful fulltime experience in a position requiring the preliminary credential

- completion of a commission-approved program of advanced study and appropriate field experience or internship (Ed. Code #44270.1).

As this text goes to press, the educational community and stage legislature are reviewing the effectiveness of requirements for the administrative services credential. It is anticipated that changes will be enacted.

PERSONNEL FILES

Most materials in personnel files that may affect employment status must be made available for inspection by the employee. The employee's review of the personnel file must take place during the normal teaching day, and the employee is to be released from duty for this purpose without loss or reduction of salary.

Materials not accessible for inspection include ratings, reports, and records obtained by the district before the person's employment. In addition, employees are not permitted to view materials prepared by identifiable examination committee members or materials obtained in connection with a promotional examination.

Information of a derogatory nature, except that mentioned above, will not be entered or filed unless and until the employee is given notice and an opportunity to review and comment on the contents of the memorandum or letter. An employee has the right to respond in writing to any derogatory materials; such comments are to be attached to and filed with the material (Ed. Code #44031).

A district may not avoid the requirements of section #44031 by neglecting to file documents or by segregating selected documents into a separate file. Rather, materials affecting employment status must be placed in an employee's single, official personnel file (*Miller v. Chico Unified School District,* 1979, 24 CAl.3d 704, 157 Cal.Rptr. 72).

SUMMARY

Most of the complex decisions related to school district personnel involve certificated employees, as this chapter has indicated. The functions performed by credentialed personnel range from teaching to school health to library services. The Commission on Teacher Credentialing has responsibility for establishing standards and procedures to enable teachers to practice their profession in our schools. Possessing the correct credential for each teaching assignment has assumed major importance in the wake of recent legislation. Other important issues discussed in this chapter include teacher evaluation and compensation.

The importance of a well-trained staff cannot be overemphasized. The chapter describes how effective teacher centers are assisting some districts to select competent staff. With many districts in a growth mode, such centers may generate significant benefits to the instructional program.

California has developed a series of programs to recruit, train, and retain a quality teaching force. The Mentor Teacher Program was one of the first. It was supplemented with The Beginning Teacher Support and Assessment Program. A recent innovation in this area is the Peer Assistance and Review Program.

Finally, the chapter noted the controversy on merit pay and salary incentives. These issues have elicited ongoing debate, not yet resolved. Linking "input" of teacher actions with "output" of student test scores has been resisted by teacher unions. To provide incentives, yet maintain fairness to employees, some districts are rewarding schoolwide, rather than individual, effort and accomplishment toward student achievement.

KEY TERMS

1. assessment center
2. Beginning Teacher Support and Assessment Program (BTSA)
3. California Basic Education Skills Test (CBEST)
4. mentor teacher
5. merit pay
6. Peer Assistance and Review (PAR)
7. SB 813
8. teacher career ladder
9. teacher certification requirements
10. Tier One and Tier Two credentials

QUESTIONS AND ACTIVITIES

1. Teacher Assessment Centers assess six critical teacher skills. List and briefly discuss the importance of each of these skills.

2. Career ladders and merit plans are being considered by many districts to reward superior teaching. What are the advantages and disadvantages of these programs?

3. If you were selected as a PAR teacher, list five ways that you could assist a below-average teacher.

4. For a teacher to serve as an administrator, he or she must obtain a Preliminary Administrative Services Credential. In addition, for continued service as an administrator, he or she must also earn a Professional Administrative Services Credential. Discuss the rationale for the professional level credential.

5. What are some tasks of certificated personnel that could not readily be tested in an assessment center? Why not?

6. In materials designed to help teachers prepare for the CBEST, locate a sample test. How would you recommend that teachers prepare so as to do their best on this test?

7. Prepare an overhead slide of a sample teacher salary schedule. Discuss in class: What does the schedule reward? Are there bonuses that might serve as an incentive for extra tasks or advanced degrees?

Chapter 7

Classified Personnel

INTRODUCTION

This chapter addresses issues related to a school district's classified staff. The California Education Code contains numerous sections relating directly to the classified service. In addition, classified staff have separate bargaining units in school districts throughout the state.

Classified staff are clearly essential to the successful conduct of school business. In 1999-2000 there were 271,721 classified employees in California, divided about equally between full- and parttime. Thus, the number of classified employees is nearly equal to the number of teachers (292,455) in the state's public schools (California Department of Education, 2000).

While the teacher is the key individual in the education of youth, his or her success greatly depends on a well-trained and efficient support staff. The first adult, outside of parents, that a child sees in the morning may well be a bus driver or school crossing guard. That bus driver or crossing guard is key to getting a youngster's day started properly. Classified employees act as an extension of the classroom teacher. They are expected to model appropriate behavior and establish standards of discipline. During each school day a child interacts with several important classified staff members. For example, in many classrooms, particularly at the elementary grades, the teacher is assisted by an instructional aide. Often, children are unaware that the aide is not a certificated teacher and respond to this individual much as they do to the teacher.

During recess and lunch students are served food by cafeteria workers and supervised on the playground by campus aides. In many districts a child who needs to go to the health office is seen by a member of the classified staff. While a child may not see the secretary or office clerk each and every day, he or she develops a close relation with these adults as notes from home are delivered and other clerical tasks are completed. In addition, the cleanliness of the classroom is dependent on the custodial staff, playgrounds are maintained by the groundskeeping department, and facilities maintenance depends on the maintenance and operations crew—all classified staff.

Certainly a committed, highly trained classified staff is indispensable. A school district that cuts back on custodians, food service, and landscape personnel soon feels the effect of those reductions on the educational program. Nevertheless, in an era of limited financial resources for school personnel, the brunt of major budget cuts often falls on the classified service.

As districts review budget reductions, they are often in a quandary as to the minimum level of support required. This becomes the critical debate at any school board meeting when budget reductions are being considered. Board members may say something like "The windows can be broken and the classroom door unlocked, yet the educational program continues." However, anyone who has tried to conduct an educational program with inadequate support personnel knows the difficulty of maintaining a suitable learning environment without their assistance.

CLASSIFIED PERSONNEL TRAINING

Programs to train and develop classified personnel, once they have been hired by a school district, have lagged behind programs in business and industry. In recent years districts have recognized that investment in such training pays off in higher staff satisfaction and reduced turnover. One program, recognized for its success, was implemented in the Albuquerque public schools. This program helps supervisors of secretaries, paraprofessionals, and educational assistants explore new management possibilities (Andreson & Durant, 1991). The authors state that the program has been of inestimable assistance in the district's training for support personnel.

All new classified employees, regardless of their background, should be introduced to their new work environment. Continuing classified employees need periodic training as new policies, procedures, and technology are introduced. For example, in many districts custodians have recently reviewed the composition of potentially dangerous chemicals used in the course of their cleaning tasks. This chapter contains excerpts from the California Education Code that identify the basis for employee compensation, work tasks, and leaves of absence.

EMPLOYMENT

The rules governing employment of classified personnel have been formulated to ensure that appropriate personnel are hired to work with and near children. For instance, persons who have been convicted of any sex offense or controlled substance offense may not be employed by a school district. To enforce this requirement, California Education Code Section #45125 requires districts to send fingerprint cards for each new classified employee to the U. S. Department of Justice, whose responsibility it is to ascertain whether the employee has been arrested for or convicted of any crime. The fingerprint requirement was discussed in Chapter 2.

No discussion of classified personnel would be complete without reference to affirmative action. A major portion of the Education Code is devoted to defining a policy of equal opportunity in employment for all persons. These sections were approved to ensure that no discrimination exists in employment with respect to race, sex, color, religion, age, disability, ancestry, or national origin (Ed. Code #44100, #44101). California school districts are required to actively seek personnel in those ethnic groups that are underrepresented in the district's workforce.

JOB ANALYSIS

A job analysis for classified employees has the same objective as for certificated personnel: determining the actual requirements for each specific job. Its importance has grown in recent years as courts have increasingly looked to this procedure in reaching judgements about various aspects of personnel selection.

Job analysis involves collecting, organizing, and evaluating information related to responsibilities and tasks. The U. S. Department of Labor (1991) suggests four dimensions for inclusion in a job analysis:

Worker functions	What the worker does in relation to data, people and things
Work fields	The methodologies and techniques utilized on the job
MPSMS	The materials being processed, the products being made, the subject matter dealt with, and the services being rendered
Worker characteristics	Worker attributes that contribute to successful job performance (education, specific vocational preparation, aptitudes, temperaments, physical demands, and environmental conditions).

An analysis of physical demands and environmental conditions is particularly important to comply with the Americans With Disabilities Act. Courts have ruled in favor of the plaintiff when a district could not prove that a physical requirement was directly related to completing a given task. For example, one employer lost a case when a job description specified that an employee must be able to use both arms when performing a particular task. One employee could not meet this requirement because his disability caused limited mobility in one arm. The court found that the essential function of the job was the ability to lift and carry a particular article, which he could do, not the ability to use both arms (Greenberg & Bello, 1992).

The actual analysis of classified positions may be performed by the district personnel director or by a consultant who specializes in job analysis. Once the analysis has been carried out, a system must be established with which the results will be reviewed regularly.

JOB DESCRIPTIONS

After a job analysis has been completed, the next step in the process is to develop job descriptions. A job description is a written, detailed outline of the duties and responsibilities of a specific job. The National School Boards Association characterizes a job description as a blueprint or guide for work to be accomplished. The description should serve both the employee's need for information about the job and the administrator's need for supervising the incumbent's performance (National School Boards Association, 1976). The job description should describe the job, not the tasks performed by the individual who happens to hold the position currently (Webb, Montello, & Norton, 1994).

Well-developed job descriptions are useful in many ways. Clear definition of tasks helps avoid misunderstandings about job expectations, with fewer grievances as a result. Job descriptions are also useful in recruitment, selection, and induction of new personnel.

A good job description shows how the job relates to the school organization. For this reason, the position title of the direct supervisor must be clearly stated.

Prior to developing new job descriptions or altering current documents, a personnel director should seek legal counsel to determine if such a step is subject to collective bargaining (Candoli, Hack, & Ray, 1992). If the district has a classified merit system, it may be necessary to have job descriptions approved by the Personnel Commission. Merit system districts are discussed later in this chapter.

JOB CLASSIFICATION

After all jobs have been analyzed, and all job descriptions revised or newly written and approved by the school board, the next task is to develop a "classification plan." Jobs with similar work requirements may be grouped into a common class. Positions within a class may differ in experience and skill requirements, or in degree of responsibility. For example, the clerical class could include positions of Clerk I, Clerk II, and Clerk III.

The classification plan undergirds the entire classified personnel program. This plan builds a foundation for employee recruitment, selection, assignment, and evaluation, as well as salary determination. It also becomes vitally important in case of layoff or reduction-in-force, in which circumstances it helps determine seniority and "bumping rights."

A title must be designated for each position in the classified service. Setting a minimum number of assigned hours per day and days per week is also required. The duties of each position must be defined; these can usually be found in the job announcement itself or in a job description that is readily available (Ed. Code #45101). Typically, classified positions are defined within the groups of transportation personnel, custodians, maintenance workers, landscape workers, food service employees, and instructional aides.

The total amount of money earmarked for classified support personnel is much less than that set aside for certificated employees. As noted in Chapter 3, legal requirements and the teachers' negotiated agreement allow little flexibility in determining the number of certificated positions to be filled. By contrast, formulas for settling on the number of staff to hire in each classification are not easily derived. Consequently, the number of classified employees in each support service is often determined by the judgment of the superintendent and the board of education, although negotiations with the classified union also play a major role. Unfortunately, during periods of economic uncertainty, classified services are often deemed expendable.

Employees may be classified in many ways. For example, a new employee is considered probationary and usually remains in this classification for a six-month period. After satisfactory completion of the probationary period, the employee is classified as permanent. This classification means that the worker has passed the required probationary period and completed all requirements of that classification (Ed. Code #45101).

Categorical funds have enabled schools to employ additional classified staff. Federal funds for disadvantaged students and state School Improvement monies have made it possible to place instructional aides in many classrooms. Media and library assistants and bilingual aides, too, are often paid from specialized categorical funds. Commonly, the classified personnel office has prospective classified employees sign an agreement acknowledging that their continued employment depends upon continuing availability of categorical funds.

COMPENSATION

The governing board of a school district is responsible to fix salaries and order the payment of all classified personnel under its jurisdiction (Ed. Code #45160). To set these salaries, boards usually compare district hourly rates with rates in the private sector and in other school districts. Typically, districts pay a lesser rate than the private sector because of the greater retirement and fringe benefits received by school employees. Of course, a board does not set compensation unilaterally, but must negotiate with the bargaining organization (or organizations) of the classified staff. The California Education Code gives boards direction as to frequency and dates of payments to employees, as well as procedures in the event of salary error, night shift work, and employees who work less than 12 months during the year (Ed. Code #42645).

The salary of a classified employee is based upon the district classification plan. In many cases classified personnel are paid an hourly wage. The principles involved in payment on an hourly basis are the same as those involved in establishing a salary schedule. These principles are as follows:

- Positions should be reviewed periodically in conformity to a pre-defined procedure.

- Fringe benefits should be considered in detail.

- The salary schedule should be made public, available to all who request it.

- All classified positions should be included in the schedule.

- The salary schedule should be internally consistent.

- Benchmark salaries should be established for each series of positions.

- Prevailing wages in the community should be considered.

DEDUCTIONS

Deductions from the gross pay of an employee include all applicable taxes, social security, payments for disability insurance, worker's compensation payments, and any payments made by the individual for group medical insurance. Deductions may be also taken for the employee union, often CSEA (California School Employees Association).

BENEFITS

Many individuals are attracted to work in the classified service, not for the salary, but for the employee benefits. All probationary and permanent parttime classified employees are entitled to sick leave and all other benefits conferred by law on classified employees (Ed. Code #45136). Fringe benefits may include medical coverage for the employee and his or her family, dental coverage, vision, and a retirement plan such as the

Public Employee Retirement System (PERS). Although employees who have never worked four hours or more per day do not contribute to PERS, legislation effective in January 1992 requires that employers set up a retirement plan for all parttime staff, regardless of the hours worked per day.

WORK TIME AND ASSIGNMENTS

The workday and the workweek of the classified employee are clearly delineated in the Education Code. The hours designated per week for the employee are 40 hours. The basic workday is set at eight hours per day. However, shorter workdays and workweeks may be established for any or all classified staff. Hours worked in excess of 40 in a calendar week must be compensated as overtime in the form of pay at time-and-one-half or time off at time-and-one-half (Ed. Code #45128). Compensatory time off shall be granted within twelve calendar months following the month in which the overtime was worked, but not at a time that would impair the services rendered by the district.

Many districts are trying to reduce overtime hours assigned to employees because of the additional cost or time off. In some districts, by way of maintaining strict control, only the director of personnel or the superintendent may authorize overtime.

LEAVES OF ABSENCE

The cost of classified personnel should always include the number of leaves that are legally due each employee. The California Accounting Manual indicates the account codes under which these expenses must be listed. "Leave" includes sick leave, pregnancy, bereavement, personal necessity, and vacation. Table 6 clarifies reasons for leaves.

PERSONNEL FILES

Rights of access to an employee's personnel file are described in the Education Code. Materials in personnel files that may affect the employee's status are to be made available to the employee (Ed. Code #44031). An employee must have the opportunity to view any derogatory information placed in his or her file and to attach a response to the document. The employee also must be notified before any negative information is placed in the personnel file (Ed. Code #44031).

Table 6
Leaves of Absence

Type of Leave	Description
Sick leave	To each classified employee who is employed fulltime, California law grants twelve days each year for sick leave; a governing board may approve additional days. These absences cover illness or injury (Ed. Code #45191). The individual employee accumulates sick leave days from year to year. In addition to regular sick leave, the Education Code allows extended sick leave of 100 days per year. These additional days may not be credited in payment at less than 50% of the employee's regular salary.
Industrial accident and illness	The governing board of the district must allow 60 days' leave per fiscal year for a single accident that occurs as a result of working in the district (Ed. Code #45192). This leave is allowed apart from regular sick leave or vacation.
Vacation	Vacation days are determined by the district, but the minimum is set at five-sixths of a day for each month in which the employee is in paid status for more than one-half the working days (Ed. Code #45197). A school district governing board may allow vacation days beyond this minimum.
Pregnancy	Boards of education may provide a leave of absence for any female employee in the classified service who takes time away from work because of childbirth. The board may also adopt rules and regulations as to the manner of proving pregnancy, the time during the pregnancy when leave may be taken, and the number of days allowed after the birth of the child (Ed. Code #45193).
Bereavement	The Education Code establishes the length of time for bereavement leave. Three days are allotted for in-state bereavement leave, or five days in case of travel out-of-state. The code defines "immediate family" as the mother, father, grandmother, grandfather, or grandchild of the employee and the spouse. The spouse, son, son-in-law, daughter, daughter-in-law, brother, and sister are also immediate family, as is any relative living in the immediate household of the employee. Governing boards may extend the length of leave or the definition of "immediate family" (Ed. Code #45194).
Other leaves	Other leaves, such as paid holidays, retraining leaves, and personal necessity, are also specified in the Education Code. Minimum amounts of time for such leaves are spelled out in law; however, a district may exceed the minimums.

39 month rule
The employee gets 39 months to take back their job.

MERIT SYSTEM

A school district may establish a classified Merit System under Education Code sections #45240 to #45320. These sections specify how the Personnel Commission is established and the rules and regulations that may be adopted in its formation. The Personnel Commission presents recommendations to the governing board regarding salary schedules, classifications, and working conditions.

Regulations governing the Merit System in a district set forth procedures to be followed by the governing board with respect to applications, examinations, eligibility, appointments, promotions, demotions, and transfers in the classified service. Other rules pertain to dismissals, resignations, layoffs, reemployment, vacations, and leaves of absence. Compensation within classification, job analyses and specifications, performance evaluations, public advertisement of examinations, rejection of unfit applicants without competition, and any other matters necessary to carry out the provisions and purposes of the Merit System are also addressed (Ed. Code #45261).

The board selects a commission (group) to set up testing, etc. Like having two boards. (Monrovia)

CONTRACTING OUT / PRIVATIZATION

Classified employees are essential for the conduct of the instructional program. The question each district administrator must answer is: What is the optimum size of the classified staff? One alternative many districts are considering is contracting outside the district for work otherwise performed by classified staff. Contracting for transportation service was one of the earliest uses of this concept. Operations and maintenance, food services, data processing, and payroll are other areas that districts may contract to an outside vendor. Proponents of contracting for school services argue that the district receives better services at less cost. Conversely, critics of privatization assert that costs are lower when a service is performed by school employees because a margin for profit is not charged. This alternative should be carefully considered by weighing the pros and cons of service from an independent contractor as opposed to service by the district classified staff.

SUMMARY

This chapter has reviewed issues related to the classified staff: classification, compensation, sick leave, industrial accident, and other laws governing the classified service. The importance of maintaining an efficient and well-trained classified staff cannot be over-emphasized. Unfortunately, in times of financial cutbacks, many classified staff lose their positions because school districts must always focus on the classroom.

As noted in the chapter, fringe benefits have assumed a major role in attracting classified personnel who might earn a better salary in private industry. In some districts fringe benefit costs are equal to the cost of the classified service.

The chapter also reviewed Merit System guidelines. A district personnel officer who finds that employees are interested in this system will find it necessary to review Sections #45240 to #45320 in the Education Code. This portion of the code describes transfers, dismissals, vacations, leaves, and competition for employment under the Merit System.

KEY TERMS

1. classification plan
2. compensatory time off
3. contracted services
4. custodial formulas

5. job analysis
6. job description
7. Merit System
8. overtime provision

QUESTIONS AND ACTIVITIES

1. Classified personnel supplement certificated services. Name the three most important services provided by classified personnel and discuss their importance to the education system.

2. "Classification" is a major term in classified personnel administration. What is the meaning of this term? Why is it important?

3. Classified salary schedules are somewhat similar to certificated salary schedules. Discuss the similarities and differences in the two salary schedules.

4. Classified employees have the right to establish a district classified Merit System. What are the major characteristics of such a system?

5. Some California districts "contract" for services ordinarily performed by the classified staff. Name the services most commonly contracted out to private enterprise. Briefly discuss the advantages and disadvantages of contracting out.

6. In your own district or one to which you have access, compare the salary schedules of several classifications such as secretary, clerical, food services, and transportation. What are the differences in pay rates per hour? Why do these differences exist?

7. Examine the formulas issued by CASBO for calculating the number of custodians required to clean classrooms in a school. Do you agree with this formula? Why or why not?

Chapter 8

Staff Development

INTRODUCTION

The National Education Association (Colvin & Woo, 1998) estimated that the average American schoolteacher is approximately 43 years old and has been teaching 14 years. Significant societal and world changes have occurred during those 14 years. History textbooks printed in the '80s that discussed the Soviet Union and the communist bloc soon became very much out-of-date. History textbooks of the '80s still referred to the Berlin wall and a divided Germany. Few of these texts contained the name Saddam Hussein. Only a rare student could have placed Kuwait or Afghanistan on the world map.

If asked about AIDS, most teachers would have thought of a classroom instructional aide. In the early '80s the phrase "crack babies" was not part of our vocabulary; yet today these children are entering our classrooms. Surrogate mothers, laser surgery, liposuction, stealth bombers, safe sex, and condoms for students were topics unfamiliar to college graduates at that time.

During this 20-year period significant changes also occurred in American education. We learned more about how teachers might best organize their classrooms, deliver instruction, and interact with students to improve learning. A decade or two ago, collaborative learning, computer-assisted instruction, and the Internet were known in only a few of the nation's schools; yet by 2000 a school that had not embraced one or more of these programs was the rare exception.

However, many administrators and teachers are unaware of these changes except at a superficial level. Many districts have not provided staff development programs in the new skills required to teach students about computers or in organizing a class for collaborative learning. Some districts have embarked upon a course toward restructuring without fully defining the concept or developing a thoughtful strategic plan for its implementation.

These educational and societal changes, and others on the horizon, intensify the need for school districts to organize effective staff development programs. Educational leaders recognize that schooling is a labor-intensive industry and that, as a consequence, teachers, administrators, and classified employees need constantly to learn new methods and techniques to which they were not exposed during their training or education. Today, it is literally impossible for an individual to enter any trade or profession and remain in it without upgrading and learning new skills and knowledge throughout his or her career.

Paradoxically, change has become a constant in American society, and schools reflect the values of that society. Societal needs have imposed and will impose new mandates on schools, creating constant need to introduce new services. All staffs will be required to become familiar with new information, new instructional materials and equipment, new instructional strategies, and new modes of assessment. As these demands escalate, so does need for staff development programs. Somehow, school systems must commit additional resources to satisfy societal demands for a well-trained, knowledgeable staff.

STAFF DEVELOPMENT AND EDUCATION REFORM

The most important resource in any organization is its personnel. With staff committed to the expectations of the district, well informed and well trained, and high in morale, great things happen in schools! Michael Fullan, in an address and followup session at the 1998 conference of the Association of California School Administrators, underscored the importance of staff development as a tool for large-scale reform. Indeed, he argued that although large-scale reform calls for decentralization, higher levels of the education organization must take responsibility for "investment in local capacity." That is, all adult members of the school community, parents as well as staff, need support in gaining the understandings and becoming skilled in the strategies necessary to help students achieve. Assessment literacy, according to Fullan, is at the top of the priority list for such development, if the profession is to respond to rigorous external accountability systems—which he also regards as a necessary component of large-scale reform. This heightened local capacity can only come into being if schools become professional learning communities focused on student achievement (Fullan, 1998a, 1998b). Here Fullan echoes the work of Peter Senge, who argues for learning organizations and, in *The Fifth Discipline Handbook* (Senge, Kleiner, Roberts, Ross, & Smith, 1994), offers strategies for creating them.

Along similar lines, Sparks and Hirsh (1997), in a publication sponsored by the Association for Supervision and Curriculum Development (ASCD), speak of a "paradigm shift." They propose that staff development must not only affect knowledge, attitudes, and skills, but must also "alter the cultures and structures of the organization in which those individuals work." They, too, see student outcomes as the ultimate tool for evaluating the success of staff development efforts.

DEFINITIONS

There is much confusion regarding the definitions of "inservice education" and "staff development." A workable differentiation is that inservice education imparts specific skills or knowledge, while staff development promotes ongoing professional growth through a cumulative process. Thus, inservice education has been associated with short-range goals yielding specific objectives, whereas staff development has consisted of series of experiences leading toward long-term outcomes.

For example, most teachers with ten or more years' experience have had little university training in computer technology. An effective inservice program gives staff the competencies to assist students in working with computers. The objectives of the program would be stated quite precisely and inservice activities scheduled within a relatively short period of time.

Training a staff to be bicultural and bilingual, on the other hand, exemplifies a staff development undertaking with complex learnings to be mastered only after long and consistent effort. In other words, inservice education may be viewed as a subset of staff development, although the terms are sometimes used interchangeably.

LEGAL REQUIREMENTS

The California state legislature recognized the need for professional growth activities for teachers and approved legislation requiring an ongoing professional development program to achieve this objective. The legislature's direction to school districts is set forth in Education Code section #44670.1:

> The Legislature recognizes the necessity for school development which results in direct improvement of instruction to pupils. The Legislature intends to give all those who work with pupils ongoing opportunities to strengthen subject matter knowledge, instruction, and support through locally designed school development plans.

The code section gives teachers a wide range of options for completing a minimum of 150 clock hours of participation in activities that contribute to competence, performance, or effectiveness in the profession of education. For a teacher to maintain a clear teaching credential, this requirement must be completed every five years.

Several other Education Code sections refer to inservice training programs. For example, sections mandate specific training for teachers; these include AIDS prevention instruction, discriminatory practices, and hate violence.

STATE SUPPORT FOR STAFF DEVELOPMENT

The state of California has given financial support for staff development by several means. School Improvement funds, now in nearly every elementary school and a significant portion of secondary sites, have been a major source of funds for teacher, classified staff, and parent education for more than 20 years. The California mentor teacher program, established as part of education reform legislation in 1983, was replaced in 1999 with Peer Assistance and Review, already discussed in Chapter 6. Recent legislation has addressed standards-based curriculum in core subject areas, support for underachieving schools, and administrator training. Unfortunately, as this book goes to press, funding reductions may hamper the implementation of some of these programs.

Release Days

Before 1998 districts were allowed to excuse students from attendance for a maximum of eight days each year to conduct inservice programs. This practice was eliminated by SB1193, the Instructional Time and Staff Development Reform Program. Implementation of alternatives in the wake of this legislation was fraught with problems. Requiring staff to participate necessitates changes in collective bargaining agreements. Voluntary participation often fails because key people choose not to attend.

Subject-Matter Projects

Nine subject matter projects—arts, foreign language, history-social science, international studies, literature, mathematics, physical education and health, science, and writing—have involved teachers across the state in curriculum and staff development. Following legislation to establish statewide norm-referenced tests with the requirement that 90% of students become grade-level proficient, these subject matter projects were directed by law to conform to the statewide academic standards then being prepared for adoption by California's State Board of Education.

Bilingual Teacher Training Program (BTTP)

The Bilingual Teacher Training Program was legislated in 1981. The program established a baker's dozen of BTTP centers to train teachers in second language acquisition in bilingual and monolingual settings. Upon completion of this program a teacher receives either the English-only (CLAD) or Bilingual (BCLAD) Cross-Cultural Language and Academic Development certificate.

NEEDS ASSESSMENT

The first step in organizing and planning a staff development program should be an assessment of district and school needs. Too many well-intentioned programs overlook the real needs of the employees and are, therefore, destined for failure from the beginning. A careful needs assessment provides accurate information to be utilized in decision-making and planning prior to embarking on the program. Needs assessment is a systematic approach to determining whether an organization's objectives are being satisfactorily accomplished. Building on that information, the process leads a planning group to identify staff development requirements.

Needs assessment is concerned with "what is" as compared to "what should be." An effective needs assessment asks: What is the real problem? What must be done to fix it? What is the best solution? If needs exceed available resources, as is often the case, priorities are established. Then action plans are developed and resources allocated accordingly.

As noted in an earlier chapter, an effective needs assessment may be as simple as revisiting the district's mission statement. However, in other circumstances it may require a very detailed review of the organization's educational philosophy, objectives, and practices. The assessment process should be ongoing and related to the district's goals and objectives.

In summary, the needs assessment should be guided by established goals and objectives. If a goal has been set for student achievement, then information about student achievement must be gathered. If a goal has been set to improve the skills of bus drivers, then one must inquire into the skills of bus drivers. An effective assessment instrument enables a district to set priorities, allocate resources, and provide direction for the staff development program within the vision and goals of the organization.

IMPLEMENTING A STAFF DEVELOPMENT PROGRAM

Maintaining and improving the quality of a school staff is top priority for educational leaders. Improved quality of administrative and teaching staff has also become a concern of national leaders, including the President, most governors, and legislative bodies at both state and national levels. Wirt and Kirst (1989) estimated that more than 250 state task forces had sprung up during the '80s to study every aspect of education and to recommend changes. Most of their reports called for improvement in the quality of teachers. Proposed reforms included teacher competency testing, career ladders, mentor teachers, schools of choice, and restructuring of decision-making. Every one of these programs demands new training and retraining for those involved.

Margaret Fitch and O. W. Kopp (1990) identified five elements of a quality staff development program:

- building common knowledge and concepts

- developing a shared vision among participants

- identifying desired changes in values and beliefs

- supporting new values and beliefs by translating them into specific objectives or behaviors

- systematically managing change to obtain desired results.

These elements aggregate to a systematic move toward a goal of the organization. The overriding goal of staff development is to assist staff members to perform their duties more effectively as they meet the needs springing from an inconstant environment. Thus, the primary purpose of a staff development program is to increase the knowledge and skills of employees, thereby increasing the potential of the organization to achieve its goals and objectives.

An important consideration is state mandates. For example, in California a student testing program was enacted as law in 1997. This new assessment program replaces the long-standing California Assessment Program (CAP), which had been replaced briefly by the California Learning Assessment System (CLAS). The 1997 program carries the acronym "STAR"—Standardized Testing and Reporting. The system includes norm-referenced testing (the SAT9) and matrix testing aligned to a new generation of state standards.

In addition to these instruments, districts may develop a combination of two or three assessment instruments to determine whether students have reached grade-level proficiency. Like its predecessors, STAR requires training for teachers and administrators. Staff development must address test administration and reporting as well as communicating results to parents, school site councils, and school boards. Most important will be teachers' ability to use both norm-referenced data and performance-based assessments to improve curriculum and instruction. This is the "assessment literacy" called for by Michael Fullan (1998a, 1998b).

ADULT LEARNING

The concept of lifelong learning spurred new research in how adults learn. Since the participants in staff development include classified personnel and parents, as well as certificated staff, an early step in effective implementation is to review the literature on adult learning. Malcolm Knowles (1970) is generally credited with having coined the word "andragogy" (the art and science of teaching adults), as distinct from "pedagogy" (the art and science of teaching children). Andragogy is based on the notion that adults are self-directed learners who are unique as a consequence of their personal experiences. Their need to learn results from their desire to face the challenges they encounter throughout life. Knowles identified four critical characteristics of adults and their patterns of learning:

- As a person matures, his or her self-concept moves from dependency to self-direction.

- The mature person accumulates a growing reservoir of experience that provides a resource for learning.

- The adult's readiness to learn becomes increasingly oriented toward the developmental tasks of his or her social roles.

- The adult's time perspective changes from future to immediate application of knowledge; accordingly, his or her orientation toward learning becomes problem-centered, rather than subject-centered.

More recent work by Speck (1996) established a list of elements essential in an adult staff development program:

- Adults need real-world applications.

- Adults want to be treated as competent professionals.

- Adult learning involves egos.

- Adults need constructive feedback on their efforts to learn and apply new skills.

- Adults benefit from participating in small-group activities.

- Adult learners are unique individuals with a wide range of skills and experiences.

- Transfer of learning must be facilitated.

- Coaching and follow-up support are needed to help adult learners transfer learning into daily practice.

Programs consistent with adult learning theory make for success. The superintendent, coordinator, or principal who reviews these principles when planning and implementing a program can avoid much of the current criticism of staff development.

METHODS OF PRESENTATION

Presenters of staff development programs must model the best principles of effective teaching. Designing a program involves more than simply finding a university professor or independent consultant who is interested in offering a workshop on a particular topic. Using persons with various, but relevant, backgrounds enriches a staff development program. A major source of presenters should be the senior or mentor teachers in the school or district itself. Often these presenters possess credibility with a staff and enjoy a built-in trust that contributes to program success.

Those charged with organizing the program must have a profound understanding of the psychology and conditions required for effective learning. In far too many programs, presenters do not practice effective teaching skills. Even though a presenter may be eminently knowledgeable of subject matter, if he or she does not exhibit effective teaching, the audience will be cynical about the content of the message.

Like a teacher of children, the session leader must consider the skill and knowledge level of the participants. Although educational leaders constantly express their belief that every learner is different, this principle is often ignored when they plan staff development activities. At each district or school site, teachers have different needs, interests, learning styles, and abilities. Teachers often complain that staff development activities have been a waste of time because no effort was made to match learning activities with learning needs.

Placing elementary and secondary teachers into separate groups to address some objectives is sometimes advisable. For instance, in preparing teachers for a completely new testing program, it may not be productive for secondary teachers to learn the mechanics of scoring a third-grade test. Beginning teachers may best be grouped apart from more experienced staff. Burden and Wallace (1983) suggest that sessions for beginning teachers should follow a structured, directive approach, while teachers with more experience prefer a program that adds variety to their teaching and, therefore, favor a collaborative approach.

Showers and associates (1987) identified four steps for a successful inservice session:

- presentation of theory

- demonstration of a teaching strategy

- initial practice

- prompt feedback.

The more complex the behavior being taught, the greater the need for a program that incorporates all four elements. Practice and feedback appear to be particularly important when the desired behavior is unfamiliar to the learner (Sparks, 1983).

By designing a staff development program around felt needs, carefully structuring the program based on the principles of adult learning, and selecting effective presenters who model excellent teaching practice, most criticism of staff programs can be averted.

BEYOND PRESENTATIONS

Although much staff development will no doubt continue to rely upon skilled presentations followed up with collegial feedback, Sparks and Hirsh (1997) point out that constructivism is applicable to adult learning, as well as to children. Indeed, many of the practices suggested by constructivism resemble those developed earlier by Knowles and others in the field of andragogy. Moreover, staff development should model the instructional practices that teachers are expected to use with their pupils—and many of these, too, recognize that learners continually construct and reconstruct their understandings. Consequently, Sparks and Hirsh recommend "job-embedded learning," designed so that new ideas are immediately applied and adapted. Such activities as action research, study groups, and journal writing are described as successful staff development strategies.

TIME FOR STAFF PARTICIPATION

A critical element in staff development is to arrange the time necessary for employee participation. Moore and Hyde (1981) divide teacher time for staff development into four categories:

- "Salaried work time" includes all hours during which teachers are on duty.

- "Release time" means periods during which substitutes are employed to release teachers from teaching duties.

- "Stipend time" is time outside of regular work hours during which teachers participate in staff development activities and receive a salary supplement. This type of work activity is often scheduled during the summer months—or off-student-schedule for those schools that operate year-round.

- "Personal time" is after the school day, that is, the teacher's personal, non-contract time. A teacher's personal time is the least costly for the district, but may also be the least productive or effective.

Too many programs fail because they are scheduled after a full day of teaching when employees are tired and display built-in resistance. No teacher, administrator, or classified employee can assimilate new ideas when fatigued. More than 25 years ago Davies and Armistead (1975), asserted that the common practice in business and industry of scheduling staff development programs during the work day or on "company time" should be emulated in education.

Unfortunately, California's commitment to that recommendation has suffered a setback with the shift from the possibility of eight release days during the school year to three staff development days, probably voluntary, outside the instructional year. Other options include negotiated work days—over and above the teaching schedule—for staff development and dismissing school early in the afternoon on a given number of days each week or month for this purpose.

STAFF DEVELOPMENT FOR CLASSIFIED EMPLOYEES

Much of this chapter has specifically addressed staff development programs for teachers and other certificated employees. However, many of the same principles apply when establishing a strong program for classified staff. There is growing awareness that instructional associates, campus supervisors, secretaries, bus drivers, and other members of the classified staff are as much in need of inservice training and staff development as their certificated counterparts. For example, all new classified employees need an orientation period during which they learn the expectations of the school or district and the requirements of their new assignment.

These employees are so important in supporting the certificated staff that investment in their continued training is also essential to efficient and effective schools and districts. Consider, for instance, that schools reflect society in the ever-expanding place of technology. A secretary with 10 or more years' service may not have been trained on the use of the computer for word processing, budget control, or attendance accounting. Similarly, a custodian may require training in the use of new cleaning materials and equipment, while maintenance staff may need to learn how to repair new and more complicated machinery.

WHY STAFF DEVELOPMENT IS SOMETIMES INEFFECTIVE

Much has been written criticizing staff development programs currently provided by schools and districts. Perhaps the most serious criticism is found in such teacher comments as, "The presentation was interesting and gave me a 'great idea in theory,' but it won't work in my classroom." This criticism is most often heard when a speaker attempts to teach a new idea or skill with a heavy dose of theory and little opportunity for practice. Joyce and Showers (1988) make a strong case that other learning components must be included for a successful program:

- Only five percent of learners will transfer a new skill into practice as a result of theory alone.

- Ten percent will transfer new skills into practice as a result of theory and the demonstration of the new learning.

- Twenty percent will transfer a new skill into applied practice if theory, demonstration, and practice of the new learning are conducted within the training.

- Twenty-five percent will transfer a new skill into practice if the use of theory, demonstration, practice, and feedback are provided during the training.

- Ninety percent will transfer a new skill into use if theory, demonstration, practice, feedback, and ongoing coaching are provided as elements of the professional development program.

STAFF DEVELOPMENT AND THE INTERNET

A relatively new and exciting opportunity for teacher and administrator staff learning is becoming available on the Internet. Articles by noted academics, task force reports, and effective teaching and learning practices are all available via computer. At the most informal level, teachers can participate in professional discussion through e-mail, discussion forums, and online "chats." At the next level, a variety of university courses is now offered on almost any topic of interest to a teacher or administrator. Then, too, nearly every professional education association has developed a Website or is in the process of doing so. A list of Websites for teacher and administrator exploration is contained in Appendix A.

EVALUATION

A final component of an effective staff development program is an evaluation system to determine whether objectives are being met. Staff development and inservice activities must be evaluated intensively to ascertain whether they are worth the cost and effort invested in them. Wade (1984/1985) writes that four outcomes should be measured to evaluate effectiveness of a staff development program. They are:

- teacher reactions

- teacher knowledge

- teacher behavior change

- increased student learning.

Evaluation of staff development may range from a simple perception-based approach, such as asking participants to comment on or to rate the value of the program, to a complex format with elaborate statistical analysis. Guskey and Sparks (1991) write that evaluation findings should be used to improve a program, not merely to make judgements about its effectiveness. Important elements to consider in program evaluation go beyond participant outcomes to organizational and student outcomes. Sound evaluation procedures follow up to determine whether change has taken place in the classroom or on the job, and not just in an artificial practice session. If participants and organizations do not meet the targeted objectives of the staff development program, then it is impractical to expect improvement in student learning. Thoughtful planning and ongoing evaluation should serve to ensure the effectiveness of a staff development program. Effective evaluation yields guidance both in assessing program effectiveness and in developing plans for future training.

SUMMARY

Effective teachers are lifelong learners; therefore, effective staff development and inservice programs are critically important to good schools. Change is a constant condition in American society: new technology, the latest research, and legislative mandates impact schools almost at once. Schools need highly competent teachers, administrators, and support staff to implement these changes. No employee can remain highly qualified without ongoing education and training. No longer can a district employ a teacher, administrator, or classified employee and feel confident that the skills and competencies at employment will continue to meet the needs of a changing environment. *Interesting...*

Staff development is designed to advance the knowledge, skills, and understanding of teachers and other staff members so as to produce better performance. Staff development should be designed to update subject area skills and knowledge in order to improve instruction. It must also consider and respond to societal demands and changes. The updating of skills and dissemination of research and new knowledge designed to improve instruction will continue to be a high priority. Programs will also be required to inform staff of new policies and procedures and ensure compliance with new state mandates. An effective program involves top-level leadership—including superintendents and principals. Successful programs grow out of careful planning, attention to the needs of the adult learner, and a carefully designed evaluation system.

KEY TERMS

1. adult learning
2. andragogy *– adult learning*
3. company time
4. inservice
5. needs assessment

6. pedagogy
7. personal time
8. released time
9. salaried work time
10. staff development
11. stipend time

QUESTIONS AND ACTIVITIES

1. Fitch and Kopp (1990) identified five elements of a quality staff development program. Briefly discuss each element and state why it is essential in a quality program.

2. The first step in organizing and planning a staff development program should be an assessment of district and school needs. Discuss the procedures involved in completing a needs assessment.

3. Staff development programs are often criticized by teachers. What is the usual reason for this criticism? How might it be avoided?

4. Obtain a copy of three school districts' master plans for staff development. Meeting in a small group, compare similarities and differences.

5. Invite to your class or district a personnel officer from a private business that is noted for its effective staff development program. Take advantage of this opportunity to compare purposes, resources, and program designs in the private sector with those in schools.

6. In a small group, brainstorm the areas in which you feel staff development is most urgently needed in many school districts. Select one area, agree upon one or more outcomes, consider the options, and outline several inservice experiences toward the identified outcome(s).

7. Interview one teacher from each grade level in an elementary school or one member of each department at a secondary school, Elicit their suggestions for improving staff development programs in their school.

8. Develop a needs assessment survey that could be administered in your school or district to gather perceived staff development needs.

9. Interview your principal or superintendent to learn what they see as top priorities for staff development in your school or district. Do you agree? Explain.

10. Review your school or district budget to determine the amount of funds allocated for inservice or staff development. Is this amount adequate? Discuss.

Chapter 9

Organizational Culture and Climate

INTRODUCTION

When Deal and Kennedy published their book *Corporate Cultures* in 1992, they identified such organizational features as heroes and heroines, tribal habits, and wizards and scribes. Many readers thought they had picked up a copy of Tolkien's *Lord of the Rings*, rather than a book about organizations. But the longer one ponders an organization, the more one can actually identify its "heroes," its "villains," its "dinosaurs," and those who—writing or talking about organizational history—act as "scribes" or "wizards."

The players who make up an organization shape the organizational culture. That is, as they work within the culture, their behavior, attitudes, and beliefs make up the organizational climate.

What is the difference between *organizational culture* and *organizational climate*? "Organizational culture" is defined as shared philosophies, ideologies, beliefs, feelings, assumptions, expectations, attitudes, norms, and values (Kilmann, Saxton, & Serpa, 1985). "Organizational climate" is the total environmental quality of an organization; it is the "feeling tone" of a company or school. Organizational climate may be characterized as open and warm; as hostile, rigid, and closed; as impersonal or informal. The twin concepts of organizational culture and organizational climate are key to understanding the nature of schools. Moreover, school culture and climate can determine success or failure in achieving successful student outcomes.

This chapter addresses the issues of organizational culture and organizational climate in school settings. The discussion begins with the nature and characteristics of organizational culture. Next, we describe how organizational cultures are created, changed, and maintained. We take an unusual example, a funeral parlor, to explain the science of "semiotics." A comparison is then made between organizational culture of schools and that of business organizations. The topic of organizational climate follows. Finally, we discuss similarities and differences between organizational culture and climate—particularly in the school personnel arena. The chapter closes with our contention that these concepts, properly understood and applied, can help create excellent schools.

ORGANIZATIONAL CULTURE

If you walk about a school and note its symbols, behaviors of the staff, and manifestations of staff beliefs and feelings, you are observing the features of that school organization. To describe organizational culture, you must perceive the school's shared norms, values, assumptions, ideologies, and philosophies. Edgar Schein (1992) emphasizes that the things a group holds in common constitute the common culture. These commonalities might include customs, traditions, group norms, espoused values, game rules, shared meanings, habits of thinking, mental models, and integrating symbols. He feels that a useful way to think about culture is to conceptualize it as "accumulated shared learning" of a given group. Implicit in this definition is a period of time necessary to build the culture and relative stability in a membership group.

We can draw an analogy by meandering through the aisles of a well-known department store. Nordstroms, originating from Seattle, Washington, has a distinctive culture. The attitude of the salespeople, the layout of the store, and the liberal quality of its merchandise return policy all contribute to the "Nordstrom Culture." If you walk into Nordstroms today, you "feel" the climate, you detect the helpful (yet assertive) attitude of its salespeople. The story may be apocryphal, but it is said that Nordstroms actually accepted a "return" of an automobile tire (although the store does not sell tires), based simply upon the customer's explanation to the clerk. Obviously, the customer or client is given the highest consideration in this store.

INDICATORS OF ORGANIZATIONAL CULTURE IN SCHOOLS

It takes longer to sense the organizational culture of a school. We would need to observe a faculty meeting, listen to faculty in the lounge, and talk to staff, parents, and students. What particular indicators might contribute to our understanding of school organizational culture? Who are the "teacher-heroes"? According to parents, how difficult is it to find the office? Is the vision of the principal communicated clearly? If this is a high school, does the principal, like Mike Matthews, the principal of Malibu High School, teach a class? Does this action communicate something about this principal's resolve to remain close to students?

Although there are many indicators of organizational culture, five characteristics seem key in observing and analyzing any organization. Researchers such as Edgar Schein have been instrumental in observing organizations and discovering the culture within, whether obvious or "hidden." Indicators of organizational culture in schools include interpersonal behavior, "newcomer" guidelines, vision/mission statements, values, and norms.

Interpersonal Behavior

How do people treat one another? Is there evidence of team teaching or collaboration among teachers? For example, do teachers cooperate to use multimedia in lesson presentations? Even overall school layout may indicate how teachers interact with each other. For instance, how far apart are the classrooms?

Social interactions also play a large part in establishing the school culture. For example, do teachers eat their lunch or work during the lunch period? Do they develop close personal relationships or view the school as just a place to work? Does a staff member using the copy machine turn to a person waiting and ask, "How many copies do you need?" This may be a small act, but it reflects positively on the staff and suggests a courteous and considerate culture.

"Newcomer" Guidelines

Most newcomers in schools devote much time and attention to "learning the ropes." But when a newcomer has a problem with a student, do colleagues encourage or discourage him from discussing the problem with the principal?

Vision / Mission Statements

Most school districts have devoted significant time and effort to drafting vision or mission statements that are intended to appear in all district documents. Such a statement embodies the philosophy of the district. It is intended to guide the ways employees treat students and administrators consider employees. It describes how schools are expected to relate to parents, the community, and to educational standards. In some schools the district vision is well known among students, staff, and the community. In other districts, a puzzled look appears on the faces of individuals quizzed about the district's vision or philosophy.

Values

Many phrases used by schools and districts sound platitudinous because they are not practiced. The degree to which they are more than slogans is the degree to which these phrases capture something that employees really believe about the organization. If these phrases become central to an organization's philosophy, they may be called its "core values." For example, many companies and schools rely on their employees' desire to "do a good job." Those in positions of power institutionalize core values by creating task forces, by listening to ideas, and by rewarding those who visibly put the values into practice.

Norms

Usually a norm, whether spoken or unspoken, sets a standard. In many organizations, for example, the notion of "a fair day's pay for a fair day's work" is the norm, the way people work. The issue becomes more complex when law becomes involved. In California, for instance, state law specifies that a teacher must report to work 30 minutes before school opens. Consequently, the norm for teacher working time typically kicks in at the close of the school day, when teacher time is more flexible. Thus, the *maximum* time given each work day is largely determined by "norms." Group norms have strong impact and are a major force governing employee behavior.

Although the above indicators of organizational culture may be difficult to identify, they exist at every school site and in every district. Moreover, organizational culture has a major effect upon organizational outcomes. Thus, to assess how successfully a school is operating, one might examine the dropout rate, scholastic achievement, or student attitude. An educational organization typically uses such feedback to improve its performance. But these outcomes may be influenced by drives or constraints that originate in the school's organizational culture. In this case, it becomes necessary not merely to devise a new procedure or program, but to modify or re-create the culture itself.

CREATING ORGANIZATIONAL CULTURE

Many how-to books advise managers on creating a positive organizational culture. Such texts may extol the importance of values. And indeed, values lie at the very soul of any organization. But a school will not carry out the stated mission or vision if the staff does not "buy into" the formulation.Rather, in addition to the stated values of the school, its people—its heroes and heroines—largely determine its culture.

Southwest Airlines: A Different Drummer

A good example to illustrate how one individual can create a unique culture in a large corporation is the leadership of Herb Kelleher, the CEO of Southwest Airlines. In a world that prizes corporate homogeneity, Southwest dares its employees to be different, and Kelleher models that difference. A lawyer who became the corporate leader of the low-fare carrier, Kelleher rides into company cook-offs on a Harley Davidson. The company selected "LUV" as its stock symbol, and Kelleher is famous for hugging and kissing employees. This chain-smoking, bourbon-swilling legend recruited Raquel Welch look-alikes to be his hot-pants-clad flight attendants. Although flight attendants usually wear shorts, they have been known to dress in elf costumes and serenade passengers with Christmas songs. The company is famous for offering customers a choice of several meals—as long as the meal is peanuts.

However, in spite of his playful image, Kelleher has a serious leadership style. For example, he states that Southwest works a lot harder at hiring than most companies. The company may interview a hundred candidates to select one flight attendant. Kelleher is looking for that special person, a person with a sense of humor and a strong sense of service.

The company's success proves that the culture works. Kelleher and Southwest have carved a powerful niche for the carrier. The company grew from four planes with no profit in 1971 to sales of more than $6 billion in 2001. The company's philosophy and management style have been described in a book published by Bard Press, entitled *Nuts! Southwest Airlines' Crazy Recipe for Business and Personal Success.* The book notes that at Southwest, sassy and flamboyant marketing has always overshadowed a fierce corporate discipline. Managers at Southwest take no guff. When a rival laid claim to the industry's customer service crown in 1992, Southwest responded with a print ad declaring, "After lengthy deliberation at the highest executive levels and extensive consultation with our legal department, we have arrived at an official corporate response to Northwest Airlines' claim to be number one in Customer Satisfaction: 'Liar, liar, pants on fire!'" (Groves, 1996).

Kelleher offers excellent advice that would well serve a new superintendent or principal who wishes to change the district or school culture. If you were to try changing a culture, you would need to eliminate the keepers of the old culture. If you choose to redefine the culture, you must change unbelievers into believers.

The Case of the Funeral Home

Even though a funeral home may be an unusual example of creating organizational culture, a major study accomplished this goal. Stephen Barley (1983) used the science of semiotics (signs) to analyze creation of culture in a funeral home. This study is useful because it takes us out of the school, forcing us to view cultural change in another milieu. It is also important because it shows how a business (the funeral home) works subtly to create an atmosphere that attracts clients without their awareness.

"Semiotics" is the use of symbolism to portray a vision or "idea" of how things should be. For example, "crown" is used to denote something regal or kingly. Barley's study was designed to apply the basic units of semiotic analysis. He studied a funeral home for three months. The home was operated by two brothers, both of whom were funeral directors, having inherited the business from their father.

He found that the goal of the staff was to make live visitors at home as well as to create a "natural" atmosphere for all. In addition, the deceased would be hidden as much as possible unless he or she were shown in a natural or "sleep-like" state. How did they accomplish this?

To create a sleep-like appearance, the corpse is dressed with cosmetics. The body is also arranged in the casket so that the public perceives that the body may be "sleeping."

Then, to create a home-like atmosphere, the funeral director furnishes each room in the home with comfortable stuffed chairs and couches, similar to those found in the living rooms of private homes. The furniture is upholstered in light colors and the carpets of the rooms match the upholstery.

The funeral director also creates a culture in the manner of removing a body from a home. Our society is uncomfortable about viewing a dead body. Therefore, the director asks all interested parties to congregate for coffee in the kitchen while the body is being removed. He then carefully removes the body and leaves the bedroom as pristine as possible. The strategic rearrangement of the room is intended to reconstruct what the room may have looked like before it became a death room and to suggest that a removal did not occur.

All these signs indicate a particular culture—a culture designed to intimate that death is natural, calm, and peaceful, and to reflect a family orientation. Each symbol is used to project these images.

Corporate Heroes

One well-known heroine who is responsible for building an organization in which the culture is well articulated is Mary Kay Ash. She founded Mary Kay Cosmetics—a company that inspires its workers to carry out the company's vision ever more energetically. As a reward to her workers, Mary Kay offers diamond bumblebee pins; these signify that anyone has the ability to rise above what might be expected. (Mary Kay people are told again and again that the bumblebee's ability to fly defies aerodynamic principles.) Other well-known business leaders who were perceived as "heroes" at certain points in their careers include Tom Watson at IBM, Lee Iacocca at Chrysler, Sam Walton at WalMart, Dane Thomas, founder of Wendy's Hamburgers, and Ed Carlson at United Airlines. Schools, too, have their heroes and heroines. Rituals, rites, and communication networks are among the means by which these individual influence their organizations.

The Disney Way

Every school child, teacher, and parent knows about Disneyland. As a matter of fact, many school administrators have adopted Disney's renowned way of controlling crowds. School cafeteria managers have embraced the "snake like" cafeteria line that seems so much shorter than a long, continuous line. However, most school people probably are not aware of a highly successful management program taught by the Disney Corporation.

Can you imagine the reaction of a school board if the superintendent requested to send her management staff to Disney World for a management training program—a three and one-half day seminar at a cost of $2,500 each? If the board were to approve such a request, school personnel would be joining some 60,000 people who are enrolled in a course in leadership, people management, and quality service. The Disney Corporation began sharing its management philosophy in the late 1980s, after the company was profiled in Tom Peters' *In Search of Excellence.*

The management philosophy of Disney is to make every moment magical for the customer—What a concept! What a difference it would make if every school strove to make every child feel that each school day is a magical moment! The Disney program emphasizes the importance of setting expectations about job performance and making the company's goals clear to employees. Valerie Oberle, Vice-President of Disney University Professional Development Programs, has said, "It's easy for other institutions to adapt Disney's culture to their businesses" (Applegate, 1996). In addition to its adaption by business and industry, the model has been successfully implemented in hospitals. Schools may be next in line.

Rituals and Rites

Both everyday activities and special celebrations may fulfill the function of rituals and rites. They are key tools with which to create an organizational culture. Teacher of the Year, Model School, and California Distinguished School awards are processes that form part of the ritual picture in education at state and national levels. Similarly, in many companies birthdays are given special attention. At Southwest Airlines the CEO leads a cheering crowd of employees as a regular ritual during company retreats. Strong cultures create deep meaning for many employees.

Coaches, music directors, and speech/drama teachers exemplify rituals and rites in schools. These teachers set clear standards of student success and celebrate with letter awards, banquets, and scholarships.

Networks of Communication

Each institution has "storytellers" who keep organizational stories in oral history. These stories, sometimes in the form of gossip, embellish the "heroes" of the organization and their past exploits, thus playing a key role in building and maintaining the organizational culture. Every faculty has a senior teacher who enlightens the staff with great stories about previous principals, staff members, and students. The importance of these information communication networks cannot be overstated. Feeding and reading them is one reason that "leadership by wandering around" is such an important concept.

The Principal's Office

A powerful influence that establishes the culture and climate of a school is the location and environment of the principal's office. First, where is the office located? Is it near the main entrance to the school? This location may connote an open and friendly invitation to parents and visitors. A central location with a window where the principal can observe students in the quad or playfields establishes a different priority.

Next, we move to the entrance to the principal's office. What a difference in the atmosphere of the school if the office is easily accessible to students, staff, and the public without gates and counters and layers of secretaries and clerks. The first impression, and often lasting impression, of a school is established by the first person with whom a parent or community member comes in contact, and that is often the secretary. One could write pages describing how that person's demeanor establishes the perceived values of the principal and the school.

Once inside the office, a strong message is sent by the placement of the principal's desk. A large imposing desk with two chairs placed across from the desk may send the message, "This is a very formal place; state your business, and be quick about it." Even the type of chair sends a message. Hard, unpadded chairs do not create an invitation to relax, take your time, and solve a problem together.

Some principals place their desk on one side of the office to establish a work space. Having a table, couch, and comfortable chairs in another area of the room provides a friendlier atmosphere for discussion and problem-solving. The decoration of the office also reflects the image the principal wishes to establish. Some offices have barren, military decor, devoid of photographs or personal mementos. Other principals have the walls covered with their degrees, recognition letters of achievement, or photos of family and students. The way the office is decorated reflects the principal's personality and leadership style. Each of these images contributes to establishing the school's culture and climate.

MAINTAINING SCHOOL ORGANIZATIONAL CULTURE

Once a school or business is a viable entity, mechanisms come into play to maintain consistent patterns within the organization. For example, one process that can be structured to encourage consistency is that of choosing and inducting new employees. Richard Pascale (1985) identifies seven steps in personnel selection and orientation that are important to maintaining a strong culture. Although some of his steps may not be applicable to a professional setting such as a school, the following points may be helpful.

- Encourage senior staff to share organizational values and experiences with new employees

- Recognize successful performance that contributes to the goals of the organization

- Consistently follow the transcendent values that make it worthwhile to work in the organization

- Keep alive the stories ("folklore") that remind employees of the goals and values of the organization.

Much of the work of organizations, including schools, revolves around the processes of "culture maintenance." To this end, both public and private schools and districts maintain elaborate rituals and communications networks, including public meetings, newsletters, television presentations, and radio conversations.

CHANGING THE CULTURE OF AN EDUCATIONAL ORGANIZATION

Sometimes outside forces provide impetus for change in an organization. At other times, the organization itself determines that it must change. Frost (1985), who has studied the factors that initiate change in organizations, notes the following:

External enabling atmosphere	Many external elements can trigger change within an organization. For example, the success of the Japanese car market in the early 1980s provided the impetus for American automobile companies to make major changes in their manufacturing and design operations. Other external forces that trigger change in schools include SAT or other test scores, a new program such as the Peer Assistance and Review legislation, or other changes in policy or law.
Internal ready conditions	At times, an organization may be ready for change. The major players must have the ability to note the time for change and have the ability to cooperate and even lead change. For example, new faculty or major turnover in other staff might trigger change in a school.
Precipitating pressures	Stakeholders may exert pressure for change. These stakeholders might be parents, teachers, or members of an interview team selecting a new principal. Fear of the voucher movement might act as precipitating pressure on a school.
Triggering event	A special education law such as PL 94-142 or Title IX may trigger changes within the school district as policies are modified to accommodate the new law. Or a school district may receive funding for a new project such as Reading Recovery.
Cultural visioning	Leaders continually survey the beliefs, assumptions, and values of the organization, enabling them to create a vision of the new and preferred school or organization. Perhaps raising test scores is a key element in the overall vision of the group.

Cultural
change
strategy

Good school leaders spend time creating a new vision of a pre-ferred school or organization. To accomplish this, they must be very sensitive to the existing culture. They become aware of this by making sure they know what is happening at the school site.

Action plans—> Intervention implementation—> Reformation of culture

School leaders seek to sustain positive change despite cycles of staff change and external forces. As each change is assessed, evaluation feedback is used to guide adjustment of school operations. At times, changing one faculty member may alter the culture of the school. For example, if the union president is a member of the school faculty and moves to another school, then the climate is likely to change at the first school.

ORGANIZATIONAL CULTURE AND THE EXCELLENT SCHOOL

To maintain an excellent school, many writers, including Thomas Peters and Nancy Austin (1985), suggest that a leader must employ a "hands-on" approach at the school site. In addition to maintaining this style of leadership, the recent literature suggests that a school principal should:

- maintain actions at the school that clearly support the mission and, further-more, relate all measurements to the main goals of the school or district

- insist that the school know its clients and "stick to its knitting"

- make important decisions that affect the school with input from those who "know the territory."

Most recent school leadership books include variations on the above themes. They consistently advocate that the organizational leader stay close to her customer and maintain a vision for the future. For example, advocates of Total Quality Management (TQM) focus on the client as the centerpiece of organizational leadership. The TQM, or Deming, model contains fourteen points that help the principal or manager stay close to the customer and change the organization quickly as change is needed. These points were outlined in Table 3, Chapter 1.

ORGANIZATIONAL CLIMATE

As already defined, organizational climate is the total environmental quality within an organization. This climate can be described as hostile, rigid, warm, or open. Of the many instruments available to measure organizational climate, the following exemplify two approaches:

- Wilbur Brookover (1984) *School Learning Assessment Instrument*

- NASSP (1987) *Comprehensive Assessment of School Environments.*

Other tools are available at Websites listed in Appendix A, especially the ERIC database at http://searcheric.org

The Brookover *School Learning Assessment Instrument*

The Brookover assessment clusters seven factors that have been found significant in the leadership of a school. These seven factors are administrative instructional leadership, emphasis on achievement, expectations and evaluation of students, using test data to evaluate programs, safe and orderly environment, grouping for instruction, and attention to time-on-task during instruction. Practitioners and researchers have used the Brookover instrument to evaluate school environments. The instrument has been validated with data collection from Michigan and Tennessee elementary schools.

The National Association of Secondary School Principals (NASSP) Comprehensive Assessment of School Environments (CASE) Instrument

The NASSP survey instrument to judge school climates was validated in pilot and normative studies of 1,500 teachers, 4,400 parents, and 14,600 students. The assessment measures level of student activities, parent and community relationships, student attention to achievement, security and maintenance, teacher-student relationships, and administration. The CASE battery facilitates monitoring and analysis of outcomes-based data. These data are then available to guide decisions about the school site.

SUMMARY

The culture and climate of a school are significant to its success. A desirable climate is the environment that emerges from an efficiently managed, instructionally effective, and caring group of employees at the school site. The principal is clearly key in identifying intended outcomes and keeping the vision before the teaching staff. It is only when the organizational climate and culture fuse in a school that all the stakeholders have an idea of what will happen next day, next year, and the year after. An effective school climate provides an environment in which students and teachers feel comfortable in working toward their goals.

KEY TERMS

1. Brookover School Learning Assessment Instrument
2. heroes and heroines
3. NASSP Comprehensive Assessment of School Environments
4. norms
5. organizational change strategies
6. organizational climate
7. organizational culture
8. rites and rituals
9. semiotics
10. Total Quality Management
11. values

Current Issues

Inst. Leadership

Emphasis on achievement

Data Driven

Safe Campus

Grouping for instruction

Time on Task

Program evaluation

QUESTIONS AND ACTIVITIES

1. There is general agreement that the culture of a school affects student learning. Discuss three specific instances to show how this occurs.

2. Every organization has "norms." Identify three specific norms and discuss how they affect student learning at the school where you teach or work.

3. Pascale discussed seven steps in personnel selection that are important for a school or district that wants to maintain its culture. Select three of the seven steps and explain why they are important in maintaining organizational culture.

4. A school principal plays a very important role in establishing the culture of a school. Analyze three specific examples that show how a principal's leadership style affects a school's culture.

5. Several instruments have been developed to measure school climate and culture. Discuss one of these instruments and indicate how it could be used to improve student learning.

6. Explain the difference between organizational culture and organizational climate.

7. Applying an organizational climate instrument to a school with which you are familiar, analyze the components of its climate. What recommendations do you draw from this analysis?

8. Read one of the references cited in this chapter. Summarize ways in which this material furthered your understanding of organizational culture or organizational climate.

Chapter 10

Collective Bargaining

and District Employee Organizations

INTRODUCTION

The labor movement in the United States began in response to undesirable management practices in industry. It soon spread to include employees in the public sector, such as government workers and teachers. Today, if there is one document that the California personnel director should know to every paragraph, word, and comma, it is the Rodda Act—the most important document drafted for school employee bargaining in California.

The impact of collective bargaining upon school employee organizations has been immense. Organizations that began as teachers working together and meeting socially, the National Education Association (NEA) for example, began to acquire the trappings of organized labor as collective negotiations won more rights for employees. More than 80% of the nation's teachers belong to either the NEA or the American Federation of Teachers (AFT) (Webb, Montello, & Norton, 1994).

Many students of personnel history would agree that collective bargaining has affected the employee/employer relationship more than any other single issue. Working conditions, hiring practices, and salaries, as well as the minute-by-minute tasks performed daily by each district employee—all are influenced by collective bargaining. Both school superintendents and personnel directors list the collective bargaining process among the most important issues facing education (Norton, 1989). Many surveys have shown that much of the time spent by personnel officers and superintendents involves grievances brought under the collective bargaining agreement.

This chapter defines "collective bargaining" and describes the process, addresses the history of collective bargaining, identifies laws that have accelerated collective negotiations, and analyzes the impact of labor negotiations. The chapter concludes with a brief review of the major employee organizations that are active in California school districts.

COLLECTIVE BARGAINING DEFINED

At one time the terms "professional negotiations" and "collective bargaining" described two different activities. "Professional negotiations" was the phrase used in connection with professional educators, whereas "collective bargaining" connoted bitter disputes between management and labor in business and industry. In the personnel literature today, and in this chapter, the terms are used interchangeably.

The American Association of School Administrators (AASA) defines collective bargaining as "the process by which teachers, through their designated representatives, negotiate with the board of education, or its designated representative(s)." Negotiations cover salary, working conditions, and other matters of interest to employee groups (Redfern, 1967). As expected, NEA's definition of negotiations was more generic: "negotiate on matters of mutual concern" (NEA, 1991).

HISTORICAL PERSPECTIVES

Collective actions by employees began in medieval times. Craftsmen banded together in Europe to bring grievances as a group, rather than as individuals. Even at that time the power of group action came to be recognized. Today, complaints of organized groups are widely disseminated by the media, a tool available to unions to touch the sympathies of society.

Collective bargaining has become an accepted part of the educational system. The first labor contract in public education was negotiated in 1962 with teachers in New York City after a bitter teachers' strike. Since that time most state legislatures have enacted collective bargaining laws for the public sector. Because personnel expenditures constitute more than 80% of school budgets, virtually every aspect of the system has been influenced by negotiations between employees and the board of education.

In the 1970s many educators bewailed the anticipated encroachment of collective bargaining (Lieberman, 1979). Many individuals stated that teachers should not be given the right to strike and that teacher representation rights should be reduced. Many articles in *Phi Delta Kappan,* a respected education journal, opposed the collective bargaining process. The authors predicted that collective bargaining would weaken the public's perception of the teacher as a professional.

Regardless of the position of these educators, the negotiations process is here to stay. Collective bargaining lies at the heart of the personnel process. Whenever employer-employee relationships involve a union, collective bargaining establishes, administers, and enforces agreements between the parties.

Collective Bargaining in the Private Sector

Table 7 indicates the major laws enacted by the federal or state government in the 19th and 20th centuries that influenced employment agreements of public and private educational institutions.

All relevant federal legislation has influenced personnel policies and collective agreements between employee groups and the boards of education of private and public institutions. Prior to the move of collective bargaining to the public sector, however, four major congressional acts set guidelines for negotiations in the private sector: the Norris-LaGuardia Act of 1932, the National Labor Relations Act of 1935 (Wagner Act), the Labor-Management Relations Act of 1947 (Taft-Hartley Act), and the Labor-Management Reporting and Disclosure Act of 1959 (Landrum-Griffin Act). A brief discussion of each of these laws follows.

The year 1932 saw passage of the **Norris-LaGuardia Act.** Before this legislation, employers had almost unlimited freedom in preventing workers from organizing unions. After this act was passed, however, workers had the right to organize and form unions if they desired. The act also placed restrictions on the power of courts to issue injunctions to suppress labor activities. The Norris-LaGuardia Act stipulated that, should an employer refuse to negotiate with representatives of employee groups, this action constituted an unfair labor practice subject to intervention by the courts.

This legislation established the first public policy on labor unionization. No longer was the "yellow-dog" contract in effect; that is, no longer could an employer require employees to sign as a condition of employment a document stating that they were not members of a union and would not join a union as long as they worked for that company. This law was a breakthrough in the history of employee-employer relations and served as the "foot in the door" for laws that would follow.

The next major piece of labor legislation was the **Wagner Act**, or the National Labor Relations Act, passed in 1935. It is generally agreed that the Wagner Act was the most significant legislation to further the goals of the labor movement. This act applied only to employees in the private sector, excluding all public workers. In the Wagner Act, Congress established the right of workers to negotiate with their employers on matters pertaining to conditions of employment, job-related benefits, and wages. It strengthened the guarantee that workers might organize and join labor unions for the purpose of collective bargaining with employers. The Wagner Act also prohibited several actions on the part of employers:

- Employers could not refuse to bargain with the representatives selected by the employees. The National Labor Relations Board (NLRB) was established and given responsibility for conducting elections to determine union representation.

Table 7

Major Laws Relating to Current
Public and Private Personnel Collective Agreements

Year Enacted	Legislation
1866	Civil Rights Act of 1866
1871	Civil Rights Act of 1871
1883	Pendleton Act (Civil Service Commission)
1923	Federal Civil Service Classification Act
1931	Davis-Bacon Act
1932	Anti-Injunction Act
1935	National Labor Relations Act (Wagner Act)
1935	Social Security Act
1936	Walsh-Healey Public Contracts Act
1938	Fair Labor Standards Act
1947	Labor-Management Relations Act (Taft-Hartley Act)
1959	Labor-Management Reporting and Disclosure Act
1962	Work Hours Act
1963	Equal Pay Act
1964	Civil Rights Act
1966	Freedom of Information Act
1967	Reemployment of Veterans Act
1967	Age Discrimination Act
1968	Garnishment Provisions, Consumer Credit Protection Act
1972	Equal Employment Opportunity Act
1972	Title IX of the Education Amendments of 1972
1973	Rehabilitation Act

Table 7 (contrd)

Year Enacted	Legislation
1974	Employee Retirement Income Security Act
1974	Privacy Act
1974	Vietnam Era Veterans Readjustment Assistance Act
1975	California Rodda Act
1978	Age Discrimination in Employment Act Amendments
1978	Civil Service Reform Act
1978	Pregnancy Discrimination Act
1984	Retirement Equity Act
1990	Americans with Disabilities Act
1991	Civil Rights Act
1991	Omnibus Transportation Employee Testing Act
1993	Family and Medical Leave Act

● Employers were forbidden to discriminate against an employee who filed charges or gave testimony under the act.

● Employers could not discriminate against an employee because of union activity.

● Employers were prohibited from interfering with employees in exercising their rights to join labor unions and bargain collectively.

Other acts governing collective bargaining were passed after the Wagner Act. Although most of these acts followed the same general guidelines, some later legislation, such as the Taft-Hartley Act, took a somewhat different direction.

The **Taft-Hartley Act** of 1947 further expanded and clarified workers' rights in the negotiating process. However, it also sought to prevent unfair labor practices on the part of unions. For example, it protected an individual's right *not* to enroll in a union and included provisions to prevent unfair treatment of employers by unions. No longer would the closed shop be allowed. The federal government could seek an injunction to prevent work stoppages for 80 days if a strike were seen as injurious to the national welfare. Union funds could not be used in national elections. Moreover, union officers were required to swear that they were not members of the Communist party. Other restrictions on unions forbade the following:

- excessive initiation dues

- participation in a conflict between two or more unions over the right to complete certain types of work

- forcing an employer to pay for services that were not completed

- participation in secondary boycotts to bring pressure upon an employer not involved in the original dispute

- forcing an employer to discriminate against a worker who was refused membership in or expelled from a union

- refusal to negotiate collectively with an employer.

The **Landrum-Griffin** legislation, or Labor Management Reporting and Disclosure Act of 1959, created additional procedures to monitor union operations. Corruption in unions had become widespread before the passage of this act. Under this law union members were granted such rights as secret ballots, freedom of speech at union meetings, and protection against improper disciplinary action or dues increases. In addition, the law covered the right to sue in case members' rights were violated, guidelines for participation in union affairs, and governance practices such as voting rights. Financial reporting procedures, expense accounting, election of union officers, and "democratic practices" were included. The following amendments were included in the Taft-Hartley Act.

- Union shops with required membership after seven days' employment were authorized in the construction industry.

- Practices in which employees seek to bring economic pressure on another employer by refusing to handle, use, sell or move products were restricted.

- The right of the striker to vote in union representative elections was guaranteed.

- The act prohibited picketing by a union when a rival union had been selected to represent employees or an NLRB election had taken place within the previous 12 months.

- States were granted authority over cases outside the jurisdiction of the NLRB.

- Union administrators were no longer required to take a non-Communist oath.

Teacher groups were still excluded from the provisions of this law.

Collective Bargaining for Public Employees at the Federal Level

The executive order that opened the door for bargaining by federal employees occurred in 1962 with Presidential Executive Order 10988. Issued by President John Kennedy, E. O. 10988 provided to federal workers the right to join organizations of choice and recognized that organizations might engage in negotiation. This order required federal agency managers to meet and confer in good faith with recognized employee organizations with respect to personnel policies and conditions of work. It defined unfair labor practices, set up a code of conduct for labor organizations, prohibited a union shop, and forbade strikes by federal employees. Finally, E. O. 10988 established advisory arbitration of grievances.

Owing to this order, employee unions in the public sector began to flourish. The order had a "domino" effect on state and local employees, who sought collective bargaining rights that would match or exceed those of federal workers.

In 1968 improvements to E. O. 10988 were recommended. Subsequently, in 1969, President Richard Nixon issued E. O. 11491 to supersede the previous directive. The purposes of E. O. 11491 were to standardize procedures among federal agencies and to bring federal labor relations more in line with the private sector. The Assistant Secretary of Labor was given authority to determine appropriate bargaining units, to oversee recognition procedures, to rule on unfair labor practices, and to enforce the standards of conduct for labor organizations.

Negotiations in Local and State Governments

E. O. 11491 opened the door to labor negotiations in the public sector. Some 40 years later over three-fourths of the states have mandatory or permissive statutes governing the rights of public school employees to negotiate, organize, exercise sanctions, and strike. These laws differ in many, sometimes major, ways. Since laws are organic in nature, they are subject to judicial interpretation, repeal, and possible amendment.

Growth of Teacher Unionism

The roots of teacher organization are found in the National Teacher Association (NTA), founded in 1857. In that year 15 states had teachers' associations, among them those in New York, Massachusetts, and Rhode Island, organized in 1845 (Wesley, 1957).

A preponderance of teachers at that time were women. As early as 1870 women comprised two-thirds of the national teaching force; by 1900 they numbered three-fourths (Warren, 1989). With the exception of David Tyack of Stanford University, historians have sadly neglected the feminine aspect of educational history.

Despite their large numbers, career success and power within the system often eluded women teachers. "Schoolmen" (a favorite nineteenth century word) refused to make any allowances for long-term female teachers. They believed that all women would leave the profession after a short while. Thus, women were assumed to need neither equal pay nor equitable pensions, since teaching was only a way station until they married. A 1907 New York *Times* editorial on the issue of equal pay commented: "There may be detected occasional exceptions, who may seem destined for a life of celibacy and possibly school-teaching. But one does not legislate for exceptions." The *Times* editors further argued, "How can anybody expect that they are going to take their provisional method of making a living as seriously as the male who takes it for life?"

In 1870 the National Teacher Association (NTA) merged with the Normal School Association and the National Association of School Superintendents to form the National Education Association (NEA). Later, in 1916, the American Federation of Teachers (AFT) was established. Since that time, NEA and AFT have competed for members and for the role of teachers' exclusive representative at the bargaining table.

Against this backdrop, one of the first agreements between an organized teachers' group and a school system was negotiated in Illinois in 1934. This agreement included a contract, a grievance procedure, and regulations for issuance of salary checks.

Gradually, concern for education employees began to intensify in the states. By 1947 NEA resolutions reflected concern for the economic conditions of teachers. In 1962 NEA promulgated a policy insisting on the right to negotiate with boards of education.

Collective bargaining activities and agreements proliferated after this pronouncement. Despite criticism of the "unprofessionalism" of teacher negotiations, collective bargaining became an accepted activity in most school districts after 1965. Several factors contributed to the growth of negotiations in education:

- Teachers, who felt that their wages were not on par with other professions, increasingly expressed discontent with their salary levels.

- After 1966 NEA assumed a much stronger role in strike actions than had previously been the case.

- As negotiated agreements emerged in school systems, other districts began to follow suit, thus creating a "domino" effect.

- Competition intensified between NEA and AFT for new members and influence in the negotiations field.

- The announcement of Executive Order 10988, the directive issued by President Kennedy in 1962, set a federal precedent for negotiations in the public sector.

- In 1960 the United Federation of Teachers (UFT) began an active drive for control of collective bargaining in New York City. After a strike on November 7, 1960, the board of education sought a resolution to teacher demands. The conflict culminated in appointment of a fact-finding committee to investigate issues and present recommendations to the board.

- In 1978 the case of *Norwalk Teachers' Association v. Board of Education* (138 Conn. 269, 83 A. 2nd 482) strengthened the legal right of teachers to engage in collective bargaining (Peterson, Rossmiller, & Volz, 1978).

From the 1960s to the 1980s these events escalated interest and intensity in the public sector labor movement, with the outcome that concerted actions by public employees gained momentum. Between 1975 and 1980 strikes occurred in 900 school districts.

THE RODDA ACT IN CALIFORNIA

Prior to 1960 discussions about working conditions and salary were accomplished through the genteel scenario of the "sit and chat" Winton Act. But teachers began to tire of this process when, after hours of sitting and chatting, significant changes in working conditions and salaries were not evident. Then, from the 1960s and through the 1980s, in California and throughout the United States, teachers and boards of education relied on the collective bargaining process to an ever greater extent to work through issues and resolve their differences. As a result, teachers in California and other states prevailed on lawmakers to adopt job security laws and retirement packages by statute.

In 1975 the Educational Employment Relations Act (EERA), also known as the Rodda Act, furnished the vehicle through which California teachers and classified employees gained the right of collective bargaining (Murphy, 1991). The act guarantees school employees the right to form a bargaining unit and to choose an organization as their exclusive representative in contract negotiations with the board of education as to conditions and terms of employment. Employees engaged in such activities are to be free from negative action by the school district.

The statute accommodates management rights by stating that any rights not mentioned in the act are reserved to management. Such rights include determining annual budget, hiring and establishing duties of employees, setting criteria for job performance, and establishing the educational goals of the school district.

IMPLEMENTING THE LAW

The Process of Collective Bargaining

No matter what definition is used for collective bargaining, negotiations between employee groups and the board of education typically involve the following steps.

- Formal acknowledgement by a board of an employee organization to represent all employees of that jurisdiction (members and nonmembers) signals acceptance by the board of the collective bargaining principle.

- Collective bargaining in the public sector gives the employee the right to participate through a chosen representative in determination of personnel policies and practices that affect conditions of employment.

- If more than one personnel unit is recognized by the board of education, each such unit separately designates its bargaining representative. Large school systems may have one bargaining unit for teachers, one for maintenance personnel, another for secretarial and clerical workers, and so on.

- Collective bargaining imposes restrictions on the system and on the personnel association or union. The system must bargain with the official bargaining unit or units.

- Representatives of the local association and the board of education meet to negotiate salary, fringe benefits, and working conditions.

- Failure to reach agreement leads to an impasse, after which specific procedures involving outside persons come into play.

Impinging upon the Rodda Act and the technical terms contained throughout its provisions are the many philosophies of players at the district level. Some feel that the collective bargaining process should be a "win-win" proposition in which everyone benefits. Others believe that the process is the worst thing that has ever happened to education and that no positive gains from the process are ever realized.

Collective bargaining may take many avenues, depending upon the direction of the board and the philosophy of the superintendent. There are some "givens" in the process. For instance, on the management side a district's bargaining team relies in its negotiations upon the parameters and guidelines of the school board as a whole. These must be developed thoroughly before negotiations begin and must be clearly communicated to the team or teams that bargain with both classified and certificated groups. Key questions that must be answered by the board are:

- Should the contract be negotiated as a multi-year or a single-year agreement?

- What are the financial limitations of the district?

- What in the previous contract should be changed? what maintained?

- In this time of fiscal uncertainty, with management and union far apart on wage offers, might such non-economic issues as binding arbitration or agency shop be negotiated?

Some of the strategies used in the negotiations process include deferring tough issues, prioritizing remaining issues, planning for fallback positions, selling a position, and working toward agreement by repackaging.

Even if negotiations are conducted in good faith, a move into impasse and fact-finding becomes necessary if progress ceases. Usually, the first stage of fact-finding identifies remaining issues, followed by a request for mediation. The second phase involves the fact-finding procedure itself, working through five steps:

- meeting with a mediator to review issues at impasse

- restructuring proposals with the aid of the mediator

- working slowly toward the last and final offer on remaining issues

- making the last and final offer through the mediator, followed by

- agreement on a new contract or continuation of impasse.

Successful negotiators keep everyone informed through regular updates in writing and by telephone. Helpful communications strategies reduce tension by

- separating the people from the issues

- clarifying interests, not positions

- knowing and showing respect for the other side

- honesty

- allowing the other side "a way out."

The Typical Collective Agreement

Although there is no set pattern for an employer-employee agreement, certain sections usually appear. These sections are outlined below:

Management rights	Certain subjects cited as management prerogatives are excluded from compulsory bargaining.
Union security	The union seeks to protect its position by including union security provisions in the contract. Either union shop or a modified union shop may be described.
Working conditions, hours, wages	Hours of work, compensation, and benefits usually take center stage in the bargaining agreement.
Contract duration	The term of the agreement is set. Employers usually favor such a clause so as to stabilize the district and minimize disruptions from slowdowns or strikes.
Grievance procedures	Usually, grievance procedures describe in careful detail the grounds for a grievance and the steps required for their processing.
Fringe benefits	The scope and level of fringe benefits are specified in the collective bargaining agreement.

| Leaves of absence, vacation days, and sick leave | Leaves are authorized and minimum levels established in the California Education Code. These code provisions are usually mirrored in the agreement, although districts may negotiate more liberal leave provisions if they choose. |

Salaries

The paycheck is undoubtedly the most important issue at the bargaining table for both certificated and classified groups although, as noted in the next section, the hidden cost of the benefits package may be a critical issue on the management side. As noted in Chapter 6, salaries in California are high, 14% above the U. S. average. The state's ranking was eighth in 1999-2000 (American Federation of Teachers, 2000). Nationally, teachers' average annual salary in 1999-2000 was $ 41,820, while California teachers earned $ 47,680. Of course, the value of income is relative, not only to the cost of living, which is high in California, but also to the quality of life one expects to enjoy.

In the classified service districts must establish a salary range for each position (Ed. Code #45101). The law for Merit System districts provides that the Personnel Commission, whose members represent both the board and the employees, sets the relationships among the salary ranges, and that the board, although it may approve, amend, or reject the salary recommendations from the commission, may not alter those relationships. The principle of "like pay for like service" is to be built into the Merit System schedule (Ed. Code #45268).

The Merit System operates much like civil service. Thus, it does not deal with merit pay, defined as differential pay based on performance. Rare at the negotiations table, but frequent in the literature, are discussions of merit pay in this latter sense, an issue already raised in the chapter on certificated staff. Quite ordinary in certificated contracts, however, are provisions dealing with extra pay for extra duty. These extra duties may mean hourly projects outside of the regular work day, such as service on curriculum committees or attendance at inservice workshops, or they may be stated as a particular responsibility with expected, but unspecified, additional time. Examples of the latter include department chair or grade-level team leader, athletics coach, and parent education coordinator.

In practice, both certificated and classified salary schedules typically have two dimensions—one for years of experience and the other for (in the case of certificated) college units of credit or (in the case of classified) level of classification. In constructing such a schedule, the rows and columns usually bear a uniform percentage relationship to one another. Although a negotiated salary increase is most often applied equally to every cell in the salary chart, modifications are sometimes agreed upon, most often to raise the salaries of those at the lower end of the schedule.

Fringe Benefit Costs

Employee benefits paid by the employer became popular as a way for employees to obtain compensation free of income tax, along with protection from certain financial risks. Health care costs continue to escalate throughout the United States, and benefit costs in California schools follow that pattern. Spending on health care in the United States was projected to exceed $1.3 trillion during 2000 (Kemper, 2000). In the past decade health care costs have risen more than 300%. Rising costs have led many managers to seek alternative fringe benefit plans (Fromach, 1992). Building in employee contributions, limitations on dependent coverage, cost containment programs, flexible benefit plans, and large deductibles are considered very seriously in the bargaining process.

Other benefits, too, have risen in cost. Worker's compensation, life and disability insurance, and mileage allowances benefit the individual directly. Preventive programs in safety, hazardous materials, and training are less visible, but also expensive. Few employees realize that an additional amount ranging from 20% to 40% of their salary (for parttime workers, sometimes the equivalent of their paycheck) accrues to them in health and welfare benefits, insurance packages, and other benefits (U. S. Chamber of Commerce, 1990). Because these costs are skyrocketing, fringe benefits and cost containment have become important issues at the bargaining table.

PROFESSIONAL ORGANIZATIONS

Professional organizations play an important role in collective bargaining. Organizations for teachers and classified employees seek to represent their constituencies at the bargaining table. Organizations for administrators and board members offer workshops and publications on legal, financial, strategic, and practical aspects of contract negotiations and administration.

National Education Association (NEA)

The National Education Association (NEA), with 2.5 million members, is the largest of the teacher unions. The NEA consists of classroom teachers and specialists in schools, colleges, and other educational agencies. After its formation in 1870, the NEA provided an avenue for organized groups of teachers to present their concerns to educational boards. In response to competition with the American Federation of Teachers (AFT), the NEA has become immersed in actions strongly supporting teacher welfare and rights. NEA takes the position that "the right to strike" must be an integral part of the collective bargaining process (National Education Association, 1991).

NEA sought a unified profession that would not split into opposing interest groups or engage in public conflict over resources. The group concentrated its efforts at state and national—rather than local—levels, thus leaving the individual district lower in its priorities (Wirt & Kirst, 1989). The group has an extensive bureaucratic structure. Policy is developed by a board of 92 directors and an 11-member Executive Committee.

Each year the Political Action Council of NEA expends hundreds of thousands of dollars supporting political candidates at the state and national levels. The differences between the AFT and the NEA are clearly reflected in their political efforts. The AFT has had more success in big cities, while NEA has been more effective dealing with state-level politicians.

The American Federation of Teachers (AFT)

The American Federation of Teachers (AFT) is the second largest teacher union with 1.2 million members. AFT, affiliated with the AFL-CIO, was formed in 1916. The stated objectives of the AFT are as follows:

- to bring associations of teachers into relations of mutual assistance and cooperation

- to obtain for teachers all the rights to which they are entitled

- to raise the standards of the teaching profession by securing the conditions essential to the best professional service

- to promote such a democratization of the schools as will enable teachers to equip their pupils to take their places in the industrial, social, and political life of the community

- to promote the welfare of the childhood of the nation by providing progressively better educational opportunity for all.

The AFT has taken a very aggressive stance advocating that teachers should take control of their own profession. Albert Shanker, longtime president of the AFT, once commented that "there is recognition that some teachers are excellent, some are very good, and some are terrible" (Currence, 1984, 1).

AFT-NEA Merger

The two unions, the National Education Association and the American Federation of Teachers, after many years of discussion, developed a blueprint for merging the two organizations. The first step in the process was scheduled for the summer of 1998 with a vote of representatives to the annual conventions of the two organizations. On July 7, 1998, the delegates to the NEA convention rejected the merger by a 58% vote. The AFT, only one month later, voted in favor. However, the vote by AFT members was primarily symbolic, in view of NEA's rejection.

If approved, the merger would have linked 3.7 million members and created a national affiliation with the AFL-CIO labor union. The merger would have taken place in 2002. With its rejection by NEA, the future of the proposal is uncertain. Perhaps local chapters of the two organizations will unite. This concept is not new; Los Angeles NEA and AFT teachers merged in 1970 to form United Teachers-Los Angeles (UTLA).

California Teachers Association (CTA)

The California Teachers Association (CTA) is affiliated with the 2.5-million-member NEA. The two groups conduct joint studies to extend understanding of educational issues. CTA was founded in 1863 under the name California Educational Society. The name was changed to California Teachers Association in 1875. CTA is a statewide organization that wields tremendous influence among the rank and file teachers in the state. The organization has staff who consult with teachers at the local level in negotiations with boards. CTA also assists its members with decisions regarding retirement and fringe benefits. The CTA uses its influence to bring sanctions against districts and district boards of education.

For many years teachers exerted only minimal political influence and were widely viewed as submissive. Teachers had traditionally hesitated to use collective actions against boards. For their part, school administrators played down the collective role of the teachers' organization, encouraging negotiations by individual professionals instead. However, with CTA, teachers became strong in institutional power. Their power potential increased as education became big business.

CTA represents 295,000 members, including public school teachers and supervisory certificated personnel. In addition, approximately 9,000 community college instructors and 20,000 instructors and professors in the 20-campus California State University System are CTA members. An achievement of which CTA is especially proud is its work on Proposition 98, which provides minimum state funding for education. These funds have helped teachers during periods of shortfall in state revenue. CTA members collected more than 70,000 signatures and contributed more than $7 million to pass the 1988 initiative.

Concern about wages motivated teachers to organize for collective bargaining on salary and other matters. Insistence on rights was seen in the strengthening of the National Education Association (NEA), as well as the rise of the American Federation of Teachers (AFT). These groups became more active in party politics and began to endorse presidential candidates beginning with Carter in 1976.

Classified School Employees Association (CSEA)

The Classified School Employees Association (CSEA) is the primary organization for support of service employees in the state of California and represents approximately 190,000 employees. Employees who are represented by CSEA include custodians, clerks, bus drivers, cafeteria workers, maintenance staff, and instructional aides. Classified employees typically have an organized bargaining unit that negotiates a collective bargaining agreement between themselves and the district board.

CSEA often negotiates a bargaining agreement that parallels the contract with the teachers' organization as to wages, fringe benefits, and working conditions. Portions of the contract are different in response to different sections of the California Education Code for classified personnel.

American Association of School Administrators (AASA)

Most school superintendents are members of the American Association of School Administrators (AASA). Moreover, AASA enrolls a large number of other administrative personnel. AASA was founded in 1865, when a group of approximately 50 city and state superintendents formed the National Association of School Superintendents. In 1870 the National Association of School Superintendents became the NEA's Department of School Superintendency. The name was changed in 1937 to the American Association of School Administrators.

Today, AASA is an independent professional organization for more than 14,000 educational leaders across the United States and Canada and in many other parts of the world. Its mission is to guarantee the preeminence of American education and ensure learning for all students through visionary and effective leadership. Unlike NEA, AASA historically has opposed teacher strikes and has encouraged administrators to keep school open during a strike (Webb, Montello, & Norton, 1994).

National Association of Secondary School Principals (NASSP)

The National Association of Secondary School Principals (NASSP) was organized in 1916 and became a department of NEA in 1927. The association has 40,000 members, with control vested in an executive committee. NASSP publishes a journal, the *NASSP Bulletin*, that contains practical, up-to-date information about school management and is used as reference in many studies and articles. Now an independent association, NASSP sponsors the National Association of Student Councils, the National Junior Honor Society, and the National Honor Society.

National Association of Elementary School Principals (NAESP)

The National Association of Elementary School Principals (NAESP) is analogous to the National Association of Secondary School Principals. The NAESP was founded in 1921, and in 1970 was a department of the NEA. It numbers 28,500 members. NAESP sponsors the National Distinguished Principals Program, Presidential Academic Fitness Program, American Student Council Association, Blue Ribbon Schools Program, and National Teacher of the Year.

Association of California School Administrators (ACSA)

ACSA is the administrative group located in California. Issues of interest to California administrators are presented in the ACSA publication *EdCal*. Monthly job listings are also included in this publication. In addition, ACSA publishes a journal for school administrators, *Leadership*. ACSA conducts seminars, academies, and annual conferences of interest to site and district administrators. It also maintains staff to assist administrators threatened with demotion or dismissal.

California Association of School Business Officials (CASBO)

CASBO is the primary organization for school business employees. Both school accountants and business managers attend monthly meetings at which available resources are discussed. In addition, CASBO has furnished managers with recommended formulas for operations and maintenance staffing. CASBO issues a monthly printout listing all school business jobs available in California and publishes a professional journal for business managers, superintendents, and school boards.

Note on Professional Organizations

The public sees conflicts among professional educators and believes that these divisions are irreversible. The media, at times, seek to overemphasize these divisions. Nevertheless, past traditions of a unified profession and the common training and teaching experience of educators have led to agreement on certain common values. Both principals and superintendents have typically been employed as teachers. Many education personnel must complete some kind of licensing or certification procedure to work in California schools, so that educators may be bound by the common experience of having attended the same trade school, college, or university.

Support personnel have traditionally experienced different jobs before they assumed their district positions. Therefore, they are more attuned than certificated staff to comparing job conditions and wages with comparable positions in the public and private sectors. Unfortunately, with recent budget cutbacks in California, negotiating groups have been pitted against one another in competition for scarce funds. Salary rollbacks have occurred from previously signed-off employee agreements. These circumstances have generated major pressures upon employee groups as well as the management side. Furthermore, these conflicts will not be resolved unless California's fiscal situation improves. Thus, California educators are torn between joining together in common cause and battling over scarce resources.

SUMMARY

This chapter has reviewed the history of collective bargaining in the United States in both the private and public sectors, culminating in the Rodda Act in California. It specifically outlines the development of collective bargaining in teacher organizations, which progressed from social get-togethers to unions negotiating salary and working conditions. Even though many writers railed against the passage of the Rodda Act, this law has quickly become entrenched in the system and provides a framework for all employee negotiations, including the stages of mediation, arbitration, and impasse.

Several employee organizations are active on the collective bargaining scene as participants or as sponsors of workshops. These include the National Education Association, American Federation of Teachers, California Teachers Association, American Association of School Administrators, and the Classified School Employees Association.

It is apparent that collective bargaining has become an integral part of the educational system. Depending upon the philosophies of the individual district employee group and the local school board and administration, this process may be extremely negative, leading to bitter, long-lasting hostility—or highly positive, with "wins" for both.

KEY TERMS

1. agency shop
2. American Federation of Teachers (AFT)
3. arbitration
4. California Teachers Association (CTA)
5. concerted activities
6. Executive Order 10988
7. fact-finding
8. fringe benefits
9. grievance procedures
10. impasse
11. management rights
12. National Education Association (NEA)
13. Norris-LaGuardia Act
14. Rodda Act
15. scope of negotiations
16. Taft-Hartley Act
17. Wagner Act

QUESTIONS AND ACTIVITIES

1. Many students of personnel history agree that collective negotiations have affected employee/employer relationship more than any other single issue. Do you agree or disagree? Support your answer with specific examples.

2. During the 1930s and 1940s three major federal laws were passed by Congress and signed by the President: Norris-LaGuardia Act, Wagner Act, and Taft-Hartley Act. Briefly discuss each of these acts and explain its contribution to the labor movement.

3. Although teacher unionism traces its history to the 1850s, it did not become a major force in public education until the 1960s. What major factors in the 1960s resulted in an increase in the influence of teacher unions?

4. The Rodda Act has had major impact on collective bargaining in California. What are the major components of this legislation? Why did it have such a powerful effect?

5. A major teacher professional organization is the California Teachers Association (CTA). Discuss three primary strategies utilized by this organization to benefit students and teachers.

6. Analyze a teacher contract by listing those portions that were not in the previous year's contract. In your opinion, did the changes make improvements for teachers? for management? for students?

7. Collect three separate classified and three certificated salary schedules. What is the percent of increase from one year (step) to the next? Are advanced degrees or other training rewarded? Which would best attract new employees? Which has a long-term fiscal advantage?

8. In a small group, discuss the advantages and disadvantages of union membership.

9. Attend a board of education meeting in which a collective bargaining agreement is introduced to the public. Report your impressions of this meeting.

Chapter 11

Collective Bargaining: Negotiations

INTRODUCTION

The previous chapter discussed collective bargaining, including the history of collective bargaining in the public sector and a review of major public school employee organizations in California. Collective bargaining was defined as the process of negotiations between the school board and employees on terms and conditions of employment. Collective bargaining has gained wide acceptance as a means of settling issues of salary and working conditions between school districts and unions. Between 1962 and 1980 more than 40 states and the District of Columbia enacted legislation regarding collective bargaining in the public sector (Education Commission of the States, 1980). Union membership has grown over the past 40 years from 10% to about a third of public sector workers—almost exactly the reverse of union membership in the private sector (Hick, 1994).

Because personnel expenditures constitute approximately 75% to 85% of school budgets, virtually every aspect of education has been influenced by collective bargaining. Thus, collective bargaining has had a major impact on the operation of school districts. Norton (1989) found that school boards, superintendents, and personnel directors consider collective bargaining among the most significant issues and challenges in education.

This chapter continues the discussion of collective bargaining and negotiations. California's collective bargaining started with passage of the 1975 Rodda Act. This legislation had an impact upon public school and community college governance and terms and conditions of employment far beyond that anticipated by Senator Rodda, its sponsor.

The traditional/adversarial model of negotiations has dominated the negotiations process in most school districts, both in California and nationally. This chapter first outlines the steps in the traditional model of collective bargaining. The importance of including principals as part of the district's negotiating team and the necessity for successful management of the approved contract are also explained.

Due to the adversarial nature of the traditional collective bargaining model, several alternatives have been developed. The generic name for several of these alternative models is "collaborative bargaining." The collaborative approach takes many forms. A summary of several collaborative models is included in this chapter.

THE TRADITIONAL / ADVERSARIAL MODEL

The process of collective bargaining has typically utilized the traditional, or adversarial, model to negotiate union contracts. Early in the development of collective bargaining, education adopted the industrial model of unionization with little adaptation specific to the profession of teaching (Smith, 1990). This model focuses on three basic assumptions:

- Each party operates on the perception that gains to one side must be achieved at the expense of the other.

- Each party must seek detailed protection against every negative act that might conceivably be committed by the other during the life of the contract.

- The process must be seen as adversarial in order to satisfy each party's political constituencies (Abbott, 1990).

The process itself typically includes activities intended to demonstrate employee solidarity, while administrators and board members are often perceived as intentionally deceiving the bargaining unit to gain a negotiating advantage (Wagner, 1991).

Traditional bargaining is characterized by official bargaining teams and a formal exchange of initial positions within a narrowly defined scope of bargaining. This approach involves proposals and counter-proposals, usually in an adversarial atmosphere. Both sides expect a moderation of the initial positions on issues until a compromise settlement is reached.

In the traditional model a chief negotiator and team are appointed by the school board. Likewise, the union appoints or elects a team and chief spokesperson. Negotiations are characterized by face-to-face bargaining interspersed with caucuses for consultation among members of both teams. The process is widely perceived as a series of adversarial postures in which each side attempts to prevail over the other.

Often, traditional bargaining leads to mistrust and gamesmanship, with each party attempting to gain advantage and power over the other. When management receives the union's initial proposal, school boards frequently see the terms of the proposal as an attempt by the union to erode the power of the district's elected policymaker. Likewise, union members see the bargaining process as an avenue for sharing power with the school board, while also diminishing the power of administrators.

The very nature of the model is prone to conflict and mistrust. Even when an agreement is reached, adversarial bargaining tends to lead to a win-lose conclusion between the parties. If negotiations break down into a serious impasse, the probability of a lose-lose outcome increases. In this situation, not only are the parties frustrated from achieving a satisfactory agreement, but students may be adversely affected.

When adversarial bargaining occurs, the teaching-learning environment may be disrupted by hostility between the parties. Parents, students, and the community become upset when the school is unable to function properly because of unsettled disputes between the school board and its employees (Jones & Walters, 1994). In these situations, the aftermath is likely to be marked by grievances, poor staff morale, and continued distrust between the employees and the leaders of the school district (Gates, 1985).

However, even though traditional bargaining often leads to an adversarial relationship between the school board and the unions, this is not always the case. Traditional bargaining has led to satisfactory contracts in many districts. In these situations, the adversarial process has worked with a minimum of conflict between the board, management, and the union. This situation has been most common in small districts where an open, trusting relationship exists among the board, administrators, and employees.

Scope of Negotiations

The phrase "scope of negotiations" refers to those matters that are negotiable. In some states public sector negotiations are limited to salaries, while other states permit literally hundreds of issues to come to the bargaining table. Inclusions and limitations concerning the scope of negotiations depend, in large part, upon state statutes and previous court rulings. Consequently, laws governing issues that fall within the scope of negotiations vary from state to state.

The Rodda Act, which established collective bargaining in California, limited scope to matters relating to wages, hours, and other terms and conditions of employment. However, the definition of scope in California has been greatly extended since passage of the enabling legislation in 1975. These extensions have arisen over the years largely through decisions of the Public Employment Relations Board (PERB), which was established by the Rodda Act to administer its provisions. PERB rulings have defined "terms and conditions of employment" to include health and welfare benefits, leaves, transfers, and reassignment polices. The definition has also been extended to safety conditions of employment, class size, procedures for evaluating employees, procedures for processing grievances, and layoffs of probationary certificated employees.

In addition, unions have gained the right to consult on definition of educational objectives, content of courses and curriculum, and selection of textbooks. The causes and procedures to be used by a district when disciplining employees with actions other than dismissal have also been included within the scope of negotiations. Procedures for layoffs of certificated employees are subject to negotiations. In addition, a district that is considering certificated merit pay must meet and negotiate that issue prior to changes in the salary schedule.

The Negotiating Teams

To bargain these issues, the school board and union each selects a negotiating team. Ordinarily, the superintendent recommends makeup of the board's team. The union team usually includes the local union president and other members elected or appointed to serve.

There is no universally accepted practice in forming negotiating teams. A determining factor seems to be the size of the school district. In small school districts, the superintendent or a board member often conducts negotiations with the certificated and classified unions. The size of the team also varies from district to district, with smaller districts likely to have smaller teams. The team usually consists of an odd number of persons to avoid the possibility of a tie vote on issues (Rebore, 1998).

In medium to large districts, the director of employee relations or the assistant superintendent for personnel usually serves as the chief negotiator for the board. The chief negotiator is typically assisted by district and site-level administrators who serve as part of the team. Districts find it a genuine advantage to have principals on the team, as they are first-line supervisors who will be expected to interpret and enforce the contract, once it is signed. Principals live with the contract on a daily basis and know its weak and strong points. They are also largely responsible for managing the contract. An additional advantage to including principals on the team is that union representatives frequently have a more favorable opinion of principals than of central office staff. Consequently, a principal's presence may reduce tension and hostility.

Some larger districts employ an outside negotiator, usually an attorney who specializes in school law or an experienced labor relations specialist. The advantage of employing a negotiator with this background is that the district gains the experience and expertise of the individual. The disadvantage is that, since the individual is not a district employee, he or she may be viewed with suspicion and distrust by district employees. Employees may also be critical of the amount of money paid to this individual. The salary for an outside negotiator is usually set at an hourly rate ranging from $125 to $300 per hour. Occasionally, the outside negotiator is given a yearly contract at a cost of several thousand dollars. Employees often refer sarcastically to such a negotiator as a "hired gun."

Because it is important to have financial information available to team members, the district's chief financial officer is often a member of the negotiating team. Many districts that do not employ an outside negotiator nevertheless include an attorney specializing in school law. If an attorney is not included, one should be consulted regarding technical proposals that may need clarification.

As mentioned earlier, some boards negotiate directly with the union. In other districts, one or more board members may serve as a team member. The advisability of the board's direct involvement on the negotiations team is subject to debate. Although board members have served on many negotiating teams, some experts advise against this practice (Gonder, 1981). This advice is based on the reality that board members rarely have been trained as school administrators or as negotiators. A board member at the bargaining table may also dominate negotiations or come into conflict with fellow board members. Regardless of the makeup of the district's team, all board members must be kept well informed about the issues and the progress of negotiations.

The union's team also may include an attorney, or an executive who represents the union. In smaller districts, this executive may lead negotiations for unions in several districts. In larger districts, he or she may be a fulltime, paid employee of the union of that district.

Preparation for Negotiations

Once the district's team has been selected, the important process of preparing for negotiations occurs. If personnel matters are well managed, this process will have been ongoing in the district. Problems or concerns with the current contract will have been analyzed and new language developed to deal with these issues.

An analysis of the prior year's grievances is a good place to start. Were several grievances filed over a particular section of the contract? For example, was the wording regarding personal leave open to various interpretations?

The negotiating team needs a clear understanding of the board's objectives prior to the start of negotiations. It is also important to determine the objectives of the union. Knowledge of the objectives of both school board and union enables a district's team to be proactive, rather than merely reactive, at the table. Kennedy (1982) suggests that a district's objectives be prioritized as follows:

1. objectives that must be achieved

2. objectives that the team intends to achieve

3. objectives the team would like to achieve.

Establishing priorities helps the team determine tactics and strategies during negotiations.

Budget projections for the year are of major concern to the board and its negotiating team. A number of important questions must be addressed in planning for negotiations. Some of the questions include:

● Will student enrollment for upcoming school years increase or decrease?

● Will funds be available for new educational objectives of the board?

- Will funds be available for salary increases?

- Will there be a major increase in the cost of fringe benefits?

The answers to these questions help establish goals for the negotiating team.

Ground Rules

Once preparation for negotiations is completed, the next order of business is to establish ground rules for negotiations. Ground rules consist of statements and agreements that govern the conduct of negotiations sessions. Developing ground rules may require several meetings between the district and union representatives.

By establishing specific ground rules, bargaining teams increase their chances of reaching an agreement acceptable to the district and the union. Ground rules should include:

- the time and place of sessions
- the number of participants at the table
- a target date for completing negotiations
- a policy on press releases
- an agreement on impasse procedures
- procedures for each side to use in ratifying the agreement.

Initial Proposal and Trade-Offs

Bargaining takes place in face-to-face meetings between management and union representatives. At the first of these sessions an initial proposal is presented by both parties. After initial proposals, numerous additional proposals and counter-proposals are exchanged in an effort to reach a settlement between the two parties.

Tradeoffs are those items that are included in the initial proposals by both board and union negotiators, but with little hope that they can be attained or even, at times, with little desire to do so. These proposals are sometimes referred to as "poker chips" placed on the negotiating table. For example, the union may include binding arbitration in its initial proposal as a tradeoff. At some point in the negotiating process, the union's chief negotiator will offer to drop this proposal in exchange for, let us say, an increase in fringe benefits. An example of a board tradeoff may be a proposal to give the board ultimate authority to transfer an employee involuntarily to a different school site. Again, the board's chief negotiator may offer to take this proposal off the table in exchange for agreement to an item that holds high priority for the board and management.

The downside of utilizing tradeoffs at the bargaining table is that the concept tends to lead to gamesmanship and distrust. For instance, while the union's bargaining team may understand that the district is not serious about involuntary transfers, employees may become angry and frustrated if the board and superintendent make such a proposal.

Caucus

A basic principle of negotiating is that only one person—the chief negotiator—speaks at the bargaining table. Other members of the bargaining team remain quiet. They may be assigned such tasks as taking notes, watching body language of opposing team members, and developing further bargaining strategies. Members of the bargaining team are also asked to monitor the chief negotiator's language to ensure that he or she is not inadvertently agreeing to a proposal that may be negative for the district or the union.

A caucus is a private meeting of bargaining team members. Some ground rules permit the calling of a caucus at any time; others specify the frequency, duration, or other conditions for a caucus. A caucus gives team members an opportunity to discuss, in private, any proposal or counterproposal presented by the other side. A strategically called caucus also may help defuse "heated language" between the two chief negotiators. A caucus is also used by a team to take a break from the stress of negotiations.

Unfair Labor Practices

The Public Employment Relations Board (PERB) has jurisdiction over unfair labor practices. Section #3543.5 of California's Government Code specifies five district actions that fall within the category of unfair labor practices:

- imposing or threatening reprisals on employees or interfering with, restraining, or coercing employees who have exercised their rights

- denying employee organizations the rights guaranteed to them

- refusing or failing to meet and negotiate in good faith

- dominating or interfering with the formation or administration of an employee organization or contributing financially or encouraging employees to join one organization in preference to another

- refusal to participate in good faith in the impasse procedure.

This definition of unfair labor practice has been very broadly interpreted by PERB decisions, to the detriment of district boards and administration.

Section #3543.6 of the Government Code identifies four specific actions on the part of an employee organization that fall within the purview of unfair labor practices:

- causing or attempting to cause a public school employer to commit an unfair labor practice

- imposing or threatening reprisals on employees or otherwise interfering with, restraining, or coercing employees because of the exercise of their rights

- refusing or failing to meet and negotiate in good faith with the school board's representative

- refusing to participate in good faith in impasse procedures.

Either the union or the district can file an unfair labor charge. Such a charge is filed with PERB and must be in writing. The charge must be specific as to the statute upon which the charge is based. Once PERB determines that a charge meets statutory requirements, a determination is made to amend, dismiss, or issue a complaint based on the charges.

If a complaint is issued, the case is assigned to an administrative law judge (ALJ), who conducts an informal hearing between the two parties. At the hearing, the ALJ assesses the strengths and weakness of the charge, acts as a mediator, and encourages settlement of the unfair labor charge.

If settlement is not reached at this level, a formal hearing is scheduled by PERB. At this hearing, evidence is presented, and witnesses give testimony for each side. Subsequent to the formal hearing, the ALJ renders a written decision on the charge. Once a decision is reached on charges of an unfair practice, a precedent is established that may subsequently be cited by other parties in similar disputes.

Impasse

If negotiators believe they cannot reach an agreement, they may declare an "impasse." Although the term has not been clearly defined, an impasse arises in practice when one or both sides feel that normal negotiation procedures have been exhausted. An impasse can only be declared after negotiators have met in good faith and attempted to resolve the issues. It may be declared independently by the representative of the board or of the union, or jointly by both.

Twenty-two states have established some variant of a public employment relations board to assist and provide direction to districts and unions in resolving negotiation issues.

In California the Public Employment Relations Board (PERB) has the final say as to whether an impasse exists. If PERB determines that negotiations have truly reached an impasse, it is required to appoint a mediator to assist with negotiations.

Mediation

Mediation is the most commonly used procedure for resolving an impasse. In California, PERB has responsibility for appointing a mediator when a district or the union has declared a genuine impasse. Once a mediator has been appointed by PERB, he or she meets with the members of both negotiating teams and tries to persuade them to resolve their differences and reach an agreement.

mediator

The role of the mediator is advisory. Therefore, the mediator has no authority to dictate a settlement. Rather, his or her role is to assist the two teams in identifying common interests that would lead to agreement.

The mediator may meet with the teams jointly or separately. Joint sessions may assist in determining the actual status of negotiations. The joint session is also used by the negotiator to ascertain the degree of difference between the two parties.

Separate meetings with members of the two teams are also scheduled by the mediator. These meetings give the mediator an opportunity to resolve any personal differences among members of the two negotiating teams. During these sessions, the mediator may also guide the negotiators to focus on major contract issues, rather than secondary concerns.

Factfinding

advisory only

If the mediator cannot settle the controversy, the next step in the bargaining process is factfinding. If the mediator has not been able to bring the two sides together within 15 days and declares that factfinding is appropriate, either party may request that their differences be submitted to a factfinding panel.

Factfinding is a procedure in which a neutral panel reviews evidence and makes recommendations for settling the dispute. The panel usually consists of three to five members. As its name implies, the purpose of the panel is to determine the facts in the case. The financial condition of the district is the most frequent source of conflict. The district states that it does not have sufficient funds for a salary increase. The union takes an opposite position and argues that there are sufficient funds for the increase.

So that the factfinding panel can complete its task, it has power to issue subpoenas, to require the attendance of witnesses, and to compel both parties to submit evidence. Government Code section #3548.2 establishes seven factors to be considered by the factfinding panel:

- state and federal laws that are applicable to the employer

- stipulations of the parties

- the interests and welfare of the public and the financial ability of the public school employer

- comparison of the wages, hours, and conditions of employment of the employees involved in the factfinding proceedings with wages, hours, and conditions of employment of other employees performing similar services in comparable communities

- the Consumer Price Index for goods and services, commonly known as the cost-of-living adjustment

- overall compensation presently received by the employees, including direct wage compensation; vacations, holidays and other excused time; insurance and pensions; medical and hospitalization benefits; the continuity and stability of employment; and all other benefits

- other facts that are normally or traditionally taken into consideration in making such findings and recommendations.

Upon completion of <u>factfinding</u>, the <u>panel submits</u> its findings and recommendations to the board and union. The factfinding report and recommendations are presented to the school board in an open session and made available to the public. The recommended terms are advisory and need not be accepted by either party. However, each side has an obligation to consider the findings and recommendations of the panel.

The district must consider whether the union's most recent proposal warrants acceptance or rejection. If the district decides the union's position is unacceptable, the district may implement its last and final proposal. However, a district's implementation of its last and final offer may be interpreted by PERB or the courts as refusal to bargain in good faith, as in a case involving Modesto City Schools (1982, 136 CA1.App.32d 881, 186 Cal.Rptr.634.)

Arbitration

Arbitration is the process of submitting a dispute between a board and a union to an impartial third person or panel of persons. Arbitration can be either compulsory or voluntary. Compulsory arbitration must be established by statute. Nineteen state legislatures have approved compulsory arbitration. The National Education Association has supported this process in the belief that it will curtail long and costly strikes (National School Public Relations Association, 1979).

Strikes

In CA, must show serious health/ safety problem to strike.

If negotiations, mediation, factfinding, and arbitration do not resolve the conflict between the board and the union, a strike is the union's ultimate weapon. Strikes are actions that result in stoppage of work and services rendered by an employee group. Federal law prohibits strikes by teachers. Most states have passed similar laws; however, California law does not expressly prohibit strikes by public employees unless the district can show that the strike creates an imminent threat to health or safety.

Even though teacher strikes are illegal in many states, it is rare that teachers are sent to jail for violation of the law. However, teachers in the Middletown, New Jersey school district received nationwide attention when a judge sentenced teachers, in alphabetical order, to jail. The teachers had disobeyed a court order to return to the classroom.

By the ninth day of the strike the judge was up to the "r's" in the alphabet and more than 200 of the district's 900 teachers had been placed behind bars. The strike was primarily over the district's insistence that teachers make a greater contribution toward paying their health benefits. Middletown teachers earned an average salary of $56,000 in the 2001-2002 school year and were among the highest paid in New Jersey (Wilson & Goldman, 2001).

Because the question as to whether California public employees have a legal right to strike has not been clearly settled, most districts attempt to place a no-strike clause in the negotiated agreement. Such a provision puts the union on record against going out on strike and involves the union in enforcing laws prohibiting strikes. In addition, a no-strike provision usually permits management to impose monetary damages on employees who engage in an illegal strike.

These are very uncommon

NONTRADITIONAL BARGAINING MODELS

As a result of the potential for conflict and disharmony created by the traditional model of collective bargaining, some school boards and employee organizations have abandoned that model in an attempt to achieve more positive results. The new models have collectively been referred to as "collaborative bargaining." Collaborative bargaining focuses on activities intended to identify, enlarge, and act upon common interests of the school board and the union. Its objective is to increase gains for both parties, the "win-win" outcome.

Collaborative bargaining attempts to reduce the adversarial nature of labor negotiations. Its goal is to foster problem-solving, positive communication, consensus-building, cooperation, respect, and trust. Collaborative bargaining is built on the premise that school boards and union leadership want to cooperate to achieve a satisfactory contract settlement.

A number of bargaining strategies grow out of the concept of collaborative bargaining: trust agreements, win-win, and the getting-to-yes Harvard model. Other models include the interest-based model of the California Teachers Association and the California Foundation for Improvement of Employer-Employee Relations (CFIER) model. An overview of several collaborative models follows.

Trust Agreements

A "trust agreement" is a negotiated compact between the board and the union that enables employees to work with the district on those issues that fall outside the collective bargaining contract. The goals of a trust agreement are:

● to develop new roles for personnel

● to develop new relationships between administration and the employee association

● to build new coalitions

● to alter the way decisions are made

● to establish a common ground upon which to resolve problems.

Trust agreements incorporate goals and objectives in areas that typically are inaccessible to teacher decision-making groups. Three steps are followed:

1. identifying and prioritizing the educational problems or opportunities most in need of attention during the period specified in the trust agreement

2. determining required resources and identifying those responsible for meeting the desired goals

3. implementing and then assessing the outcomes of the trust agreement.

A trust agreement is similar to a contract in that it specifies work procedures and responsibilities and includes steps to ensure effective implementation. On the other hand, trust agreements are unlike contracts in that contracts specify rules, while trust agreements develop shared goals. Whereas contracts mandate certain behaviors and create specific rights for employees, trust agreements define the purposes of teaching activities and identify resources to be utilized in pursuing those purposes. Rather than emphasizing accountability for mandated actions, trust agreements underscore joint planning (Mitchell, 1986).

The advantage of developing a successful trust agreement is that it can structure school district labor relations so that energy and effort are released for educational concerns. It may also help resolve conflicts between employees and the district. The disadvantage is that failure to develop the trust agreement may lead back to traditional bargaining with even greater animosity between the board and employees.

Win-Win Model

Another example of the collaborative model of bargaining is referred to as "win-win." This model was developed by Irving Goldaber, a sociologist who specializes in conflict resolution (Goldaber, 1987). This model seeks to develop a partnership between the employer and the employee. Like other collaborative models, win-win tries to establish effective communication and trust. The model encourages exploration of creative ideas and solutions to meet the needs of both sides (Prasad, 1993).

The win-win model is built on three basic tenets:

● The entire school board negotiates directly with the officers of the employee organization under strictly defined rules, or protocols.

● Each side independently develops problem statements.

● Specific issues are identified and referred to committees representing both the board and union. After the committees complete their work, the resolutions are brought back to the total group.

An additional characteristic of win-win bargaining is appointment of a facilitator. The role of the facilitator is to keep the process moving in a positive direction, to enforce agreements on rules, and to assist with mediation.

The win-win process specifically avoids compromise, as compromise entails loss of something prized by one side or the other. Instead, a serious attempt is made to reach consensus. The goal of win-win is to have both sides buy into a solution, with neither side forced to give up its desired goals. Hamilton (1988), an advocate of the win-win approach, believes that this model permits open discussion of problems and can result in creative solutions without the perception that the board "gave away the farm."

The advantage of the win-win model is that it gives participants an opportunity to hear the other side and understand its viewpoint. The emphasis on creativity also generates solutions that may not have been thought of in traditional bargaining. When win-win is successfully accomplished, a positive, trusting relationship among board, administrators, and employees can be developed. Advocates of win-win argue that if agreements cannot be reached, participants will at least have a rare opportunity to listen to and consider issues and concerns expressed by the other party.

The Getting-to-Yes Harvard Model

Roger Fisher and William Ury (1981) describe their model in *Getting to Yes . . . Negotiating Agreement Without Giving In*. This bargaining model was developed by the Harvard Negotiation Project. The Harvard process is a collaborative model derived from an interest-based approach to negotiating. The five major tenets of this model include:

- separating the people from the problem, thus assuming that relationships are independent issues to be managed separately

- focusing on interests, not on positions (because a position is something one has decided upon, while an interest is the reason for the position)

- assuming multiple possibilities

- inventing options for mutual gains, thus fostering cooperation and giving both parties opportunity to seek many answers

- using objective criteria, thus deciding on outcomes by agreed-upon standards, rather than through a contest of will (Fisher & Ury, 1981).

The getting-to-yes model attempts to motivate each participant to consider what is good for all the stakeholders, as opposed to what is good for a single individual or group.

A basic premise is not to bargain over positions. The key is to separate the people from the problem, then focus on interests, not positions. Like win-win, getting-to-yes bargaining advocates the concept that both parties can win and that it is the obligation of both parties to help the other win. As is the case in all the collaborative models, getting-to-yes is based on mutual trust among all participants. If trust is elusive, then the system breaks down.

California Teachers Association (CTA) Interest-Based Bargaining Model

Another collaborative bargaining model is the California Teachers Association (CTA) model. The philosophy underlying this model is that successful bargaining rests on the ability of the parties to achieve shared goals without undermining either party's ability to attain its own goals or to protect traditional rights and responsibilities. The CTA model is eclectic in that it incorporates concepts from several other collaborative models.

The model was developed by CTA and the California Department of Mediation Services. Although CTA utilized Fisher and Ury's getting-to-yes model as its primary source, the CTA adaptation also incorporates several unique qualities. The model's primary goal is to improve relationships with the board and its negotiators so as to enhance bargaining skills and the outcome of negotiations. The model is intended to increase participants' awareness that successful bargaining depends on developing a positive, ongoing relationship between the parties. Like other collaborative approaches, the CTA model aims to facilitate communication among negotiators, improve relationships, build a team spirit, and reach for consensus. Emphasis is also placed on identifying interests and exploring options and alternatives in the attempt to reach consensus.

California Foundation for Improvement of Employer-Employee Relations (CFIER)

In 1987 California's Public Employment Relations Board (PERB) began researching how the agency could assist negotiations teams in resolving their disputes and bargaining problems (Chisholm, 1993). This research resulted in PERB's 1989 sponsorship of a pilot project to provide training and facilitation designed to improve the effectiveness of labor-management relationships.

In 1991, at the direction of the California Legislature, the California Foundation for Improvement of Employer-Employee Relations (CFIER) was established as an independent, nonprofit foundation to continue the program. CFIER membership includes representatives of school districts and unions. Neutral individuals and groups are also included. All the major labor organizations dealing with public school employees—PERB itself, the California School Boards Association (CSBA), the California Department of

Education, and other education and labor organizations—are represented on the CFIER board.

CFIER trains, facilitates, and consults with public school employer and employee bargaining teams to support interest-based approaches to negotiations. The training fosters a form of the collaborative model and emphasizes identification of interests common to both board and union. All participants are encouraged to focus on alternative solutions to problems. The parties study issues jointly, focusing on the issues themselves, rather than on bargaining positions. The training program incorporates lectures, case studies, negotiations simulations, role reversals, creativity, and team-building.

Like the CTA model, the CFIER approach is eclectic in nature, combining concepts from several other collaborative models. It places greater emphasis on the study of change than do other collaborative models. Thus, Lewin's change theory is included as part of the training (Wishnick & Wishnick, 1993). Lewin's formula for organizational change describes processes of unfreezing, moving, and refreezing. As applied to collective bargaining, "unfreezing" is the commitment of team members to change the current state of the organization to one more desired. "Moving" is defined as the team acquiring new beliefs, attitudes, and behaviors. "Refreezing" is the solidification of new behaviors.

The CFIER model also draws from the interest-based negotiations model developed by Fisher and Ury. Team members are encouraged to focus on needs and interests underlying their bargaining positions so they can move to mutual development of solutions. This model is similar to other collaborative models in that necessary elements include effective communications, positive labor-management relations, and trust-building.

Advantages and Disadvantages of Collaborative Bargaining

Collaborative bargaining is an attempt to reduce the adversarial role of collective bargaining. As noted above, its goal is to foster problem-solving, positive communication, consensus-building, cooperation, respect, and trust. Collaborative bargaining is built on the premise that school boards and union leadership want to cooperate to achieve a satisfactory contract settlement. When negotiations are successful, these objectives are achieved. When collaborative bargaining works, it pays off in dividends of greater mutual respect among participants and an understanding of the needs and desires of both parties.

The disadvantages of each of the collaborative models include the risk that they may hold out unrealistic expectations for success. If the collaborative technique is unsuccessful, both sides usually return to the traditional model of bargaining—which may be even more adversarial as a result of the breakdown of trust and the inability to resolve problems using collaborative strategies. An additional disadvantage is that a union runs the risk that its members may perceive that the union leadership is too close to the board and has made a deal. On the other hand, the board may also come in for criticism from a community that believes the board is too close to the union and has given away precious resources.

SUMMARY

Because personnel expenditures constitute approximately 75% to 85% of school budgets, virtually every aspect of education has been influenced by collective bargaining. Thus, collective bargaining has had major impact on the operation of school districts. This chapter continued the discussion of collective bargaining and negotiations. Since the traditional/adversarial model of negotiations has dominated the negotiation process in most California school districts, this bargaining model has been described in some detail. The procedures and steps in the traditional model include formation of negotiating teams, presentation of initial proposals, tradeoffs, mediation, factfinding, and arbitration.

Due to the adversarial nature of the traditional collective bargaining model, several alternatives have been proposed. The generic name for these alternative models is "collaborative bargaining." The collaborative approach takes many forms, several of which are included in this chapter.

KEY TERMS

1. Administrative Law Judge (ALJ)
2. arbitration
3. caucus
4. CTA interest-based bargaining
5. California Foundation for Improvement of Employer-Employee Relations (CFIER) model
6. chief negotiator
7. collective bargaining models
8. factfinding
9. getting-to-yes Harvard model
10. good faith bargaining
11. ground rules
12. hired gun
13. impasse
14. last and final offer
15. mediation
16. negotiating table
17. negotiating teams
18. PERB rulings
19. poker chips
20. proposals and counter-proposals
21. Public Employment Relations Board (PERB)
22. Rodda Act
23. scope of negotiations
24. strike
25. terms and conditions of employment
26. tradeoffs
27. traditional/adversarial model
28. trust agreement
29. unfair labor practice
30. win-win model

QUESTIONS AND ACTIVITIES

1. The traditional/adversarial model of collective bargaining is the most widely used model in negotiations between school districts and school unions. Discuss the major advantages and disadvantages of this model.

2. Successful negotiations require establishment of ground rules for negotiations. Define "ground rules" and give several specific examples.

3. The school board or the union may file an unfair labor practice against the other side. What is an unfair labor practice? What procedures have been established in the event that an unfair labor practice is alleged?

4. Some states permit binding arbitration as part of the collective bargaining process. Discuss the advantages and disadvantages of binding arbitration.

5. Several collaborative models have been used in collective bargaining between unions and school districts. Discuss four major objectives of these models.

Chapter 12

Collective Bargaining: Managing the Contract

INTRODUCTION

The community, parents, administrators, teachers, and classified employees—all breathe a sigh of relief: Agreement has been reached and a contract between the school board and teachers has been approved. Students have mixed feelings about the settlement. With the threat of a strike, some students looked forward to a few days out of class, but most students sympathized with their teachers and knew that a teacher work stoppage would be detrimental to their own education.

After this sigh of relief, what happens to the contract? It is a good bet that few employees are waiting with breathless anticipation to read through the contract, line by line. Contracts have the reputation of a "dull read." They are filled with legalese and technical jargon. Ordinarily, the superintendent and union leadership have the duty of explaining the terms of the negotiated agreement to their constituencies.

Although Americans are accustomed to contracts, we rarely read them word for word. We sign a contract when we purchase a home, buy a car, or join a physical fitness program. However, few Americans read the small print in the contract—the whereases and heretofores. Most individuals are satisfied with knowing the major points: How much are the payments and how often? If the contract involves a particularly large purchase or a complicated situation, an individual may seek the advice of an attorney before agreeing to contract terms. Generally, however, after the contract is signed to purchase the house or car, it is filed away and rarely reviewed unless serious problems arise. It is a tribute to the honesty and integrity of most Americans—and in some instances the result of extensive legislation and penalties—that contracts usually work.

This chapter continues the discussion of collective bargaining and negotiations. The focus of the chapter is on the importance of contract management. Contract management starts where negotiations end. No sooner is a contract signed than questions arise about its interpretation. These questions are usually directed to the site principal, who is expected to have ready answers.

This day-to-day monitoring, interpretation, and enforcement of the contract are referred to as "contract management." This task is equal to, perhaps even exceeds in importance, that of negotiating a fair and reasonable contract acceptable to both sides. For illustrative purposes, a discussion of an actual contract between the Association of Chino Teachers and the Chino School Board (California) is included in this chapter.

CONTRACTS

A contract between a school board and union is similar to a contract between a car dealer and an individual purchaser. However, in contrast to the private contract, a contract between school district and union is often open to multiple interpretations. A teacher may ask the principal, "Can I take a personal necessity day to visit an out-of-town friend?" The answer to that question may not be clearly spelled out in the contract and thus subject to interpretation.

Collective bargaining contracts are similar to contracts in the private sector in that they are usually complex and often lengthy. For example, the most recent contract between the Chino School Board (California) and the Chino Teachers Association is 52 pages long. The analogous contract in the Riverside Unified School District (California) has 96 pages, almost twice the length of that in Chino.

The contract, which embodies the agreements reached during collective bargaining, is legally binding on both management and the union. The general principles of contract law apply to an employment contract. Five essential elements are required for a valid contract:

- offer and acceptance

- legally competent parties

- consideration

- legal subject matter

- proper form.

Offer and Acceptance

To be valid, a contract must contain an offer by one party and acceptance by another. Until the party to whom the offer is made accepts the offer, the contract is not valid. A contract cannot be accepted by a spouse or other relative. If the board offers a contract to an individual to teach mathematics, it is not binding until that teacher agrees to the contract's terms and conditions. Similarly, the contract between the school board and the union is not valid until the last proposal and counterproposal are accepted by both parties.

Good contract practice requires acceptance in writing and within a given amount of time. Ordinarily, when agreement has been reached between the district representative and the union representative, a vote is taken by union members. This vote occurs prior to official approval of the contract by the school board. In numerous instances members of a bargaining unit have refused to ratify an agreement made by their negotiators. Only when both parties have agreed to the terms of the contract does it meet the conditions of offer and acceptance.

Legally Competent Parties

A contract is not valid unless it is entered into by two or more competent persons. This means that the persons have the legal capacity to enter into a contract. The authority to contract for a school district rests exclusively with the school board. For example, the superintendent or personnel director may recommend employment of a teacher, but only the school board is authorized to approve the contract of employment. Similarly, a buyer who negotiates a price on a new computer has made a validated purchase (contract) only upon approval of the school board.

The individual or company that enters into a contract with the school district must also be recognized as a competent party. For example, a teacher who does not have a proper credential cannot enter into a contract. In this case, the teacher would be considered an incompetent party for purposes of contracting to teach. Individuals who are mentally ill, impaired by drugs or alcohol, or under duress at the time of signing a contract also would be considered incompetent parties and precluded from entering into a valid contract.

For a contract to be valid, the board's action must also be legal. Legal board actions are possible only when a quorum of the board is in attendance at the meeting, the meeting is legally called, the meeting conforms to state legal requirements for school board meetings, and the contract was approved by a majority of the board. If the preceding circumstances do not exist, the board lacks legal status and is not considered a competent party. Similar conditions apply to the employee's union. The union must have met the requirements for exclusive representation to have legal status to negotiate for employees.

Consideration

Consideration has been defined as the "cause, motive, price, or impelling influence that induces a contracting party to enter into a contract" (Black, 1991). For a contract to be valid, it must be supported by a consideration, which is usually defined as something of value. In placing an employee on the district's salary schedule, school boards must conform to any state statutes regarding minimum salaries and must abide by the terms of any negotiated contract with district bargaining units. Also, in the absence of a merit pay program, salaries must be applied uniformly to individuals or groups of individuals who have the same preparation and experience and perform the same duties.

Legal Subject Matter

To be enforceable, a contract must pertain to legal subject matter. For example, all 50 states require a credential to teach. If a board enters into a contract with an individual who does not possess a teaching credential, such a contract is illegal and declared invalid. Another example is California's statutory competitive bid requirement. All purchases that exceed a certain amount must be open to competitive bids. Should the board attempt to enter into a contract with a vendor without meeting the competitive bid requirement, the contract would be invalid.

Proper Form

Most states require that an employment contract be in writing. However, in the absence of statutory specification, an oral agreement can be legally binding on both parties (McCarthy & Cambron, 1981).

CONTRACT PROVISIONS

Most district-employee union contracts are detailed and replace board of education policies covering the working conditions that were negotiated. Ashby and colleagues (1972) have outlined the provisions that are contained in and considered essential to a collective bargaining contract:

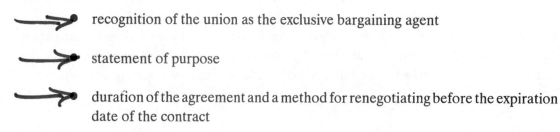

recognition of the union as the exclusive bargaining agent

statement of purpose

duration of the agreement and a method for renegotiating before the expiration date of the contract

grievance procedure

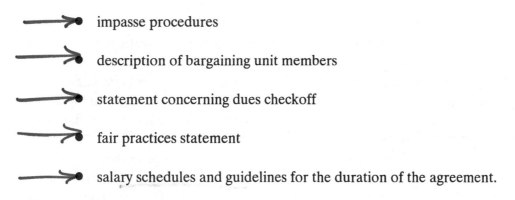

impasse procedures

description of bargaining unit members

statement concerning dues checkoff

fair practices statement

salary schedules and guidelines for the duration of the agreement.

The most problematic of these and several other common contract provisions are discussed in the following paragraphs.

Grievances

Even when principals and personnel directors exhibit exemplary interpersonal skills, disagreements may arise over interpretation of the contract. Since this reality is recognized by members of collective bargaining teams, most negotiated contracts contain a process for resolving conflicting interpretations or complaints. This contract section is usually referred to as the "grievance procedure clause." Grievance procedures reduce the cost of settling disputes for both employees and employers by keeping issues out of the courts and reducing the time required for resolution.

A grievance is a problem or complaint related to the contract agreement. It represents a violation, or purported violation, of the agreement that must be settled through the grievance procedures set forth in the contract itself. A grievance procedure is a formal system by which contract disputes are expressed, processed, and judged. The grievance clause should define what constitutes a grievance and describe the procedure for processing it. Persons eligible to initiate a grievance and the timeline to be observed in filing a grievance should also be stated in the contract (Seyfarth, 1991).

When an employee has a complaint about some act or failure to act on the part of an administrator, the employee may seek a remedy through the grievance clause. The grievance procedure has been described as a means of allowing an employee to express a complaint to management without fear of reprisal and to have that complaint addressed by successively higher levels of management until an answer is provided that the grievant can or must accept (McCollum & Norris, 1984). Teachers are most likely to grieve what they believe to be violations of contract provisions affecting job security, transfers, class size, and assignment to noncontractual duties.

The grievance process may provide three or four steps through which a complaint may be appealed. Step one typically calls for an informal hearing with the employee's immediate supervisor. If the complaint is not resolved informally, the grievant presents a formal, written grievance to the same supervisor. In this second step, the employee is required to describe the basis for the grievance; list any informal steps already taken to try to resolve the issue; state reasons why the alleged actions were unfair, arbitrary, or contrary to contract provisions; and propose actions that the aggrieved employee believes necessary to resolve the issue. Upon receiving the written statement from the employee, the immediate supervisor prepares a response. The response usually includes a statement regarding the grounds of the grievance and recommended solutions.

If agreement is not reached at this level, step three moves to the next level of supervision. The person at this level is usually the personnel director, who conducts a further investigation of the allegations put forth by the grievant. After completion of the investigation, the personnel director or supervisor renders a decision with a recommended solution. If the grievant is still not satisfied, the issue may be referred to the superintendent and/or the school board for a decision.

Arbitration

In several California school districts unions have been able to negotiate the concept of "arbitration" as the final step in the grievance procedure. A major issue facing a district and the union is the question of what "issue or complaint" is "subject to arbitration." Grievances that deal with rights granted to a board by statute are not arbitrable. Also, grievances not filed in timely fashion may not be subject to arbitration.

Most grievance policies limit the number of days that may elapse after occurrence of an event before a grievance is filed. If the allowable number of days for filing a grievance is exceeded, the grievance may be declared not subject to arbitration. An exception may be possible if the employee failed to learn of the precipitating event until after it occurred. Whether the issue is subject to arbitration also hinges on a definition of what is or is not arbitrable as stated in the negotiated contract or contained in state statutes. Certain disputes may be grievable but not arbitrable. In those situations, employees have no appeal beyond the steps provided in the grievance procedure.

Arbitrators' decisions can have considerable impact on district personnel polices. For that reason, most district administrators try through contract language to define narrowly those disputes that may be taken to arbitration. Arbitrators who review disputes between management and labor must decide whose interpretation of the contract is correct. Arbitrators use the rule of consistency and the rule of intent in deciding the accurate interpretation of contract language. Arbitrators must frequently deal with complaints that involve interpretation and application of rules. They must decide which rules apply and what actions are either required or forbidden by a rule.

One of the principles used by arbitrators in resolving grievances is past practice. Unless it is clear that the board and the union intended to institute a new practice, the arbitrator usually decides that previous practice will remain in effect.

Some superintendents never go to arbitration unless they are certain of winning. There is good basis for this guideline. Although contract language may appear straightforward and clear to administrators, there is no guarantee that the arbitrator will agree with their interpretation, and once an arbitrator's decision has been announced, it establishes a precedent that may be difficult to change.

No-Strike Provision

Most parents and educators agree that nothing is more disruptive to a school district than a strike. The repercussions in the aftermath of a strike may last for years. Federal law prohibits strikes by teachers. Most states have passed similar laws. However, California law does not expressly prohibit strikes by public employees unless the district can show that the strike creates an imminent threat to health or safety. In most cases, school districts prepare for a teacher strike by employing substitute teachers and providing them with instructional materials. These preparations avoid the threat to health or safety, and, as a result, deprive the district of the opportunity to obtain an injunction against the strike.

Because the right to strike has not been clearly settled in California, most districts in the state attempt to place a no-strike clause in the negotiated agreement. Such a provision puts the union on record against using the strike and involves the union in the enforcing the laws that prohibit a strike. In addition, a no-strike provision usually permits management to impose monetary damages on employees who engage in an illegal strike.

Zipper Clause

A zipper clause stipulates that the written agreement is the complete and full contract between the parties and that neither party is required to bargain on other items during the term of the agreement. The purpose of such a provision is to avoid continuing negotiations after the contract has been ratified.

A zipper clause does not preclude the parties from negotiating further if both agree to do so. New bargaining strategies, including collaborative or win-win bargaining, involve exceptions to a zipper clause. In most districts, collective bargaining is actually an ongoing process, with union and management negotiating continually as problems arise.

Maintenance-of-Standards Clause

Unions often seek to obtain a maintenance-of-standards clause in the agreement. When such a clause is included, the district may be unable to terminate programs that have outlived their usefulness or that it can no longer afford.

A maintenance-of-standards clause requires the district to maintain its current practices on a wide range of items, many of which are not mandatory subjects of bargaining.

For example, many high schools have a classified employee assigned to supervise the physical education locker room. If the district decides it can no longer afford this position, the maintenance-of-standards clause is probably written to prohibit eliminating the position. Moreover, a maintenance-of-standards clause increases the risk that an arbitrator will settle a contract dispute by citing past practice, usually to the detriment of the district. For these reasons, school boards generally oppose a maintenance-of-standards clause on the ground that it limits the district's options when resources or priorities change.

Just Cause

The term "just cause" is found in many collective bargaining agreements in public education and is routinely included in most union proposals. The phrase poses a danger to the school board because "just cause" has no clear definition. Thus, if the collective bargaining agreement calls for binding arbitration as the last step in the grievance procedure, then an arbitrator decides what just cause means in that case. The arbitrator's interpretation of the term may differ from management's intention.

For example, suppose a collective bargaining agreement contains the following provision: "No employee will be involuntary transferred without just cause." What does "just cause" mean in this case? Management and employees may define the term quite differently. If just cause is included in a negotiated agreement, it must be clearly defined. If the parties cannot agree on a definition, then management should insist that the clause be eliminated from discussion.

Reduction in Force

A reduction-in-force (RIF) clause is contained in most collective bargaining agreements. In most states, employee seniority takes precedence when layoffs are required. Some agreements allow for "bumping." This term means that an employee with greater seniority may "bump" or take the place of another employee in a different classification. For example, a home economics teacher with seniority who has a minor in math and is credentialed to teach that subject could take the position of a less senior math teacher. A few RIF provisions stress other factors such as affirmative action and teacher merit. Management usually tries to include these latter factors, but they are opposed by most certificated and classified unions.

Wages and Benefits

Not surprisingly, much time is devoted at the bargaining table to wage increases and fringe benefit improvements. Wage and salary increases are often stated as "across-the-board" salary increases, meaning that every employee in the bargaining unit will receive the same percentage salary increase. Generally, members of the union bargaining team negotiate for at least a "cost-of-living adjustment" (COLA). The COLA is based on the Consumer Price Index for a designated geographic area.

In addition to an increase in wages, union representatives attempt to negotiate improvements in such fringe benefits as insurance programs—life, health, vision, and dental. They may also attempt to increase the number of sick leave days and personal leave provisions in the current contract.

INSERVICE PROGRAM ON THE CONTRACT

Immediately after a negotiated agreement is signed, the superintendent should schedule an inservice program regarding any changes in terms of the agreement. It is usually wise to have members of the district negotiating team conduct the inservice program since they will have the most direct knowledge of the contract's terms.

The extent of the inservice depends on the number and complexity of changes in the new contract. If there are few changes, the inservice program may be brief; if there are many changes or complex issues, the inservice may be extensive. In addition to discussing the terms of the agreement, the inservice program should review issues raised during bargaining, explain why certain proposals were approved or rejected, and clarify any new language or new interpretations of old language (Gonder, 1981).

CONSISTENCY OF CONTRACT INTERPRETATION AND ENFORCEMENT

After principals are well versed on new terms of the contract, they need procedures for administering it. That they understand the need for consistency in interpretation and application of contract provisions is of the utmost importance. Districts experience difficulty in managing the contract when one principal administers its terms in a liberal or lenient fashion while other principals take a more conservative view.

Deviations permitted from the contract by individual principals may set a precedent that the union can use to negate part of the contract. For example, if the contract requires teachers to attend an open house and one principal excuses a teacher from attendance, this violation of the contract may set a precedent that will undermine that clause of the contract. To avoid inconsistent interpretations by individual administrators, the district should prepare an administrator's manual that contains interpretation of contract clauses, deadlines for processing grievances, and similar information.

Unfortunately, strict adherence to the letter of the law in the contract sometimes creates hard feelings between a principal and the teachers at his or her site. For example, suppose the contract requires teachers to attend a particular inservice program. Then suppose that an outstanding teacher asks to be excused and this request is denied. The teacher may be very angry with the principal. However, principals are not afforded the luxury of making exceptions to the contract out of a desire to reward a teacher's good performance. If a principal feels a provision in the contract is unfair or unjust, she should refer the question to the personnel director or superintendent.

Every administrator should know to whom contract questions should be directed when he or she is not sure of an interpretation. Employees are sometimes able to effect a change in school district operations by threatening to grieve an issue. When that happens, employees win by intimidation what they were unable to achieve at the bargaining table.

It takes great interpersonal skills on the part of an effective principal to adhere to the terms of the contract without alienating the staff. Knowledge of the collective bargaining process and of the rationale for each section of the contract assists an administrator in maintaining positive relationships with staff. The effective principal must be a good listener, treat each individual respectfully, and be sensitive to employees' feelings and needs.

CALIFORNIA CONTRACTS AND AGREEMENTS

As one would expect, collective bargaining contracts have a certain similarity. When the Rodda Act was approved by the California legislature in 1975, districts scrambled to employ attorneys who specialized in school law to assist in developing the first contracts. Therefore, the basic provisions are similar from district to district. The terms of the certificated employees' agreement with the Chino School District are included in this section as illustrative of contracts between school districts and school boards.

AGREEMENT BETWEEN THE CHINO SCHOOL DISTRICT AND ASSOCIATED CHINO TEACHERS (ACT)

The agreement between the Chino School District and Associated Chino Teachers (ACT) contains 22 articles. ACT is associated with the California Teachers Association and the National Education Association. The terms of this agreement were in force from July 1, 1998 through June 30, 2001.

Article 1: Agreement

The opening article of the contract is divided into two parts. The first part establishes that the contents of the agreement are bilateral, binding on both the district and ACT. The second part recognizes ACT as the exclusive representative for the unit. This section also protects unit members in that the district is prohibited from contracting for duties ordinarily performed by unit members.

Article 2: Negotiations Procedures

Article 2 establishes ground rules for negotiations. It includes timelines for presentation of an initial proposal by ACT and for the district's response. This article also contains the legislatively required timeline for a public hearing on the initial proposals. This public hearing is often referred to as "sunshining" the proposal. The purpose of the public hearing is to give community members an opportunity to view the proposal and offer their reactions to members of the school board and the union.

This section of the contract also contains a requirement that the district furnish copies of certain documents to the ACT. These documents may include salary schedules and employee placements on the schedule, budget information, projected student enrollment, and the like. The purpose of this information is to enable the union to fulfill its role as the exclusive bargaining representative of certificated employees.

Article 3: Association Rights

The association rights clause includes nine sections:

- the association's right to transact its business on school property

- the right to use district facilities and equipment for association meetings

- authorization to use the district's internal mail service and mail boxes

- ACT's right to place an item on a school board agenda

- a requirement that the district provide to ACT the names and work locations of all members of the bargaining unit

- the district's responsibility to provide copies of district administrative guides to the association

- the district's obligation to furnish the association with all available public information concerning financial resources and professional staffing

- the right of the association to serve on district committees

- the district's obligation each school year to provide fourteen days' released time from teaching duties for association leaders to use in conducting association business.

In addition to the nine sections in this clause, the ACT gained the right to consult with the district on definition of educational objectives, content of courses and curriculum, selection of textbooks, and methods of student evaluation.

In this section of the contract the ACT also obtained right to an "agency fee." An agency fee requires employees who are eligible for membership in ACT either to join the association or pay a fee equal to the membership fee. Under agency fee, the district is required to notify each member that his or her employment status is conditional upon joining the association or paying the fee. Provisions are made to allow members of religious bodies that have a basic tenet opposing union membership to pay a sum, equal to the membership fee, to specified charities.

Article 4: Rights Retained by the District

Article 4, referred to as the "district rights clause," gives the district all rights and powers enjoyed prior to signing the agreement. There is reference to the authority granted by the California Education Code, California Government Code, California Code of Civil Procedures, California Elections Code, California Health and Safety Code, California Revenue and Taxation Code—all containing provisions passed by the state legislature—and Title 5, the California Administrative Code.

An interesting section of this article is the statement that the association and the district shall continue to work cooperatively in converting any site from a standard to a year-round schedule or vice versa. It was understood that evaluation timelines might need to be adjusted for personnel in a school on a year-round calendar.

Article 5: Non-Discrimination

This section of the contract is a nondiscrimination clause. In addition to prohibiting the district and the association from discriminating against any unit member because of race, color, religion, sex, national origin, age, or marital status, discrimination is also forbidden on the basis of membership or nonmembership in an employee organization.

Article 6: Adult School Terms and Conditions

Article six is very specific about the terms and conditions of employment of adult school teachers. It includes a provision that adult school teachers who teach 20 hours or more per week will be members of the bargaining unit. Other sections of this clause pertain to the posting of vacancies for adult school positions, health benefits for adult school teachers, and evaluation of adult school teachers.

Article 7: Class Size

Article 7 of the contract specifies the student:classroom teacher ratios for district budgetary planning and staffing. The staffing formulas are as follows: (a) kindergarten through third grade—one teacher for every 20 students, (b) fourth through sixth—one teacher for every 32 students, (c) seventh and eighth—one teacher for every 34 students, (d) grades nine through twelve—one teacher for every 35 students.

Two interesting additional sections are included in the class size article. First, teachers who teach combination classes are paid a $1,000 stipend each year. Second, when the preferred numbers are exceeded, the teacher receives $5.00 per student for each day the number is exceeded.

This article of the contract contains specific language about balancing class size and sets forth some exceptions to the staffing ratio. These exceptions include physical education, chorus, typing, band, independent study, and team teaching. Staffing ratios for nurses, counselors, and elementary music teachers are also delineated.

Article 8: Evaluations

The goal of teacher evaluation is set forth in this article: "The intent of the evaluation program shall be to maintain and improve the quality of the instructional program." The evaluation process is to be conducted in a manner that recognizes both the teacher and the administrator as professionals and that creates an atmosphere of trust and cooperation among the participants in the process.

Timelines for evaluation are included. All permanent employees are evaluated no less than once every two years. The exception to this rule is that employees who are not performing their duties in a satisfactory manner may be evaluated more often. The section requires evaluation of probationary employees at least once a year.

Specific timelines for classroom visitations are contained in this section. The process for evaluation is also outlined. The four sets of information to be used in evaluation include:

- progress of pupils toward standards of expected pupil achievement as established by the district

- the instructional techniques and strategies used by the employee

- the teacher's use of curricular objectives as adopted by the district

- establishment and maintenance of a suitable learning environment.

Article 8 also contains procedures, requirements, and timelines for employees who receive an unsatisfactory evaluation.

Article 9: Personnel File Contents and Inspection

This section establishes the right of employees to inspect materials placed in their personnel file. Employees are also granted the right to have an ACT representative present when reviewing the contents of a personnel file. Other specifics regarding personnel files are included in this section, for example, the right of an employee to receive a copy of a derogatory letter prior to its placement in the file.

Article 10: Public Charges

The definition of a public charge is contained in article 10: "A public charge is an allegation against an employee by a member of the public (other than another employee or a student) that is deemed by the site administrator to be serious in nature." Specific procedures and timelines for processing public charges are set forth.

Article 11: Grievance Procedures

The specific steps to be followed by an employee in filing a grievance and by the district in response are contained in this article. First is the informal level, at which a grievant attempts to resolve the alleged grievance through an informal conference with his or her immediate supervisor. If the grievance cannot be resolved at this level, three formal steps are provided:

1. No later than 20 days following the act or omission giving rise to the grievance, the grievant must present the aggrieved item in writing, addressed to his or her immediate supervisor. Upon receiving the grievance, the immediate supervisor must respond to the grievant, in writing, within 10 days.

2. A grievant who is not satisfied with the decision at step one may appeal the decision to the superintendent within 10 days. The superintendent must respond to the grievant within 10 days.

3. An employee who is not satisfied with the step two decision may request the ACT to submit the grievance to arbitration.

In this district the teachers' association succeeded in negotiating binding arbitration for the resolution of grievances. Once a grievance is submitted to arbitration, the arbitrator's decision is final and binding on the association and the district.

Article 12: Working Conditions

The working conditions article contains 18 sections. A brief summary of each of these sections follows:

1. Unit members are entitled to serve on district and school committees concerned with curriculum, budget, professional inservice training, pupil evaluation, job evaluation, and educational needs assessments.

2. Teachers will have ready access to duplication equipment, clerical support, textbooks, supplies, and equipment consistent with their curriculum objectives.

Teachers are entitled to:

3. a work schedule that provides administrative support and reasonable security and protection

4. reasonable working areas for regular and special education instruction

5. facilities maintained in working order, e.g., plumbing, heating, air conditioning, and telephones

6. one emergency parking space per school site

7. physical assistance to transfer teaching materials should a teacher be required to move to a different classroom

8. adequate time for restroom visits

9. an administrator on site when students are present.

In addition:

10. When conflict develops between a teacher and an aide, the principal is required to establish a meeting to resolve the issue.

11. A teacher may choose not to have a student teacher assigned to his or her classroom.

12. Students are prohibited access to teachers' mailboxes.

13. Unit members may not be required to use their personal vehicles to transport students.

14. Unit members may not be required to perform special medical procedures.

15. The district must inform the teacher of any student who has caused or attempted to cause serious bodily injury to another person.

16. Whenever possible, the district is to provide unit members with a designated, interruption-free work space or classroom.

17. The district expressed support for a unit member's right to expect professional treatment from district personnel. Unit members are expected to conduct themselves in like manner.

18. The district must respond within 20 days to unit members' routine work orders submitted through their respective location administrative offices. In emergencies, response must come in 24 hours.

Article 13: Leaves

Article 13, dealing with leaves, is the longest article in the contract. It defines each leave provision and provides specific details regarding that leave. Leaves in this clause are available for illness, disability, maternity, parenthood, and industrial accident and illness. Other leave provisions include jury duty or court appearance, personal necessity, personal leave, and bereavement and imminent death. In addition, leave for public office service, military service, and sabbaticals are included in this section.

Article 14: Hours

Employees' hours of work are contained in article 14. The regular workday for a unit member is seven on-site duty hours or 35 hours per week, inclusive of lunch. Employees are also required to report to their work sites at least 15 minutes before the commencement of their first class and remain at least 30 minutes following the end of their last class. This section also provides that all members of the bargaining unit are entitled to not less than a 30-minute, duty-free lunch period.

The requirement that employees perform adjunct duties is also contained in this section. The specific obligations of employees include attendance at faculty meetings, parent conferences, student conferences, conferences with administrators, and inservice meetings. The contract also stipulates that additional duties are not limited to the above.

The contract specifies that such duties as campus supervision and supervision of social and athletic events and field trips will be offered to volunteers. In case of insufficient volunteers, the administration may assign such duties on an equitable basis.

An additional clause establishes preparation time for teachers. Basically, all middle school and high school teachers are provided one conference or preparation period each day. Elementary teachers are provided 150 minutes per week of conference or preparation time.

Article 15: Placement, Assignment, Reassignment, Transfer, and Vacancies

Article 15 is the second longest section of the contract. It contains five main provisions:

- definitions of placement, assignment, reassignment, transfer, and vacancy

- voluntary transfers

- involuntary transfers

- reduction in staff

- assignment or reassignment.

Article 16: Retirement Credit for Parttime Service

Contained in this section are specific provisions that allow an employee opportunity to work parttime and receive fulltime retirement credit. This option requires that a participant have reached age 55. Service under this clause is limited to a five-year period or reaching age 65, whichever comes sooner. To be eligible, an employee must have been employed fulltime for at least ten years, five of those years in the Chino district.

Article 17: Compensation and Health and Welfare Benefits

Article 17 of the contract contains the specific schedule for each of the years of the contract. It also describes the district's responsibility for health and welfare benefits.

Article 18: Children's Center / Extended Day Care and School-Age Parenting / Infant Development Programs

This article contains specific duties and conditions for employees who work in the children's centers in the district. Its sections cover class size, hours of employment, and a salary schedule.

Article 19: No Strike; No Lockout

This section of the contract contains the association's agreement that it will not encourage or engage in a strike, work stoppage, slowdown, boycott, mass absenteeism, or any other interruption of or interference with the operation of the district. If any of the above should occur, the association will be responsible for notifying employees that such action is unauthorized and promptly order its members to return to work.

In this article the association also agrees not to establish a picket line as part of the collective bargaining process. In turn, the district agrees not to engage in a lockout. A lockout is not defined in this clause, but its meaning is usually that the employer closes schools and prevents employees from reaching their workstations.

Article 20: Miscellaneous

This section is also called the "savings clause." It provides protection to the union and the district should any clause in the contract be declared illegal by a court. In that case, the offending clause is automatically deleted from the agreement, but all remaining articles, sections, and clauses remain in force.

Article 21: Completion of Negotiations

This section closes negotiations. It states that neither party shall be required to meet and negotiate any matter, covered or not covered in the contract, prior to the closing date of the contract. This section, referred to as the "zipper clause," protects the district from a forced reopening of the contract before its expiration date.

Article 22: Term of Agreement

The final clause in the contract is very brief; it simply states the beginning and ending dates of the contract and contains signatures of school board members and the ACT officers.

SUMMARY

This chapter concluded the discussion of collective bargaining and negotiations. The focus is the actual terms and conditions of the contract. Once a contract is signed by the district and the union, ongoing, day-to-day monitoring is referred to as "contract management." This process starts where negotiations end. No sooner is a contract signed than questions begin. Answering those questions is usually the responsibility of the principal, at least in the first instance. Therefore, it is of greatest importance that the district provide an extensive inservice program for district administrators and principals who have responsibility for contract management. Effective contract management results in greater harmony and accord among the board, school administrators, and employees.

Contract management is equal, or perhaps greater, in importance than negotiating a fair, reasonable contract acceptable to the school board and employees. For illustrative purposes, an actual contract between the Association of Chino Teachers and the Chino School District was summarized in this chapter.

The superintendent and his or her administrative staff must know the terms of the contract. They must possess the skill and expertise required to implement those terms. Employees should also know their responsibilities and rights under its terms. By managing the contract in a fair and consistent manner, administrators are able to focus on the educational objectives of the district. Failure to manage the contract well can only result in unhappy employees and needless distractions from instructional priorities.

KEY TERMS

1. agency fee
2. arbitration
3. bumping rights
4. consideration
5. district rights clause
6. grievance
7. just cause
8. legal subject matter
9. legally competent party
10. maintenance-of-standards clause
11. no-lockout clause
12. no-strike clause
13. offer and acceptance
14. proper form
15. public charges
16. reduction in force (RIF)
17. savings clause
18. zipper clause
19. wages and benefits

QUESTIONS AND ACTIVITIES

1. What are the five essential elements in a valid contract? List and discuss each.

2. Once a contract is agreed to by a district and union, the district should schedule an inservice program on the terms of the contract. What subject areas should be included?

3. Consistency in interpreting the contract helps reduce employee grievances. Give examples of *in*consistent interpretations that might lead to employee grievances.

4. Some districts and unions have agreed to "binding arbitration" as the final step in the grievance procedure. What are the advantages and disadvantages of this procedure?

5. Most California school boards attempt to negotiate a "no-strike" clause in the collective bargaining agreement. What are the advantages to the district of this provision?

Chapter 13

Legal Aspects of School Personnel Administration

INTRODUCTION

The nation's public schools, like all other public institutions, operate within a framework of laws. Both the federal and state legislatures enact laws that affect schools. Control and operation of schools is also subject to ordinances, rules, and regulations approved and adopted by numerous federal, state, and local agencies and government entities. The courts also exert a major influence on the operation of the schools. The modern personnel officer must have a thorough understanding of legislation and court rulings to keep a district operating smoothly without undue restrictions on policies and procedures.

THE FEDERAL CONSTITUTION AND EDUCATION

The Constitution of the United States, adopted in 1788, makes no direct reference to schools or education. Amendment X to the Constitution provides that all powers not delegated to the United States are reserved to the states or to the people:

> The powers not delegated to the United States by the Constitution, nor prohibited by it to the States, are reserved to the States respectively, or to the people.

This amendment clearly indicates that education is not a function of the federal government, but of the states. However, over the years the national government has exercised considerable power over the schools through federal legislation and decisions of the courts. The primary authority for court decisions in school matters is contained in the ten amendments to the Constitution, known as the Bill of Rights. These amendments have exerted a profound influence on the development of the American educational system.

The courts have consistently ruled that constitutional protections apply to students both in and out of school. Their rights to freedom of expression and other civil liberties are well established in law. Courts require specified procedures to safeguard those rights against abuse by institutional authority.

Amendment I

The first amendment to the U. S. Constitution expresses Congress's guarantees of freedom of religion, of speech and expression, and of the press. It also provides for citizens to assemble peacefully and to petition the government for redress of grievances.

This amendment has greatly influenced operation of the schools in the management of personnel and students. For example, school districts may not dismiss a teacher for speaking out on an issue of public concern outside the classroom. The precedent case for this situation is *Pickering v. Board of Education*. Marvin Pickering, a teacher in Illinois, had his employment terminated after he wrote a letter to the local newspaper criticizing the school board. Pickering disagreed with the board regarding the expenditure of funds for the district's athletic program. The court ruled that Pickering's letter was a matter of public concern. If a teacher's statements are not false and not knowingly or recklessly made, a statement on public matters cannot form the basis for dismissal (Alexander & Alexander, 1992).

Amendment II

This amendment provides for a militia and establishes the right of the people to keep and bear arms. This amendment has had little influence on the operation of public schools.

Amendment III

The third amendment prohibits quartering of soldiers in private homes. Like the second amendment, this has had little effect on schools.

Amendment IV

This amendment provides the right of the people to be secure in their persons, houses, papers, and effects, and protects against unreasonable searches and seizures. This amendment has often been cited by attorneys as generally prohibiting personal searches of students or of their lockers or automobiles. It has also been cited in teachers' rights to privacy.

Amendment V

The fifth amendment guarantees due process of the law. It states that no person shall be deprived of life, liberty, or property without due process of law. It also prohibits taking private property for public use without just compensation. The due process clause is often cited in personnel and student matters. The private property clause is the foundation for acquisition of land for school sites.

Amendment VI

The sixth amendment provides for judicial procedure and guarantees a speedy public trial, an impartial jury, information about the nature of the charge, confrontation by witnesses against the party, the right of the accused to obtain witnesses in his or her own behalf, and the right to have counsel. This amendment must be kept in mind if students or staff are suspected of a criminal offense.

Amendment VII

The next amendment guarantees the right to trial by jury and provides the underpinning for the country's court system.

Amendment VIII

Amendment eight prohibits cruel and unusual punishment and excessive bail. This amendment has been cited in decisions regarding corporal punishment.

Amendment IX

The ninth amendment guarantees the "rights of the people" and states that the enumeration in the Constitution of certain rights may not be construed to deny or discourage other rights retained by the people.

Amendment X

The last amendment in the original Bill of Rights states that all powers not delegated to the United States are reserved to the (now 50) states or to the people. As previously mentioned, this amendment makes education a function of the states.

Amendment XIV

Although not part of the Bill of Rights, the 14th amendment has also had a profound effect on the operation of public schools. Amendment XIV reads

No state shall make a law which abridges the rights of citizens in the United States nor deny anyone the equal protection of the law.

It further states

All persons born or naturalized in the United States, and subject to the jurisdiction thereof, are citizens of the United States and of the State wherein they reside.

Therefore, each state must guarantee to its citizens the same rights as those guaranteed by the federal Constitution. The courts have ruled that this amendment applies to all persons: adults and children.

STATE CONTROL OF EDUCATION

Since the federal Constitution does not refer to education, state governments have legal responsibility for control and operation of the schools. Thus, each state has complete authority to form a public education system.

State Constitutions

The foundation for control of schools by the state is found in all state constitutions. By 1820, 13 of the 23 states had constitutional provisions and 17 had statutory arrangements for public education (Thurston & Roe, 1957). Today, most state constitutions include firm mandates for the establishment of a public education system. California's Constitution, for example, requires the legislature to provide a "system of common schools" under which a "free school" is established in each district and, once operational, supported in each district a minimum of six months in every year. Constitutional provisions stipulate that the legislature must encourage the promotion of intellectual, moral, scientific, and agricultural improvement by establishing a uniform system of common schools.

State Statutes

Every state legislature enacts, amends, and repeals statutes, more commonly called "laws." Because public schools are state agencies, the legislature of every state has created laws governing school districts. These laws direct the control and operation of the state's public schools. The board of education and the superintendent of each district are responsible to ensure compliance with state laws.

All laws in California are codified by subject matter. For example, the Public Health Code contains all laws relating to public health, and the Criminal Code gathers all laws governing crime and penalties. All California codes, including the Education Code, are available and searchable on the World Wide Web at http://www.leginfo. ca.gov/calaw.html. The codes with background information and references to court decisions are published with yearly updates by West Publishing Company. Most laws pertaining to education are contained in the Education Code, which is, in turn, divided into three sections:

- General Education

- Elementary and Secondary Education

- Postsecondary Education.

The most important sections of the Education Code for the personnel officer are sections #44000 through #46000, which contain the laws pertaining to education personnel, both certificated and classified. A brief review of the more critical code sections follows.

CERTIFICATED PERSONNEL IN CALIFORNIA

Following are highlighted sections from the Education Code essential to administering the personnel program for certificated personnel.

Ed. Code **#44031** provides protection for information placed in an employee's personnel file. The law clearly establishes the rights of an employee to inspect all materials contained in the file. It also provides opportunity to review all derogatory comments prior to entry of the statement into the file. In addition, the employee has the right to attach his or her comments to any derogatory statement.

Sections **#44100 through #44105** establish and maintain a policy of equal opportunity in employment for all persons and prohibit discrimination based on race, sex, color, religion, age, disability, ancestry, or national origin. These sections also prescribe specific goals, timetables, and actions required in school districts to implement affirmative action programs.

#44250 through #44508 list all credentials issued in California, along with the minimum educational requirements for each. A personnel officer finds it necessary to be thoroughly familiar with these code sections. Grounds for revocation and suspension of an employee's credential are also contained in these sections.

#44660 through #44665 describe requirements for evaluation and assessment of performance of certificated employees. The key requirements for teacher evaluation are contained in section #44664 as follows:

> Evaluation and assessment of the performance of each certificated employee shall be made on a continuing basis, at least once each school year for probationary personnel, and at least every other year for personnel with permanent status. The evaluation shall include recommendations, if necessary, as to areas of improvement in the performance of the employee. In the event an employee is not performing his or her duties in a satisfactory manner according to the standards prescribed by the governing board, the employing authority shall notify the employee in writing of such fact and describe such unsatisfactory performance. The employing authority shall thereafter confer with the employee making specific recommendations as to areas of improvement in the employee's performance and endeavor to assist the employee in such performance.

This specific legislative direction requires the personnel officer, principals, and supervisors to establish a specific evaluation program and provide careful and detailed assistance to teachers who are performing in an unsatisfactory manner.

#44800 through #44929 elaborate the rights, duties, and terms of employment of certificated staff. An enumeration of duties—from the requirement of a teacher to maintain a school register to holding students accountable for discipline—is contained in this section. Criteria for employment of administrative or supervisory personnel are also presented here. Very specific requirements for the employment of every credentialed employee, from a home teacher to a school physician, are contained in these sections.

#44930 through #44988 compose the section entitled "Resignations, Dismissal, and Leaves of Absence." Very specific direction is given regarding each subject.

#45022 through #45061 give direction to local school boards on establishing compensation standards for employees. The sections are prescriptive and detailed. For example, section #45023 requires the district to print a salary schedule and make it available to each certificated employee.

CLASSIFIED PERSONNEL IN CALIFORNIA

Sections #45100 through #45460 of the California Education Code contain provisions related to classified employees. Classified employees are those *not* required to hold a credential. Selected code sections pertaining to classified employees are highlighted below.

#45100 through #45186 parallel code sections for credentialed employees in that they establish standards for administering employment, compensation, and termination of classified employees. Procedures for layoff, reemployment, and disciplinary action are described. Districts are authorized to require an employee to take a physical examination. Rules for overtime pay and length of workday are also covered in this section of the code. No minimum or maximum age limit may be established for new or continuing employment in the classified service.

#45190 through #45210 cover leaves of absence, vacation, holidays, and compensation during sick leave.

#45240 through #45320 contain the right of classified employees to establish a Merit System, or civil service system. The law provides exact procedures for instituting this system, beginning with an election among the classified employees. A majority vote in favor of the Merit System is required before such a system is implemented.

If the Merit System is approved, the governing board of the district must create a Personnel Commission, which has responsibility for administering the classified employee program. The Personnel Commission may have either three or five members. In a three-member commission, one member is appointed by the governing board, the second member is nominated by the district's classified employees, and these two members appoint the third member. On a five-member commission, two members are appointed by the board and two members are nominated by the classified employees, with the fifth member appointed by the first four members.

Once the Merit System is adopted, the Personnel Commission appoints a personnel director to administer the classified employee program. The primary duties of the commission and the director include developing salary schedules for classified employees, filling employee vacancies, and other duties associated with ongoing supervision and management of employees.

LOCAL BOARDS OF EDUCATION

In all states except Hawaii, the legislature has delegated direct supervision of schools to local school boards. These local boards have responsibility for the day-to-day operation of the schools. The duties of school boards are numerous, but principal duties include the right to establish and build schools, to employ a superintendent, to establish necessary rules to manage and govern the schools, and to raise and spend money.

This extensive delegation of power to local boards must lie within the legal boundaries of federal and state constitutions and statutes. Most school boards develop and approve board policies, which have the effect of law. The policies provide a framework for operation and management of the schools. For example, superintendents and principals rely on this authority in employing staff, disciplining students, and expending funds.

Board Policies

Limitations on the adoption of policies depend on the authority granted to school boards by the state legislature and decisions by the courts. In some states, boards may adopt any reasonable policy not specifically prohibited by statute or the state constitution. California falls into the category in which school boards are free to make any policy that is not prohibited by statute. In other states, local boards operate only within a specific statutory provision. Generally speaking, courts have tended to uphold the rule of reason, which allows boards of education to adopt any reasonable policy within the law.

The powers and duties delegated to the nation's local boards of education by the state include significant powers and duties in the arena of personnel administration. Within legal guidelines, local boards have discretionary power in selection and employment of teachers and other staff members. The development of personnel policies is an absolute necessity for competent management of a school district and its personnel department. Without written policies, a district finds extremely difficult any defense against allegations of arbitrary or capricious actions or lack of due process. In addition, well-written policies provide direction and guidelines for the administration to ensure fair and reasonable treatment for employees.

Administrative Rules and Regulations

The efficient operation of any organization requires a well-developed and well-understood set of rules and regulations. In most instances, the board of education adopts policies to provide direction and philosophy. Then the superintendent and administrative staff are allowed to exercise discretion in implementing the policy. To insure consistency of action, administration writes regulations that specify steps for policy implementation.

THE COURTS

Federal and state constitutions, statutes, and policies of local boards of education do not guarantee proper application of the law. Differences in interpretation of laws and policies are to be expected. Frequently, these differences must be decided in court. Issues that are resolved by state courts include interpretation of the state constitution and state statutes. Such issues include compulsory attendance, teacher conduct, and the use of public money.

As provided in the federal constitution, the third branch of government, the court system, provides a mechanism for an individual or group whose constitutional rights may have been violated to seek adjudication in the courts. However, courts do not automatically review laws and policies. Instead, courts settle only those disputes referred to them for decision.

The federal judicial system is composed of three levels: the Supreme Court, courts of appeal, and district courts. Special federal courts include claims court, tax court, and court of international trade. The federal courts have authority to decide cases dealing with provisions of the federal Constitution and federal laws.

The U. S. Supreme Court is the highest court in the system. It is the court of final appeal on federal law questions. For an education question to reach the Supreme Court, petitioners must claim that a state's statutes or the policies of a local board of education have violated their constitutional rights or some provisions of federal law.

Because education is a state function, state courts decide most cases involving schools. Each state has its own unique court system, but similarities exist. Many states have patterned their court system after the federal system with three levels: courts of original jurisdiction (trial courts), courts of appeal (appellate courts), and the state's highest court (state supreme court).

There are two types of courts in California: trial courts and courts of appeal, the latter including the California Supreme Court. Formerly, municipal (urban) and justice (rural) courts constituted a level of trial court below the superior courts. However, in 54 of the state's 58 counties, all trial courts have unified into a single superior court in response to Proposition 220, passed in 1998. Included within the trial court structure are several specialized courts: small claims courts (for issues that do not exceed $5,000), family and juvenile courts, traffic courts, and criminal courts (Judicial Council, 2001).

Most actions involving school districts originate in the superior court of the county in which the district is located. The most common action used by a plaintiff in an action against a school district is a petition for a writ of mandate (Port, 1998). This action is a request for a court order requiring an organization, perhaps a school district or employee organization, to take, or refrain from taking, a particular action.

Appeals from superior court decisions proceed to the courts of appeal in the judicial district in which the superior court is located. If the plaintiff appeals the decision of a court of appeal, the matter goes to the California Supreme Court. Like the U.S. Supreme Court, the California Supreme Court is not required to hear a matter and may let the decision stand as decided by the court of appeal.

Occasionally two or more courts of appeal hand down different rulings in similar cases. In a recent example, one California court of appeal ruled that charges for home-to-school student transportation are illegal, while a different court of appeal ruled that such a charge is legal. This question was appealed to the California Supreme Court, which ruled that the fees were legal. Should the Supreme Court decline to hear the case, each decision would prevail in the district where it was made. The California Supreme Court consists of seven members. A decision of the California Supreme Court is final unless the case involves federal law or the U. S. Constitution, in which situation a case may be considered by the U. S. Supreme Court.

Appeals do not move automatically from one court level to the next. The higher court may refuse the appeal; in that event the lower court's decision stands. But even when a case is accepted, the judge or justices of the higher court agree only to consider the issues; they may or may not overturn the decision of the lower court.

Case Law

The only restriction on state legislation is that it cannot contravene the state constitution, the federal Constitution, or federal laws. For example, the federal government has limited state authority over public schools through decisions on racial desegregation, teachers' and students' free speech, procedural matters, and corporal punishment. When courts resolve conflicts between state and federal government, these decisions become part of case law.

Case law is composed of principles of law derived from court decisions, rather than from legislative acts. Past appellate and supreme court decisions are considered binding on subsequent cases if the material facts are similar. This legal doctrine is referred to as "precedent." Lower courts are expected to adhere to precedents established by higher courts. State supreme courts and the U. S. Supreme Court sometimes reverse their previous positions, thereby changing the rule of law.

Personnel directors need to keep abreast of significant court decisions and case law. The federal government and state departments of education are generally reliable in notifying districts of changes in case law that may affect the operation of schools.

Lawsuits

In recent years local school boards, superintendents, and personnel directors have experienced an explosive expansion of actual and threatened lawsuits. School districts have frequently been confronted with constitutional issues, and many of these issues have resulted in lawsuits against the district or the district employee.

In many school districts the personnel officer is the contact person when the district is threatened with a lawsuit. Therefore, it is essential that this administrator have sufficient knowledge of the law to determine whether a threat is serious in nature, necessitating legal counsel. The first indication of a potential lawsuit often occurs when a parent or employee threatens to consult an attorney. Most school principals, personnel directors, and superintendents receive this type of threat on a regular basis. However, in most instances, the threat is the end of the dispute. If the parent or employee actually seeks legal counsel, he or she may be given and accept the attorney's advice not to pursue further action. The cost of legal representation may also dissuade them. In cases where legal representation is obtained, the next event is ordinarily a contact from the client's attorney. In some cases an attorney attempts to mediate the conflict, seeking a compromise in behalf of his or her client. At this point it is imperative that, *prior to* taking action, the personnel officer seek legal advice from the district's attorney.

If the complaint is not resolved on an informal basis, the plaintiff or the plaintiff's attorney may file a petition with the appropriate court of jurisdiction. At that time the plaintiff is required to set forth the cause of action, which is referred to as the allegation. A summons is then delivered by the court to a designated school official, who is required to appear in court on a given date for the purpose of pleading to the petition.

The next step in the process involves clarifying the allegation and the material facts in the charges. This process is usually accomplished by a deposition, a formal procedure in which the parties to the lawsuit answer questions developed by the respective attorneys. At this stage, if the facts do not support the allegation, the school official or defendant may file a motion to dismiss the petition. If the judge does not dismiss the petition, a trial date is set.

Torts

A tort is defined as an act or an omission, including breach of contract, that results in damage, injury, or loss to the injured person or persons. It is a civil wrong to which the injured party, or plaintiff, may seek relief through legal action. There are three major categories of torts: intentional interference, strict liability, and negligence. School employees are expected to perform their duties in a reasonable manner in such a fashion that they are not arbitrary, capricious, or negligent (Hogan, 1985). Consequently, school employees may be liable for their individual acts of negligence, for their failure to carry out prescribed duties, or the failure to carry out those duties correctly.

The personnel officer needs to be familiar with the elements of tort liability and possess the ability to recognize potential legal jeopardy on the part of an employee or the district. Negligence suits usually demand adequate evidence and contain the following elements:

- a prescribed or implicit duty on the part of the defendant for the care of the plaintiff

- an error of commission or omission by the defendant

- damage, loss, or injury sustained by the plaintiff

- indication of a cause-and-effect relationship between the error and the circumstance at issue

- absence of contributory negligence on the part of the plaintiff.

The best defense against lawsuits is proper and reasonable precaution. A personnel officer has an obligation to work with staff to ensure a safe environment for students and employees and to carefully review policies and regulations to prevent lawsuits.

ERRORS AND OMISSIONS LIABILITY INSURANCE

Lawsuits alleging misfeasance, malfeasance, nonfeasance, and malpractice are increasingly being filed against school districts and their employees. Because of their involvement with children, school teachers and administrators are particularly subject to liability in these areas. For this reason districts are required in some states, including California (Ed. Code #35208), to carry liability insurance for errors and omissions. Whether required by law or not, all school districts should be covered by liability insurance for errors and omissions. All school employees as well as board members should have this coverage. Liability insurance can be obtained from most insurance companies that specialize in providing insurance for school districts.

Professional organizations also offer errors and omissions liability insurance. The National Education Association, American Federation of Teachers, California Teachers Association, American Association of School Administrators, and Association of California Administrators provide this insurance as part of membership benefits. While this coverage is necessary for the protection of district employees, it does not cover punitive damages.

LEGAL ADVICE

Most school personnel officers have some education and training in school law. However, except in very large school districts, rarely do they have a law degree. Nevertheless, a personnel officer must have a good understanding of the legal fundamentals of personnel administration. He or she should know enough about the law to recognize a potential problem and realize when the advice of an attorney is needed. An attorney's expertise is based on his or her ability to consider the facts in a case, research relevant statutes and case law, and advise the client on a course of action.

Advice or a recommendation from an attorney must always be carefully evaluated by the personnel director. Hughes and Ubben (1994) suggest four factors in the evaluation of legal advice:

- the source of the advice

- comparison of facts and statutory analysis

- legal jurisdiction

- the school attorney's opinions.

One must keep in mind that, even though the attorney may have extensive experience in school law, rarely has he or she had day-to-day school experience. Then, too, the advice of an attorney tends to be conservative. The attorney usually advises the client to take the safe approach, which may not be in the best interest of students or the staff. Many seasoned personnel officers insist that the attorney research statutes and legal precedents in order to justify a positive course of action, rather than to take the more conservative approach of avoiding action.

SUMMARY

The nation's schools operate within a framework of laws. Federal, state, and local laws have affected the control and management of schools. The courts also exert a major influence over the operation of schools.

Since neither education nor schools are mentioned in the federal Constitution, the responsibility for education rests with the separate states. Although states have complete control over schools, the day-to-day operation has been delegated to local school boards in every state except Hawaii. (In Hawaii the state has direct control of education, and local school boards do not exist.) Each state legislature approves statutes or laws for the governance of the public schools. In California most education laws are contained in the Education Code.

Local school boards operate within guidelines provided by the state. They usually have responsibility for construction of schools, employment of staff, and the raising and expenditure of funds. School boards usually adopt board policies to provide direction and guidance to the administrative and teaching staff for the administration and operation of the district. Although school boards have considerable discretionary power, all actions must conform to federal and state constitutions and state statutes.

The provisions of federal and state constitutions, statutes, and policies of local boards of education do not guarantee proper application of the law. Variant interpretations of laws and policies are to be expected. Frequently, these differences must be decided in state or federal courts. For a petitioner to file in federal court, he or she must allege violation of a Constitutional right or some provision of federal law. Because education is a state function, state courts decide most cases involving schools.

An explosive expansion of actual and threatened lawsuits has challenged local school boards, superintendents, and personnel officers. School districts have been continually confronted with constitutional issues, and many of these issues have resulted in lawsuits against a district or an individual employee.

Perhaps no other area of school administration requires a knowledge of law equal to that in the personnel division. An effective personnel administrator must have a keen awareness of legislation and court cases. It is imperative that he or she subscribe to a legal service that provides information on recently approved legislation and court decisions that affect operation of the schools and of the district, including the personnel department itself.

KEY TERMS

1. administrative rules and regulations	6. consideration
2. Bill of Rights	7. Education Code
3. board of education	8. Merit System
4. board policies	9. Personnel Commission
5. case law	10. tort

QUESTIONS AND ACTIVITIES

1. The first ten amendments to the U. S. Constitution (Bill of Rights) have had a profound influence on the development of the American education system. Which two amendments do you believe have had the greatest effect? Explain why you think so.

2. School boards are responsible for developing policies. Why is this responsibility important? Give three examples of school board policy.

3. In addition to legislation, court decisions have influenced the course of the public education system in the United States. Discuss two examples of court cases, explaining how each has influenced public education.

4. School districts have experienced an increase in lawsuits, actual and threatened. Many of these suits charge the district with negligence in performance of its duties. Negligence suits usually contain five elements. Describe each of these elements.

5. It is important that a school district have proper legal advice. Hughes and Ubben (1994) suggest four factors in evaluating legal advice. Briefly discuss each of these factors.

6. Obtain a copy of the California Education Code. Review the sections on affirmative action and evaluation of certificated personnel.

7. Review board policies for three school districts; compare and contrast the personnel procedures covered in policy.

8. Invite a personnel officer from a merit and a non-merit school district to your class. Ask them to discuss differences in personnel administration between the two districts.

9. Ask the personnel officer in your district about his or her source of legal advice. If permissible, review the last several district court cases; list ways you think the lawsuits might have been avoided.

Chapter 14

Progressive Discipline and Dismissal

INTRODUCTION

As discussed in previous chapters, the recruitment, selection, supervision, and retention of highly effective certificated and classified employees are of primary importance to all school districts. However, even when these responsibilities are performed in an exemplary fashion, a time comes in every school and in every district when an employee is not performing in an acceptable manner. When that occurs, an administrator is faced with the difficult task of disciplining, or perhaps recommending non-reelection or dismissal, of that employee. The administrators' first responsibility is to students; their second is to staff. The second responsibility must not be allowed to override the first.

Corrective action may take the form of employee discipline or dismissal from employment. This chapter defines employee discipline and relates those procedures to the several categories of employment. The historical development of tenure is outlined, with pro and con arguments for tenure. Nonrenewal and dismissal are important responsibilities of the school administrator.

EMPLOYEE DISCIPLINE

The term "discipline" often carries a negative connotation. This negative overtone derives from the second part of Webster's dictionary definition: "punishment inflicted by way of correction and training; instruction by misfortune, suffering, and the like; correction; chastisement." The first part of Webster's definition is the positive part: "Training, education, instruction, practice; the training to act in accordance with rules; drill; method." Employee discipline refers to the expectation that employees conduct themselves according to the rules and regulations of the organization and in a socially accepted manner.

If employees do not so conduct themselves, what is the appropriate supervisorial response? It is commonly accepted in business, industry, and public service that management should react to such problems in a corrective, rather than a punitive, manner. It is also accepted that the action must be progressive if it is to withstand the legal test of "due process." For example, if a teacher releases students from class early, the principal first gives the teacher a verbal warning. If the teacher repeats early dismissal the following week, the principal gives a written warning. If the teacher's behavior continues in the third week, the teacher might be suspended from work for a few days without pay. If the inappropriate behavior continues after the suspension period, the principal must continue with progressive discipline and finally recommend dismissal of the employee from the district.

The right of the school board to terminate an employee from service is clearly established in state statutes and confirmed by the courts. The U. S. Supreme Court bestowed this authority on school boards when it held that "school authorities have the right and the duty to screen the officials, teachers, and employees as to their fitness to maintain the integrity of the schools as part of ordered society" (*Adler v. Board of Education*, 1952).

However, despite this authority, a board cannot arbitrarily discharge personnel at any time. Except when an employee has been convicted of a criminal act or has flagrantly violated board policy, the district is required to demonstrate efforts to improve the employee's performance and must also document unsatisfactory performance. To meet these requirements in cases where unsatisfactory performance continues, administrators apply progressively stronger disciplinary action.

PROGRESSIVE DISCIPLINE

When an employee is not working in a satisfactory fashion, the central question is: What action is appropriate to bring about satisfactory conduct or performance? A plethora of books and articles discuss changing inappropriate behavior by means of rewards, behavior modification techniques, and staff development programs. It is the experience and judgment of the authors that these leadership strategies work with the great majority of employees. However, a supervisor must be prepared to take disciplinary action, including a recommendation for employee dismissal from the district, when attempts to change behavior do not work.

Ethical leadership requires humane treatment of personnel. At the same time, a supervisor is duty bound, legally and ethically, to take corrective action when regulations are flouted, duties are neglected, or work is not up to standard. The process begins with setting clear expectations, providing relevant training, followed ultimately, if needed, with formal discipline and dismissal.

For example, if a district requires teachers to be on campus 30 minutes prior to the start of class, a teacher who is late one time in a semester probably would not even receive a rebuke for this violation of the employee contract. However, positive, fair, and objective measures are required when a teacher is late on a regular basis and does not respond to a verbal reminder of the importance of being in class on time.

Ruud and Woodford (1984) define progressive discipline as a pattern of gradually escalating disciplinary penalties designed to lead an employee to improve performance or change behavior. Andelson (1995) defines progressive discipline as a series of disciplinary steps, each step requiring more serious disciplinary action. He includes the following six steps in the series.

1. Oral warning/ conference

   The supervisor should state clearly the rule or policy that was violated, the expectation that the rule should be followed, and the consequence if the rule is not followed in the future. The time, date, and substance of the warning should be noted on a daily calendar or some other informal written record (not the personnel file). The oral warning should be brief and to the point and relate directly to the specific incident.

2. Written warning

   A written warning should be very similar to the oral warning and, if possible, delivered personally to the employee. One of the consequences of further violation of the rule or policy may be to notify the employee that further violation will result in a letter of reprimand to be placed in his or her personnel file.

3. Letter of reprimand

   The first two steps in the progressive discipline sequence rarely result in placing information in the personnel file. However, the next step, a letter of reprimand, is ordinarily filed with the employee's personnel records. Such a letter should restate information already presented in the oral and written notices. Employees must be notified when a document is to be placed in the personnel file and given prior opportunity to review and respond to any document containing derogatory material (Ed. Code #44031). The law does not set a specific time limit within which an employee must respond to such a document. Normally, however, the time is regulated by the collective bargaining agreement, typically allowing five to ten calendar days.

4. Unsatisfactory *Act* (evaluation)

   The requirements for evaluation are outlined in the Education Code and are generally included in the collective bargaining agreement between the district and the employee association.

5. Suspension
with pay

Suspension with pay is a nondisciplinary step often used to provide time for an investigation to determine whether discipline is justified. Suspension with pay may also accompany a second reprimand to emphasize the seriousness of the infraction. Suspension with*out* pay is used more often with classified employees, being more difficult with credentialed employees because they usually hold an individual contract. Contracts are considered a property right, and the U. S. Constitution states that one cannot be deprived of property without due process.

6. Dismissal

A later section of this chapter is devoted to dismissal.

As outlined above, progressive discipline is a system of documentation and file-building that is divided into stages, each successive stage resulting in more serious disciplinary measures. Prior to recommending dismissal from service, a supervisor is clearly responsible for working extensively with the employee in hopes of bringing his or her performance up to standard.

important

PROBATIONARY STATUS

Requirements for employee dismissal differ according to the employee's classification as probationary or permanent. A teacher is considered to have probationary status prior to achieving tenure. California teachers are classed as "probationary" during the first two years of service within a school district (Ed.Code 44929.21). During this probationary period the teacher is issued a contract valid for a fixed period of time, and renewal of the contract at the end of each school year is at the discretion of the school board.

Commonly, a probationary teacher is not entitled to know the reasons why a school board has decided to terminate the employment relationship at the end of the contract period. In most cases a probationary teacher is not given opportunity for a hearing. However, even though the school board is not compelled to inform the probationary teacher of the reasons for nonrenewal, those reasons must not violate the teacher's constitutionally or statutorily protected rights.

A school board is required to notify a probationary employee on or before March 15th of the employee's second complete consecutive school year of employment of the decision not to reelect him or her for the next school year. If the board does not give notice on or before March 15th, the employee is deemed employed for the next succeeding school year (Ed. Code #44929.21).

TENURE – teachers stay (even bad) because of tenure

Tenure is defined as a statutory right to continued employment. To remove tenure requires proof of "good cause." Tenure is defined by Black (1991) as "status afforded to a teacher or professor upon completion of trial period, thus protecting him or her from summary dismissal without sufficient cause or economic reasons." The *1992 Deskbook Encyclopedia of American School Law* defined tenure as a "creation of state statutes designed to maintain adequate, permanent, and qualified teaching staffs."

Generally, tenure granted by the state means at least two things for a teacher.

1. First, the teacher can depend upon continuing employment without necessity of annual notification.

2. Second, if employment is to be terminated, the school board must provide the teacher with adequate reasons for termination and an opportunity for an impartial hearing ensuring the attributes of fundamental fairness.

Recognition of "tenure status" is left to the discretion of the state legislature. The California Legislature has enacted such recognition (Ed. Code #44929.20-44929.29).

Purpose of Tenure

Tenure provides a teacher with security. The academic rationale for tenure is to give teachers academic freedom in the classroom—to protect them from unwarranted dismissal. Tenured teachers cannot be fired for holding and expressing, outside the classroom, unpopular political or social views. An additional purpose served by tenure is to provide equity based on seniority when staff must be reduced because of lack of enrollment or finances; length of service then becomes the criterion for dismissal.

History of Tenure

The concept of rewarding one's friends with jobs or positions of influence was inherent in early U. S. history. During this country's colonial period, the English government retained power by distributing jobs and influence to friends and supporters. This system of handing out jobs became known as the "spoils system" or "patronage."

The country's first president, George Washington, often made support of Federalist principles a test of appointment to office. When Jefferson became president, he complained of the number of Federalists he found holding jobs in the executive department and gradually replaced Federalists with Republicans. Not until the presidency of Andrew Jackson, however, were jobholders removed wholesale to make room for a president's own followers. Once established, this practice was continued by each president. During the Civil War, President Lincoln expressed his frustration over the countless job seekers who filled his appointment schedule.

The system of rewarding positions greatly accelerated after the Civil War and became a topic of national concern when President Garfield was assassinated by a half-crazed office seeker. This tragic event so excited the nation against the spoils system that Congress passed the Pendleton Act in 1883. This act allowed the President to create a "classified list" of federal offices that could be filled only according to rules laid down by a bipartisan Civil Service Commission. The Pendleton Act began the process of changing jobholding from the spoils system to the "merit system" (Bragdon & McCutchen, 1961).

Gradually, the concept that employees might gain and retain their jobs on merit spread to the states and local governments. Out of this movement developed the concept of tenure for teachers. In 1887 the proceedings of the National Education Association included "a committee report urging that the subject of teachers' tenure be given publicity in the belief that necessary legislation would result" (National Education Association, 1936).

Tenure statutes protect teachers from arbitrary actions by local boards of education. In some states and school districts, other certificated personnel also are protected by tenure statutes. The choice of positions to be covered under tenure laws lies within the prerogative of state legislators. Classifications that have gained tenure rights include school nurses, counselors, psychologists, and school librarians. In some states, selected administrative positions also gain tenure. However, tenure is rarely granted to superintendents or assistant superintendents.

Courts have upheld the constitutionality of such statutes. Certificated Tenure Act cases have concluded that tenure exists to protect competent teachers and other members of the teaching profession against unlawful and arbitrary board actions and to establish orderly procedures for dismissal of unsatisfactory teachers and other professional personnel (Teachers' Tenure Act Cases, 329 Pa. 213, 197 A. 344, 1938).

Tenure is attained by complying with specific provisions prescribed by state statutes. The nature of these provisions varies from state to state, but certain conditions are included in most legislation. Nearly all states require that teachers serve a probationary period before tenure becomes effective. Generally, a teacher's probationary period ranges from three to five years, during which time a teacher is employed on a term contract. On completion of the probation period, personnel acquire tenure automatically or by school board action. In California, this period is currently two years in most districts (Ed. Code #44929.21, 44929.23, 44929.25).

Arguments For and Against Tenure

Tenure continues to be a matter of debate in the United States. Advocates strongly believe tenure is positive for children and teachers, while opponents believe it is detrimental. Jones and Stout (1960) advanced the following arguments in favor of and opposed to tenure.

Supporting
arguments

- Tenure is a basic principle of economic efficiency.

- Tenure helps to protect the teacher from unwarranted attacks.

- Teachers are freed from anxiety of being dismissed without just cause.

- Tenure helps parents and citizens to secure better teachers because it encourages more careful selection of faculty.

- There is little evidence that tenure reduces interest in professional development.

- Tenure reduces the temptation for teachers to violate professional ethics and to yield to the whims of pressure groups.

Opposing
arguments

- Incompetent and undesirable teachers may be retained in the profession, since tenure makes it more difficult to dismiss them. *—$300,000, takes 3 years*

- It may become more difficult to supervise some teachers who know they have job security.

- Contrary to popular opinion, tenure has, in a number of instances, increased teacher turnover.

- Tenure in office is not protected by law in other professions.

- The public has, in many instances, questioned the practice of permitting teachers to hold their positions despite their failure to do a competent job.

- Competent teachers do not need to be protected by tenure legislation.

iatures   *=probs, district interns — contracted.*

NONRENEWAL AND DISMISSAL

In speaking of teachers and other certificated personnel, the terms "nonrenewal" and "dismissal" are often used interchangeably, especially with reference to termination of employment at the end of a probationary contract. "Dismissal," however, refers more broadly to termination of a contract before its expiration, including termination of a teacher who has been granted tenure. Termination is achieved through substantially different procedures in each case.

The contract of a school employee not protected by tenure may be nonrenewed for no reason, or for any reason whatsoever, providing the termination does not violate an employee's substantive constitutional rights, e.g., free speech and protection against racial discrimination. Courts have reasoned in nonrenewal cases that the contract has simply terminated, there having been "no expectancy of continued employment." Thus, nonrenewal of a contract usually requires that a school board simply give a probationary employee timely notice. In most states the school board need not state reasons for nonrenewal of a probationary teacher's contract (Hartmeister, 1995).

Dismissal, on the other hand, whether under tenure status or during an unexpired contract, is permissible only "for cause." Consequently, a tenured employee or a nontenured professional facing dismissal during a contract year is entitled to a due process hearing embodying all statutory and constitutional safeguards.

Because teachers are considered to have a constitutionally protected "property" interest in continued employment throughout the contract term, they are entitled to notification of the reasons for the dismissal and an opportunity for a fair and impartial hearing at which they may respond to or rebut all stated reasons for the dismissal. These are the essential elements of due process as provided under federal and state constitutional law.

GROUNDS FOR DISMISSAL:
CERTIFICATED STAFF

The most common grounds for the dismissal of teachers are incompetency, immorality, insubordination, unfitness to teach, and inadequate performance of duties. Other grounds for dismissal include declining enrollment or financial exigency such that a teacher's services are no longer needed or affordable. Conviction of a felony or a crime involving moral turpitude and any cause that constitutes grounds for the state to revoke a teaching certificate are further grounds for dismissal. In addition, there is normally an "elastic" clause added to this list: "other good and just cause."

Can dismiss — w/ good or just cause.

The school district has the burden of proving any of these charges and, to do so, must show persuasive evidence that the teacher being recommended for dismissal either *failed* to do something he or she *should* have done, or *did* something he or she *should not* have done.

Dismissal for Cause

Causes for dismissal are generally specified in state statutes and differ from one state to another. However, there are similarities from state to state. For example, in Kentucky tenured employees can be dismissed for insubordination; immoral character or conduct; physical or mental disability; or inefficiency, incompetency, or neglect of duty. In Illinois, causes for dismissal are listed as incompetency, cruelty, negligence, immorality or other sufficient cause. Whenever in a board's opinion a teacher is not qualified to teach, the best interests of the school require that teacher's dismissal. In Connecticut, causes are enumerated as inefficiency, incompetency, insubordination, moral misconduct, disability as shown by competent medical evidence, elimination of positions, or other due and sufficient cause.

In California, Education Code section #44932 is very specific regarding grounds for dismissal of certificated employees. Twelve reasons are cited:

- **Immoral or unprofessional conduct.** Immoral conduct must be judged within the context of local standards, but also must be reasonable and consistent with court decisions. One of the standards used by courts is the pupil-teacher relationship. Establishing a relationship with a student that goes beyond friendship and is exhibited in some form of "dating" is unacceptable. Illegal sexual acts are cause for immediate suspension. If an employee is convicted of performing such an act, his or her employment must be terminated. Unconventional sexual lifestyles, on the other hand, are not a cause for employee dismissal. Such practices as wife swapping, homosexuality, and cohabitation outside of matrimony may be unacceptable to the majority of people in the community, but do not inherently affect an individual's performance in the workplace. However, employees who advocate unconventional sexual lifestyles at work put themselves in a position in which termination is possible if the advocated lifestyles are in direct conflict with local standards.

  The phrase "unprofessional conduct" was expanded in 1977 and 1983 by Education Code section #44933. This addition allows a permanent employee to be dismissed for conduct not specified in Section 44932. In relying on the added provision, a district must specify those instances of behavior upon which the dismissal is based. This provision does not apply to districts with a collective bargaining agreement.

- **Commission, aiding, or advocating the commission of acts of criminal syndicalism.**

- **Dishonesty.** — connected w/ work.

Unsatisfactory performance. This item originally read "incompetency." The new language, "unsatisfactory performance," was approved by the legislature as Assembly Bill 729 and signed by the Governor on August 10, 1995. Appropriate supervision and evaluation are requisite if the district is to prevail in an action to dismiss an employee for unsatisfactory performance. As noted in Chapter 5, Education Code section #44664 requires evaluation and assessment of the performance of each certificated employee at least once each school year for probationary personnel and least every other year for tenured teachers. If areas for improvement are identified, the evaluation must include recommendations for improvement. The evaluator must be very specific in describing the areas for improvement.

As contained in the Education Code sections, evaluation has two main purposes:

- to determine the strengths and weaknesses of the employee so that strengths can be noted and deficiencies remedied

- to document in one place data with which to make management decisions regarding teacher promotion, dismissal, nonrenewal, transfer, demotion, withholding of salary increments, and tenure or continuing contract.

The first of these is called "formative" evaluation; the second, "summative."

Formative evaluation is a first step in improving instruction. This task is the primary function of the principal. The objective is to help each individual teacher develop to the optimum by strengthening existing skills, while discovering and correcting weaknesses in teaching. Formative evaluation is the appraisal function principals use in developing or improving teaching performance.

Summative evaluation involves many of the techniques used in formative evaluation, but goes further. It seeks to build evidence on which an educational decision can be made.

Evident unfitness for service. 44942 (Crazy)

Physical or mental condition causing him or her to be unfit to instruct or associate with children.

Persistent violation of or refusal to obey the school laws of the state or reasonable regulations prescribed for the government of the public schools by the State Board of Education or by the governing board of the school district employing him or her. Insubordination in the line of duty is always a cause for dismissal. Employees are insubordinate only if they refuse to comply with a supervisor's directive that clearly calls for something within their job expertise. For example, if a teacher is directed to attend

e.g. not turning in gradebooks

a faculty meeting and refuses, the teacher is insubordinate because teachers have a job-related responsibility in this area. However, if a teacher were asked to go to the principal's house to help with administrative paperwork, the teacher would not be guilty of insubordination as this task is not within the teacher's job assignment. The manner in which an employee responds to a directive does not usually constitute insubordination if the employee performs the task. For example, if a teacher complains about grading papers, but completes the task, the teacher is not guilty of insubordination.

Conviction of a felony or of any crime involving moral turpitude. A felony conviction is obviously a reason to terminate employment of an individual. However, there are restrictions on the interpretation of moral turpitude by the courts. Conviction of prostitution, selling of drugs, and pornography fall within the definition of crimes of moral turpitude (Rebore, 1998).

In most states, a school district employee who is found guilty of a felony is considered in breach of his or her employment contract and can be dismissed from employment. The consequences are not as clearly defined for a misdemeanor, generally considered less serious than a felony. Generally, an employee who has been arrested for a criminal offense cannot be dismissed unless convicted.

The argument for breach of contract is based on the premise that teachers are expected to be positive role models for their students. Felony convictions are not congruent with this expectation and thus are deleterious to a teacher's effectiveness. Principles of "double jeopardy" do not apply in this context. Courts have held on numerous occasions that a civil sanction, i.e., loss of employment following a criminal conviction, does not violate the double jeopardy provision in the Fifth Amendment.

Advocating communism. The applicable section of the Education Code (# 51530) reads as follows:

> No teacher giving instruction in any school, or on any property belonging to any agencies included in the public school system, shall advocate or teach communism with the intent to indoctrinate or to inculcate in the mind of any pupil a preference for communism.

The code section has a second paragraph stating that the legislature does not intend to prevent the teaching of the facts about communism, but rather to prevent advocacy of, or inculcation and indoctrination into, communism. A third paragraph in this section defines communism:

> Communism is a political theory that the presently existing form of government of the United States or of this state should be changed, by force, violence, or other unconstitutional means, to a totalitarian dictatorship

which is based on the principles of communism expounded by Marx, Lenin, and Stalin.

• **Knowing membership by the employee in the Communist Party.**

is an illness.

• **Alcoholism or other drug abuse which makes the employee unfit to instruct or associate with children.**

Reduction in Force

School districts are often faced with factors that require reductions in staff, whether temporary or permanent. The practice is commonly referred to as "reduction in force" (RIF). The conditions under which a district may use RIF are contained in Education Code section #44955.

To use this procedure, a district has the burden of documenting the reasons for the need to reduce staff. The district must establish the necessity of abolishing positions and reducing its workforce on the basis of one or more of the legislated reasons, e.g., declining enrollment, fiscal exigency, school district reorganization, or "other good and just cause."

Once the district has justified RIF, the next step is determination of the order in which to release staff. For the most part, probationary employees are released prior to those tenured. Seniority, that is, years of service in the school district or within a particular classification, is most frequently used to determine the order of layoff of employees.

DISMISSAL PROCEDURES

If a school superintendent recommends dismissal of a tenured employee, the precise requirements of the Education Code must be followed. Specific and detailed procedures are set forth. These must be followed exactly to ensure that the action is legal. The procedures basically contain three elements:

• notice of intention to dismiss by a specific date

• specification of charges against the employee (Ed. Code #44934)

Can be many many charges.

• a hearing at which the charges are discussed (Ed. Code #44944).

The procedures for notifying the employee of the hearing and the hearing process itself are more detailed than can be included in this text. Prior to recommending dismissal of a tenured employee, the personnel director and superintendent would be well advised to seek advice from the county counsel or a private attorney who specializes in school law.

Besides the procedures required in the Education Code, tenure rights qualify for constitutional procedural protections encompassed within the concepts of "property" and "liberty interests." These invoke the due process clause of the Fourteenth Amendment. Holding a teaching position qualifies as a property right if the employee has an unexpired contract or has acquired tenure; the protections of the Fourteenth Amendment do not normally extend to nontenured employees. The Supreme Court has affirmed the view of lower courts that nontenured employees have no property or liberty interests in continued employment (*Roth v. Board of Regents*, 408 U.S. 564, 1972).

A liberty interest becomes an issue in dismissal, and due process required, if evidence exists that a charge has been made that places a stigma on an employee's reputation. Such a charge would foreclose future employment opportunities or seriously damage the employee's standing in the community (*Roth v. Board of Regents*, 408 U.S. 564, 1972). A liberty interest would be constitutionally safeguarded if school board members and school administrators refrain from making public statements or releasing information that is derogatory to the employee. Even when statements are made, if they simply describe unsatisfactory performance in general, normally they are not a constitutional violation of an employee's Fourteenth Amendment rights.

Examples of charges against employees not involving a stigma include ineffective teaching methods, inability to maintain classroom discipline, and inability to get along with administrators and colleagues. Failure to award tenure does not automatically create a stigma. Examples of stigmas that qualify for constitutional due process protection include the following charges: manifest racism, immoral conduct, serious mental disorder, a drinking or drug problem, willful neglect of duty, and responsibility for the deterioration of a school.

SUMMARY

A major responsibility of every administrator is to ensure that each child is taught by a competent teacher. An administrator must have the knowledge and skills to assist teachers and classified staff to perform in a competent fashion. However, administrators also have an obligation to take disciplinary action when staff performance is unsatisfactory. An effective administrator must be well versed in progressive discipline as well as legal procedures and requirements for dismissing an employee when progressive discipline is not effective.

Terminating a teacher is a long and difficult process, especially when the teacher is tenured. It is a taxing procedure for an administrator, both emotionally and professionally. In the dismissal process, the school board makes the final determination as to retaining or terminating services of a certificated or classified employee. Since this is the case, the school board must be clear about the facts. It is the administrator's task to keep the board fully informed of the shortcomings of the employee and to responsibly and accurately present the facts gathered in the long process of documentation.

KEY TERMS

1. discipline
2. dismissal
3. evaluation
4. letter of reprimand
5. liberty interest
6. moral turpitude
7. nonrenewal
8. oral warning/conference
9. probationary status

10. progressive discipline
11. property interest
12. reduction in force (RIF)
13. suspension with pay
14. tenure
15. unsatisfactory evaluation
16. written warning

QUESTIONS AND ACTIVITIES

1. Review the steps in the progressive discipline model.

2. Develop a strong argument for the elimination of tenure.

3. What is the major difference between "nonrenewal" and "dismissal"?

4. Review the legal grounds for dismissal in California. Discuss the three you think are most serious.

5. Give examples of "incompetency" and the rationale for dismissal of the teacher in each example.

6. Define "property interest" and "liberty interest." Which of the two do you feel would be more difficult for a district to defend in a lawsuit?

7. Define "Reduction in Force." When is a district justified in using this basis for dismissing employees?

8. Find several court decisions that have dealt with teacher dismissal. What findings have serious implications for a school district?

9. Develop a chart or timeline to show key dates for employee notification and for permanent teacher layoff and dismissal.

10. Prepare a chart related to employment and dismissal of probationary employees. Include the date by which they must be notified for nonemployment the following year. Need reasons for nonemployment be given?

Chapter 15

Selected Trends and Issues in Personnel Management

The direction in which education starts a man [person]
will determine his future life.

*** Author Unknown*

INTRODUCTION

The concept of "strategic planning" has been a topic of discussion at virtually every educational administration conference over the last 10 years. Most administrators who attend these workshops are encouraged to study historical patterns and current thinking so as to project future trends. After identifying these trends, the executive is advised to base upon them all plans for the future of the school district. Not to be overlooked are the effects of these trends on a district's personnel services.

A school district personnel department is subject to internal as well as external forces. In recent years, external factors have involved continual reduction of resources—a challenge that often raises doubts about support for district office departments. As a consequence, a personnel department is continually subject to reductions in staff.

In the 1970s and 1980s personnel departments took major control of the collective bargaining process and supported a generally "top-down" educational bureaucracy. This bureaucracy maintained many services, including hiring, firing, and sometimes training and retraining employees. In the past 10 years, functions of the personnel department have shifted as a result of state and federal law, California state-level initiatives, the impact of technology, and staff reductions. Moreover, as we move into a major restructuring mode in the nation's schools, changes will continue to occur in the personnel departments of school districts. In this chapter we have selected particular personnel issues that will no doubt influence personnel departments during the next 20 years. Although many issues could be addressed, this chapter explores emerging changes in demography, economics, society, and politics—changes that impact strategic planning in schools and school districts.

OVERALL TRENDS IN SOCIETY

Researchers such as Naisbitt (1990) have identified certain trends that they feel will transform American society. Naisbitt believes, first, that we are in the process of changing from an industrial to an information society. He believes that those who are educated and can manipulate information will inevitably take positions at the forefront of such a society.

Secondly, Naisbitt tells us, the world is changing from a nationalized to a global society. A manifestation of this trend may be observed in the emergence of power in the Pacific Rim countries.

Another trend is reshaping of organizations toward a more decentralized structure in which employees have greater say in the direction that a company or organization may take. The "quality circle," allowing employees major and systematic input into an organization, is one reflection of this trend.

A fourth trend is the emergence of small, cross-disciplinary groups of employees who solve problems and generate innovative ideas by drawing upon each other's expertise. This trend is built on teamwork, rather than competition, among employees.

TRENDS IN DEMOGRAPHICS

According to records of home purchases and industrial growth, the population in the United States is moving from the North and East to the South and West. The Bureau of the Census predicted that the states of California, Texas, and Florida would account for more than 45% of the net population change between 1995 and 2025. California is projected to have 15% of the nation's population by 2025 and will remain the most populous state, with Texas second and New York third. California's population is expected to rise from 32-½ million inhabitants in the year 2000 to nearly 50 million in 2025 (U. S. Bureau of the Census, 1998).

Coupled with this trend is the "graying of America," a term that symbolizes a vast increase in the proportion of people within the population who are 45 to 64 years of age. In 1998 the Census Bureau projected that U. S. residents 65 years of age and older would increase from 31 million in 1989 to 34 million in 1997 (12.7% of the population)—then to nearly 50 million (13.3%) in 2010 and almost 62 million in 2025 (18.5%) (U. S. Bureau of the Census, 1998).

In addition to this change in age distribution, the proportions of African-Americans, Asian-Americans, Hispanic-Americans, and other minorities in the United States will significantly increase. Furthermore, the growth among minorities will be greater than in the rest of the population (United Way Strategic Institute, 1989), with Hispanics already accounting for the greatest rate of growth among minorities. One reason for this continued growth is the rise in the number of legal and illegal immigrants entering the United States. This increase will, in turn, affect California classrooms.

In addition to an influx of minorities, California will experience an increase of children living in poverty, children born out of wedlock, and children of divorce. These factors will change the way personnel administrators relate to those whom they serve in the public schools.

ECONOMIC TRENDS

It is obvious that the United States is in competition with other countries that are producing goods for foreign markets. Industries experiencing the most intense competition are mining, manufacturing, and agriculture. As firms cut costs and seek a greater market share, tight economic conditions will impact school district personnel. Faced with fewer resources, districts may reduce the number of personnel in the human resources department. Nevertheless, historical trends support predictions that recessionary times eventually cycle into an economic upturn. Thus, even though personnel departments experience cutbacks, they must inevitably maintain their significance in the organization because of their focus upon the employee and his or her working environment.

Despite this optimism as to the long-term economic future, however, the urban, minority underclass will continue to grow in California and the United States. It appears that their situation will not be improved to a great extent by general economic growth.

Privatization of Support Services / Cost-Effectiveness

Given constant monitoring of resources and expenditures, cost-effectiveness will continue to be demanded of the personnel department. Over the past two decades computers have assumed much of the burden of processing new hires, generating payroll, and tracking fringe benefits. School districts have contracted with attorneys for collective bargaining services—especially when negotiations were not moving in a positive direction. As personnel functions shift to schools, these trends toward computerization and contracting out can be expected to expand. This movement will force personnel administrators to concentrate on school administration and to facilitate site-level outcomes.

School expenditures will be examined to ensure that they are helpful to teachers. For example, rather than bringing in a series of staff development programs, principals are relying more on staff collaboration as a means of improvement. As a consequence, site administrators may wish to consider a practice found in Japanese and Chinese schools—designating a large space for teachers apart from classrooms. Teachers are assigned a desk in this room, where they spend time discussing teaching techniques with one another, preparing lessons, correcting student papers, and mentoring beginning teachers (Fullan, 1993).

A contrary position is the desire of some teachers to avoid involvement in any activities not directly tied to teaching. The school day involves just so many hours, and some teachers would prefer to leave much of the decision-making to the principal.

Computerization of Personnel Functions

The computerization of personnel functions beginning in the 1980s had a major impact on collection and organization of data. No longer was it necessary for a clerk to enter by hand all the information about an employee. Instead, a computer screen is used to collect all personnel information. Not only are such data gathered more easily, but thousands of permutations of this information can be performed and stored by the personnel department. Reports have suggested that the computer will take on more of the recordkeeping chores of schools and districts. With the advent of more sophisticated networking capabilities, personnel department staffs will no doubt need additional computer training.

Because of privacy issues, some personnel data will always be collected and maintained apart from the everyday operations of a local school. This fact, however, does not rule out the possibility of contracting out this service.

Virtual Teaching/Learning

Perhaps the most revolutionary change in education since the invention of printing is the Internet. Will school campuses, textbooks, and teachers who are assigned a classroom of students disappear within the next few years? Sounds farfetched, but perhaps not. Some $6 billion in venture capital has been invested in the education sector since 1990. The president of Cisco Systems has referred to education as "the next big killer application on the Internet" (Grimes, 2000).

Universities and trade schools have taken the lead in virtual learning, but K-12 schools are soon to follow. The University of Phoenix Online claims a virtual student body of 60,000. In elementary and secondary education, home schooling and charter schools have taken the lead; students complete their education with little direct face-to-face contact with a teacher. All the lessons, all the homework, and all the examinations are completed online.

The education community received surprising news in December of 2000 when William Bennett, former U. S. Secretary of Education, announced that he was opening a for-profit cyberspace K-12 school that would offer a complete elementary and secondary education. The surprise lay in the fact that Bennett had previously expressed concern about cyber teaching; he had written, "Keep one thing in mind: so far, there is no good evidence that most uses of computers significantly improve learning" (Helfand, 2000b). Helfand attributes the quote to Bennett's book, *The Educated Child*.

The school opened grades K-2 in September 2001 under the name K12 Inc., with plans to extend the program through high school. Initially, tuition for a full program was about $1,000 annually, with additional services to be added at additional cost. Financial analysts estimate that the market for cyber-based education is lucrative, worth billions of dollars (Helfand, 2000b).

The research and arguments, both pro and con, as to the educational value of learning online will continue unabated for some time, but thoughts of no school construction, no school buses, no textbooks, no school lunches, and no school principals will be powerful financial stimuli to make such programs work.

The Work-at-Home Movement

We are accustomed to a convention of work that entails going to a fixed place at a fixed time. There is need to rethink this traditional pattern, especially in California. New terms that have moved into our consciousness include "compressed workweek," "permanent parttime employment," "job-sharing," and "flextime." Just to drive the 405 freeway in the Los Angeles area at 6:00 a.m. or 5:00 p.m. on any weekday is to become aware of the problems that telecommuting could mitigate.

The emergence of the personal computer has opened the way to total restructuring of the world of work. These tools have become so affordable that many jobs can be performed in the home. Those occupations that have been identified as the most amenable to telecommuting are managerial: marketing manager, personnel analyst, counselor, engineer, accountant, and computer systems designer. Other occupations may include securities broker, data entry clerk, architect, computer operator, bank officer, clerical support, and secretary. Lawyers, computer programmers, real estate agents, salespersons, and travel agents, too, could work out of the home, at least parttime.

Among the benefits of telecommuting have been listed:

Improved employee retention	Telework provides more options to the employer and offers new options to employees. Mutual benefit to employer and employee can be anticipated in such situations as a key employee moving to retirement or a valued worker going on maternity leave. Such arrangements reduce the need to recruit and train new personnel, or at least facilitate that training.

Improved use of office space	In most occupations at least some office space will continue to be needed because all members of the staff need to come together at times for strategic planning or social activities. On the other hand, space can be less cluttered with equipment and, in many cases, shared. In the classroom, for instance, the same desk area can be used by two teachers who job-share.
Improved productivity	Because teleworkers spend less time on the freeway and less time preparing clothes and food for travel and work, improved productivity should follow. Because everyone has a limited amount of energy, it is assumed that energy released from travel to the place of work can be redirected to the task at hand.

Telecommuting also holds numerous benefits for workers, among them a greater sense of control over their work, reduced interruptions (thus saving salary, vacation, or leave), increased personal time for creative and rewarding family and personal activities, and savings on clothing, transportation, and food. Establishing alternative workstyles may not only relieve stress, but should also ease family obligations for the typical worker (Kelly, 1988). Instead of the tradition of "putting in the time," some companies now consider it more important to "get the job done." Flextime is not yet the usual practice, but it is slowly becoming more accepted as commuting costs and inconvenience during peak times increase.

Despite these benefits, not all workers enjoy working out of their home. Employees who need help in disciplined routines will not do well in this atmosphere. In addition, there are single workers who find that they would much rather work within the confines of the workplace and thus meet other unmarried workers within their field. And employees with young children may find they cannot concentrate on their work in the home environment.

Jobs that fit well within the telecommuting purview share certain characteristics. Such work involves:

- high daily use of either the telephone or the personal computer

- independence from other employees

- a project orientation

- information-handling of a simple nature.

Work at home is decidedly different from the pattern many of us have grown to know. Nevertheless, as we seek to clean up the air, open up the highways, and optimize our entire infrastructure, we must reexamine the 8-to-5 schedule of work. Paradoxically, working at home, an action that seems to suspend involvement with problems of society, contributes toward their solution.

Even though employees may be hundreds of miles away, personnel managers must continue to attend to sound personnel practice. Indeed, concern for human resources may be even more important, and call for more creative ideas, when workers are at a distance. Furthermore, leadership and management must adapt to the new setting. For example, strategic planning and project supervision have particular importance for managers of at-home workers.

As a district engages in strategic planning, it must prepare for this change in the work environment. Will school be conducted or classes taught via telecommuting? What about independent study or home teaching? Will the parent who is working at home have more—or less—time to play, teach, and work with the child? All these unanswered questions may profoundly affect schools and the role of the personnel department. Clearly, technology carries not only economic, but also social implications.

THE SOCIAL FUTURE

The 1960s was a period of great attention to domestic social issues. As the economic downturn occurred in the 1970s and through the 1990s, along with a massive federal deficit, revenues dedicated to social issues were sharply reduced. The social mood of a society, like a nation's economy, can be characterized as "cyclical." Thus, the cause-conscious populace of the 1960s yielded to a nonconfrontive mood in the 1990s. Social and economic trends come together in the "baby boomers," who feel entitled to the materialistic comforts of their parents, yet doubt they will ever match that level of wealth.

Already school district personnel departments are asked—and will continue to be asked—to help their employees with prevention of or treatment for substance abuse, relationship problems, and financial difficulties. In addition, fringe benefits such as life insurance and medical, dental, and vision care will assume crucial importance as these benefits become more difficult for nonemployed individuals to acquire. In California, as in the rest of the United States, childcare benefits and flexible hours will become ever more available in the marketplace (United Way Strategic Institute, 1989).

Changes in Values

Every recent decade has seen changes in values, some of them carrying important implications for personnel management. One particularly interesting change is the shift in value placed on work. To cite one statistic, among Harvard MBAs graduating between 1942 and 1978, 30% are self-employed. By comparison, 87% of the class of 1984 said they plan to start their own companies. Even though some of these would-be business owners may not succeed, this proportion—nearly triple—still represents a major increase in entrepreneurship (Plummer, 1989). Employers respond to this value by promoting "intrapreneurship" (a term coined by Peter Drucker), thus hoping to attract these individuals by offering them a creative, flexible environment within the corporate structure. Even those who prefer employment by others to building a company of their own appear more conscious of quality of life and self-fulfillment, often choosing less demanding, if also less remunerative, occupations to give themselves time and energy for personal pursuits.

Changes in attitudes toward health and diet also reflect a change in societal values. Such changes have practical implications, too, as witness the phenomenal rise in sales of diet drinks and foods within recent years. For instance, by the early 1990s "light" beers—not even in existence a few years earlier—constituted 33% of all beer consumption in the United States.

Other paradigm shifts include a new focus on individuality in the corporate setting, renewed expectations for high ethical values in political figures and employers, a reaching out for extended background through personal travel, and a move toward cradle-to-grave education. As individuals weigh these new value orientations, they find it necessary to rethink their total conception of life and work.

Male and Female Roles

The changing paradigms include new perceptions of the roles of males and females—perceptions that are breaking down barriers to entry of women into higher-paid, male-dominated occupations. More women than ever before are preparing for and entering these occupations, rather than the traditional feminine fields of teaching and nursing. This shift has contributed to the dramatic change in the nation's teaching force noted below.

These same trends, while luring women away from teaching, may result in greater numbers of women filling school administrative roles that are stereotypically masculine. In particular, the combination of substantial numbers of administrator retirements, an increasing proportion of women securing administrative credentials, and the new view of gender roles may increase representation of women in decision-making positions (Pounder, 1990). Moreover, the reforms of the '80s—teacher empowerment, instructional leadership, and the school effectiveness effort—have moved women to the fore of educational management. Perhaps there is need for a different type of administrator—for an instructional diagnostician rather than an "executive manager"—and perhaps the former role is more comfortable for women.

Three forces are most likely to impact the future of men and women at work (Powell, 1989). They are:

Equal opportunity	What are the regulations, how extensively are they enforced, and how closely are they monitored?
Socialization experiences	How are men and women socialized? How are their occupations influenced by their experiences?
Work and family issues	How do couples learn to balance their work and family responsibilities? How do organizations help employees meet their family needs?

Related demands, such as child care, will also impinge upon the knowledge required of personnel managers, whose role will become far more complex as they cope with these changes in gender roles and family arrangements. School personnel officers, like their counterparts in the private sector, will play a major role in establishing policies and procedures to address these issues.

Change and More Change

Thus far, and for the remainder of this chapter, the discussion points to change. A recent book proposes that the changes before us are not superficial, but threaten the very fabric of our society. As reviewed by Hertsgaard (1998), *The Future in Plain Sight* by Eugene Linden discusses global warming, severe storms and drought, population growth, and consumerism. These will lead to breakdowns in banking, food production, and disease control as well as unemployment, large-scale relocation—perhaps "massive social collapse." Indeed, Hertsgaard believes that Linden has understated the risks before us.

Of course, this is not the first time that futurists have predicted doom. Twenty years ago a flurry of reports from the Club of Rome and other futurists warned of imminent disaster as a result of uncontrolled growth and greed, depletion of energy resources, environmental wastage, and overpopulating. For some time we heard such slogans as "zero population growth" and "small is beautiful." Then optimism reasserted itself. In any case, it is obvious that the growing complexities of human resources development only mirror complex issues in the larger world.

POLITICAL TRENDS

In the past decade the attitudes of American citizens have undergone a major shift with respect to the notion that government should solve societal problems. This shift has created pressure on state and local government. Coming at a time of economic downturn and reduced resources, demands for more services create a nearly unresolvable contradiction. Although political trends are difficult to predict, it appears that the economy prevails, and that courts and the federal government are assuming a more limited role in social activism. But who would have predicted the political upheavals in Eastern Europe? the attack on the World Trade Center with its economic and political fallout? Such events emphasize the reality that political changes may come suddenly and unexpectedly.

SITE-BASED MANAGEMENT

Some 35 years ago, in 1968, Redfern was already predicting that classified staff and teachers would become increasingly involved in the decision-making processes of school districts, a prediction that has become reality. As district offices have experienced annual reduction of personnel and as various constituencies have demanded a stronger voice in school governance, decisions have increasingly been transferred to school site leaders. This nationwide movement toward site-based management has been under way for the past decade and will continue to gather momentum. Students, staff, and parents now participate in policy decisions at the school. This trend has created a school that is less insulated from the external environment than was the case 50 years ago.

The professional literature suggests that schools should pursue decentralization in an effort to accomplish higher levels of flexibility, accountability, and productivity. Several assumptions undergird this school improvement movement. Most important among these are that:

- meaningful change is more likely to occur at the school level than at the district level, and

- for change to occur, flexibility must be granted with regard to regulations.

Increased decentralization, coupled with collective bargaining, has made the job of a personnel officer more complex and increased the number of functions to be performed. Consequently, today's personnel officers must be better prepared in grievance resolution, personnel law, and contract negotiations than ever before (Metzger, 1988). They must be able to communicate to site staff the information they need to make legally and ethically defensible decisions. They must understand the staff development implications of participatory management, which calls for such skills as collaborative planning, decision-making, consensus-building, and conflict management. And they must model these skills in their daily work.

The Learning Organization

Peter Senge's concept of the "learning organization" (1990) fits within the context of site-based management. Senge speaks of everyone functioning as members of a "great team." He discusses creating an atmosphere, in this case in a school, where groups of teachers enhance their ability to further their capabilities and skills. Senge places great reliance on the primacy of considering the "whole school" as a single system rather than concentrating on its parts. He cautions us not to "tinker" with any subsystem—staff, students, or parents—unless we consider the effect on the whole.

Teacher leadership is essential to the learning organization. As an overburdened district office transfers administrative tasks to school sites, teachers have been called on to exert leadership among their peers. As a result, teachers serve more in such roles as team leader, mentor, peer coach, staff developer, and curriculum collaborator. In California, state law provides resources to enable mentor teachers to work with new and experienced teachers, to design programs and curricula, and in other ways to enhance the educational enterprise.

As more quasi-administrative tasks are assigned to teachers, we will see a stronger push for graduated salary scales. Teachers in leadership roles may be granted a title like "master teacher," empowering them to assist new teachers, create staff development programs, and coordinate peer evaluation processes.

The Charter School

If one attends a conference concerning personnel issues, many of the sessions involve the concepts of "charter school" and "voucher." Why are these sessions so popular? The reason lies in broad interest in school autonomy. Many school officials feel that they would rather have power over the resources necessary to run their schools than to depend upon district administration. These principals believe that they can allot funds and apportion staff more efficiently than a fiscal or personnel director working at the central office.

The California legislature passed a law to allow, beginning in January 1993, the establishment of 100 charter schools within the state. Five years later, in 1998, Governor

Wilson signed AB544, which lifted the 100 charter school limit. This legislation authorized 250 charters in 1998-99 and allowed 100 more in each subsequent year. Even though a district school board is still ultimately responsible for a charter school, the guidelines in the enabling legislation are extremely flexible.

The greatest challenge for charter schools may lie in creating the learning communities proposed by Senge and colleagues (1994) and Fullan (1998a, 1998b). Perhaps inadequate progress toward that concept is related to the findings of a study released by the University of California, Los Angeles, in the closing weeks of 1998 to the effect that

> most charter schools have no way to measure whether their students are doing better, have too much control over who attends them, rely too much on private outside funding and are not being required to reflect the racial-ethnic mix of their districts ("Charter Schools," 1998).

In 2001 the Rand Corporation was unable to find conclusive evidence of either merit or harm in attending charter schools. The study concluded that a student's education in a charter school depends on the type of school or program and the population the school services. The study reports that 2,400 charter schools were operating in the U. S. in 2001 (Colvin, 2001).

TEACHER / PERSONNEL HIRING ISSUES

Recently, a dramatic change has been noticed in the nation's teaching force. It appears that new recruits to teaching may be less academically qualified than those who are leaving the profession. Even though teacher shortages have occurred before, new circumstances may intensify the predicament. For one thing, expanded opportunities in other fields, especially for women and minorities, have made teaching comparatively less attractive. That salary ranges in teaching cannot compete with starting pay in many other professions merely compounds the problem.

This shortage may necessitate new procedures for recruiting teachers. Employment policies may need to be rethought and changes introduced in search procedures. Creative programs will be important also to retain teachers. For this latter purpose, the first few years of a teacher's employment are critical. According to a survey by Louis Harris and Associates in 1991, teachers reported that the following would help them most in their first two years:

● a skilled, experienced teacher assigned to provide advice and assistance

- more practical training, such as a year's internship before having their own classroom

- better training with students and families who represent a variety of ethnic backgrounds.

California's class size reduction legislation, which provides funding to decrease class size to 20 or fewer students in kindergarten through third grade, has thereby significantly increased need for additional teachers. This legislation, combined with the large percentage of teachers who leave the profession during their first few years of teaching and the number of California teachers who are reaching retirement age, promises to exacerbate the shortage of teachers in California schools. Thus, several thousands of new teachers will be needed in the state in the next several years.

In hiring staff other than teachers, an interesting trend is that personnel are not being hired permanently, but rather that many employees work on a "just in time" basis. These individuals may be hired to perform a task, only to be let go by the school district when the job has been completed. This practice represents a significant departure from past practice in employing classified and support staff.

SUMMARY

A review of demographic, economic, social, and political trends has been presented in this chapter. Clearly, forces such as the nation's economy are crucial to the school district personnel department, yet difficult to predict. Economic trends may impact a vast array of personnel issues, from an employee's base salary to a shortage of teachers. Restructuring may range from job restructuring among those—both male and female—who wish more time in the home or with their children to institutional restructuring through participatory management.

Shifts forecasted in the labor force that will have major impact upon the personnel function include increased numbers of minority workers and female managers. Additional resources will be needed to care for the physical and mental health of all employees; programs in stress management, nutrition, and exercise will expand.

In addition, human resources management will be seen as increasingly important within the larger frame of strategic planning. While generating many new problems, this recognition will also provide human resources administrators with opportunity to use their expanded expertise to make a richer contribution to the educational enterprise.

Forecasts are difficult to formulate. The tendency for "soothsayers" is to focus upon critical societal problems of the moment. Furthermore, one must recognize at the outset that solutions arising from traditional concepts are almost certainly wrong. No one can predict with certainty the innovations that will actually solve the nation's problems. Indeed, many solutions have not yet been considered, or even invented.

KEY TERMS

1. affirmative action
3. bilingual teacher shortage
3. Charter Schools
4. class size reduction
5. flextime
6. global society
7. learning organization
8. over-enrollment
9. Proposition 187
10. site-based management
11. strategic planning
12. telecommuting

QUESTIONS AND ACTIVITIES

1. Naisbitt (1990) identified three societal trends that will change American society: changing from an industrial to an information society, changing from a nationalized to a global society, and restructuring of organizations toward decentralization. Assuming that these trends continue, how will each of them affect education?

2. The "English for the Children" ballot proposition that was passed in 1998 raises many questions, especially in view of federal court decisions calling for non-English-speaking students to have access to the core curriculum. Using your "crystal ball," predict what bilingual education will look like in the year 2010.

3. A trend in the nation and in California is the work-at-home movement. How will this trend affect public education?

4. The growth of technology is continuing to accelerate in the U. S. and around the world. How will technology affect public school education in the year 2010? Give specific examples to support your answer.

5. The California Superintendent of Public Instruction has advanced the notion of freeing schools from the requirements of the Education Code with the objective of improving instruction. Give specific examples of laws that restrict educational improvement. Discuss several ways education could be improved without the constraints of Education Code requirements.

6. Select a journal, such as *The Futurist,* that deals with global futures. Select three topics from the journal and extrapolate ways in which these issues may affect future personnel issues in California.

7. Review an article and write a five-page analysis of the effect of changing sex roles upon the workforce of the future.

8. Which careers in personnel administration will be affected most as male and female roles become equalized? Explain.

9. Many individuals feel that the work-at-home movement will be a major force in the 1990s. List all the occupations that you feel might be practiced successfully at home.

10. Consider your occupation and the occupations of those you know. Could these jobs be accomplished at home or by computer? Why or why not?

11. What might be some reasons *not* to rely on telecommuting in the workplace?

12. Interview a Director of Personnel or Assistant Superintendent of Personnel. From the interview, predict the nature of this position in 20 years.

13. Analyze a school in your district. Determine activities the staff are involved in now that might enable this school to become a "learning organization."

Chapter 16

Career Advancement

We judge ourselves by what we feel capable of doing, while others judge us by what we have already done.

• • • Henry Wadsworth Longfellow

INTRODUCTION

This chapter is not limited to the interests of personnel officers, but is of interest to teachers aspiring to administrative careers and to entry-level administrators who hope to advance. It is included in this book because the authors believe that teaching institutions have an obligation to help their students obtain a position in which to apply their learnings. Since advancement into administration is a personnel issue, a textbook on personnel management seems the most appropriate place for this topic. It is also true that candidates often seek advice and feedback on career pathing and promotion from personnel directors.

The opening years of the 21st century will continue to offer extensive opportunities for individuals seeking a career in school administration. It is projected that student enrollment in California's public schools will increase by 200,000 students each year. One way to estimate the number of new administrators needed for this increased enrollment is to calculate one administrator for every 500 students. This calculation is based on a staffing pattern of one principal for each elementary school and one administrator for every 500 students at the secondary level. This figure is relatively conservative, given the large number of small schools and districts in the state. Based on this projection, student growth will require an additional 400 administrators each year.

Another way of estimating the vacancies for administrative positions is to apply the administrative-teacher ratio in Education Code section #41402. The maximum ratio of administrative employees to teachers is 9:100 in elementary school districts, 8:100 in unified districts, and 7:100 in high school districts. Taking the same growth factor of 200,000 students per year and assuming a ratio of one teacher for every 30 students, 6,666 additional teachers will be added to California's teaching ranks annually. Again, using the staffing ratio allowed by the state and dividing 6,666 teachers by an administrative ratio of eight, 833 additional administrative vacancies will occur. This number is probably more realistic than the 400 calculated in the preceding paragraph.

In addition to the approximately 800 administrative positions needed each year to accommodate growth in student enrollment, vacancies will be created by administrators who leave their positions for other job opportunities or for retirement. Estimates indicate that over one-half of all California administrators will reach retirement age within the next five years. This factor will create a significant need for assistant principals, principals, directors, assistant superintendents, and superintendents to provide leadership to California schools.

With this in mind, another approach to estimating opportunities for advancement into a management position is to review administrative job vacancy announcements. The most complete list of administrative vacancy announcements in California is contained in *EdCal*, the official newspaper of the Association of California School Administrators (ACSA).

EdCal is published 40 times per year and, in addition to articles of interest to school administrators, each publication contains Job Information Survey (JIS), a list of administrative openings in California. One issue in July 2001, announced 5 vacancies for superintendent, 4 administrative positions at county schools, and 19 vacancies at district offices. In addition, there were 26 vacancies for high school administrators, 16 announcements for middle school positions, and 30 openings at elementary schools. There were also 2 openings for classified management positions and 5 announcements for special education administrators. This total of 107 administrative vacancies in a one-week period is fairly representative of each issue of JIS. Using the openings advertised in this publication, a quick calculation suggests approximately 4,000 vacancies for school administrative positions in California in 2001-2002.

The administrative vacancy announcements contained a broad range of district size and locale. For those interested in a small rural district, Bear Valley Unified School District in San Bernardino County, with an enrollment of 850 students, was seeking a high school principal. If the large city and large district held an attraction, Garden Grove District, with an enrollment of 49,000, was also seeking a high school principal. Compensation for the administrative positions also varied greatly from a minimum of $61,372 for an elementary school principal in the Amador County Unified School District to a maximum of $130,000 for an assistant superintendent, business services, in the East Side School District, located in Santa Clara County.

This information about administrative openings would lead one to believe that administrative positions are readily available for the aspiring assistant principal, principal, director, or superintendent. The authors believe there are administrative jobs for all qualified candidates who truly want a leadership position. There is one caveat: the aspiring administrator must be willing to take the necessary steps, and even make sacrifices, to obtain a principalship or superintendency.

SELF-ASSESSMENT

Advice in obtaining an administrative position is often difficult to obtain. Often, the only suggestions one receives come from his or her principal or superintendent. Universities prepare students enrolled in educational administration in the basic skills required for the credential and the position. However, assistance in preparing a letter or application or putting together a résumé is not a standard part of the curriculum.

Landing one's first administrative position is often more difficult than getting that first teaching job. Perhaps an individual had been able to choose among a wide choice of teaching positions and cannot understand why his or her teaching experience is not adequate preparation for an assistant principalship or principalship. However, administrative positions are less plentiful and, hence, more competitive. As a result, a candidate may find it necessary to take a position that is not the preferred choice just to get the proverbial foot in the door.

Most often this compromise involves geography. A candidate who is restricted to a limited geographic area is at a real disadvantage in obtaining that desired position. For example, in California the search for an administrative position in a beach community is highly competitive, since many highly qualified candidates prefer that setting.

The first step in obtaining an administrative position is to complete an assessment of one's experience, training, and characteristics as measured against the requisites for effective leadership. The second part of the assessment calls for a review of the required tasks and abilities necessary to obtain the position. The third part of the assessment examines the personal objectives that must be considered when seeking an administrative position. This latter assessment should consider lifestyle requirements and family preferences. For example, is one willing to relocate from the suburbs to the inner city or to a rural community to obtain that promotion?

Townley (1992) devised an instrument to assist the potential administrator in completing a self-assessment. This form is in two parts: Table 8 includes items of experience, training, and leadership characteristics necessary for effective leadership, while the second part, Table 9, includes tasks and abilities that are necessary to obtain the position. This table also facilitates a self-assessment of lifestyle requirements and family preferences.

Table 8

Administrative Candidate's

Self-Assessment Instrument

Part 1

Experience — Training — Leadership Characteristics

	Circle one number in each box				
	Low				High
1. Experience qualifying you for the promotion	1	2	3	4	5

2. Education (choose one)
  a. master's degree
  b. enrolled in doctorate
  c. completed doctorate
	1		3		5

3. Communication skills—oral	1	2	3	4	5
4. Communication skills—written	1	2	3	4	5
5. Decision-making skills	1	2	3	4	5
6. Noted for good judgement	1	2	3	4	5
7. Noted for excellent organizational skills	1	2	3	4	5
8. Judged as personable and enthusiastic, a likable personality	1	2	3	4	5
9. Reputation as a hard worker	1	2	3	4	5
10. Ability to lead a committee or group to consensus and completion of a task	1	2	3	4	5
	Add numbers circled for TOTAL SCORE _____				

Experience

Requirements vary greatly, depending on the job in which the applicant is interested. For example, an opening for superintendent in a district with small student enrollment may require experience as a teacher and possibly experience as a principal, whereas a district with large student population usually requires experience as a principal and assistant superintendent.

Aspirants to an entry-level administrative job should gain experience teaching at as many levels as possible. This statement is particularly true of candidates in elementary schools. Secondary teachers are advised to teach a variety of subjects. The aspiring administrator who has only taught, for example, third grade is at a disadvantage in competition for an elementary principalship as compared with candidates who have taught at several grade levels. This same principle applies to secondary applicants who have taught only one or two subjects and are competing with candidates with more varied background.

In addition to teaching experience, an applicant must have completed a wide variety of administrative tasks. Having acted as principal when the administrator is away from campus, service on curriculum task forces, and participation in committees dealing with students are a plus when interviewing for an administrative position. Demonstration of leadership is a prerequisite for selection as assistant principal or principal; positions as mentor teacher, student activities advisor, athletic director, subject matter coordinator, as well as grade-level chair at the elementary level or department chair in secondary schools exemplify activities viewed as showing leadership. The aspiring administrator needs to seek such experiences to gain a competitive edge in obtaining a promotion.

Education

Most administrative jobs require a master's degree as the minimum educational qualification. However, an individual seeking a career in school administration must decide for himself whether a doctoral degree is also necessary. Many superintendents do not have this terminal degree and yet have pursued successful careers. However, the doctorate is essential for particular positions or locations. It is decidedly a consideration in upper income communities where many parents hold advanced degrees.

Even where the degree is not crucial, enrollment in a program leading to the doctorate in educational administration makes one more competitive for a principalship or district-level position, particularly in larger metropolitan districts. Obviously, possession of the doctorate is a plus, especially for the superintendency.

Many school administrators also teach at a college or university, often in addition to their regular jobs. In addition to the extra compensation, these individuals find university teaching a way to keep current with new trends and curriculum innovations. The doctorate is usually a requirement for consideration as a university instructor.

Communication Skills

The word "communicate" comes from the Latin *communicare*, meaning to "share" or "make common." Effective communication is perhaps the most salient characteristic of a successful leader. An administrator spends approximately 80% of his or her time engaged in oral or written communication. Bennis and Nanus (1985) write, "Leaders communicate at all times, and the more effective the communication, the more effective the leadership." A candidate weak in this area should plan a program of self-improvement, both to attain an administrative position and to succeed, once a position is attained. Gorton (1986) suggested five strategies for better communication:

Paraphrasing	Restate the main ideas of others to clarify those ideas. One might say, "Let me see if I heard that correctly . . . "
Perception checking	Check to see that your perception of what has been said is accurate, for example, "Are you saying that the budget must be balanced by next week?"
Relating to personal feelings	Communication sometimes breaks down because receivers misunderstand or have a negative reaction to statements. We may offend unknowingly or unintentionally. These feelings should be confronted when they occur, either by restating ("That is not what I meant to say") or by acknowledging one's own response ("That statement made me angry").
Objective descriptions	Highly subjective words or terms that imply personal values hurt open communication. Rather than such expressions, use objective terms to describe behaviors so that people are less likely to say, "I don't disagree with what you say, but with how you're saying it."
Feedback	Give and accept constructive and honest feedback to keep communication channels open among all parties.

A major prerequisite for the successful administrator is developing topflight communication skills. The successful principal or superintendent must be highly committed to effective and open communication, and the aspiring administrator needs a strong rating in this essential skill. A personnel officer must model effective communication above all, as scarcely an hour will pass in which that individual is not engaged in sensitive oral or written communication.

Decision-Making Skills

Another prerequisite for a successful career in administration is the ability to solve problems quickly and decisively. In a typical day an assistant principal or principal may be required to solve as many as 50 problems, ranging from helping a student who has lost his lunch money to deciding whether to evacuate the building because a bomb threat has been received.

Lest a poor decision have dire consequences, a new administrator must be proficient in problem-solving the very first day on the job. Therefore, coursework for the administrative credential and master's degree should include a significant component of situational problems and provide students opportunities to assess a situation, look at alternatives, and make defensible choices. Role-playing and simulations are also effective teaching strategies for improving problem-solving skills. Such strategies allow future administrators to experiment and attempt creative solutions to problems in a non-threatening environment.

Judgement

Judgement is critical in a leadership position. An administrator must make decisions that are wise, reasonable, and valid. Good judgment is often determined after the fact: did you do the right thing? Self-assessment must include an evaluation of your ability to reach those well-thought-out, wise decisions. It may be beneficial to seek an honest evaluation of your ability in this area from trusted friends and colleagues.

Organizational Skills

The successful administrator is able to establish priorities and complete tasks in timely fashion. One must know how to take a complex task or problem and analyze it step by step. Successful task completion calls for skill in delegating responsibilities, evaluating progress, and getting the job done.

Personality or Charismatic Leadership

Charismatic leaders may or may not have a high IQ, may or may not be attractive, may be tall or short. They are not necessarily outgoing, assertive, or dominant. As a matter of fact, there is no single distinguishing characteristic of the charismatic leader. Charismatic leadership is marked by the response of other individuals who are attracted by, identify closely with, and like or respect the person who exercises power. Gorton (1986) listed assumptions about this source of power:

- The greater the perceived attractiveness of the person exercising power, the more likely the identification with the leader.

- The stronger the identification with the leader, the greater the likelihood that charismatic power can be successfully utilized by the leader. Often the charismatic leader is perceived to have some special gift, even supernatural power. Examples of charismatic leaders in politics include John F. Kennedy and Winston Churchill. Other instances include movie stars, professional athletes, and some tele-evangelists.

Charismatic leaders express goals and values that are lofty, broad, long-term, and difficult. They energize subordinates to pursue these goals, often beyond their own expectations. One could attribute this type of leadership to Ross Perot, who in 1992 galvanized millions of Americans to his candidacy for the presidency without ever becoming specific as to the programs he espoused.

Charismatic leaders show concern for subordinates' welfare and faith in their ability to realize those lofty goals. They use symbolism and imagery to enhance their influence as leaders, and encourage and inspire their followers to develop a sense of mission. The charismatic leader exclaims passionately, "This is a tough task, but I *know* you can do it."

Most leaders are quite human and experience the same range of human emotions as those who are led. People are more likely to respond positively to a leader who exhibits enthusiasm, friendship, trust, and high ethical standards. Perhaps the best way to estimate your power as a charismatic leader is to ask yourself, "Do people enjoy my company?"

Reputation as a Hard Worker

A very old saying declares, "She doesn't ask us to do anything she wouldn't do." Teachers and classified employees alike appreciate a boss who works just as hard as they do. The successful candidate for an administrative position needs a reputation as one who is willing to put in the time and effort necessary to get the job done!

Leadership

Increasingly, educators have recognized the importance of administrators as a key element in the overall effectiveness of schools (Austin, 1979; Brookover and Lezotte, 1980; Lipham, 1981). Tannenbaum, Weschler, and Massarik (1961) defined leadership as "interpersonal influence, exercised in a situation, and directed, through the communication process, toward the attainment of a specified goal or goals." A necessary characteristic of the successful administrator is the ability to provide leadership to a staff. Simply stated: Leaders must have followers. In assessing one's own leadership ability, ask "Do I really enjoy endlessly working with and constantly being with people?"

The search for a precise understanding of the factors contributing to effective leadership has been at the center of virtually every study of organizations. People are always fascinated with the enigma of determining the precise characteristics of effective leaders. Without looking for specific characteristics, since they are still unclear, one's self-assessment should include the questions: Do I like to be in a leadership position? Do I often take this role in my school or district?

Scoring

After giving careful thought to the administrative position or promotion that would be right for you and keeping that position in mind as you respond to the items in Part 1 of the self-assessment, score this part of the evaluation by adding up the numbers you have circled. Assume that you scored 40 or higher on this assessment of your experience, training, and leadership characteristics. You are now ready for that principalship or superintendency. However, in addition to having the experience, training, and leadership skills to do the job, you must still land the position. Preparing for this task is the subject of the second part of this chapter.

GETTING THE JOB

Many excellent teachers have the necessary leadership skills to be equally fine administrators. However, many of these individuals never receive an administrative appointment. This statement could also be made of assistant principals who would like to become principals, and of assistant superintendents who aspire to the superintendency. It is not enough to be able to provide capable leadership to a school or district; one must be selected for the position after competing with many other well-qualified candidates.

This second task entails a set of skills that overlap leadership skills in part, but are distinctive in part. It also demands personal decisions, some of which may be difficult. The self-assessment in Table 9 is related to applying and interviewing for a position and the personal decisions needed before accepting a promotion.

After completing a master's degree in school administration and receiving an administrative credential, the next step is to acquire the administrative job—and this may not be an easy task. An aspiring administrative candidate writes, "I would learn the rules. I would overcome all obstacles!" (Oliphant, 1990). Oliphant writes that after many years of teaching, she decided to seek an administrative career. Five years later she was still in the classroom and had not achieved her objective. Why would a successful teacher who had completed all the necessary work for a doctorate in school administration have failed to receive that promotion? A major reason may have been insufficient knowledge of the second element in receiving a promotion—the actual task of applying and interviewing for the position.

Table 9

Administrative Candidate's

Self-Assessment Instrument

Part 2

Application — Interview Skills — Personal Decisions

	Circle one number in each box				
	Low				High
1. All references rated "outstanding"	1	2	3	4	5
2. Two or more references written within the last year	1	2	3	4	5
3. References on file at college	1	2	3	4	5
4. Quality of letter of application and résumé	1	2	3	4	5
5. Personal appearance	1	2	3	4	5
6. Specific information about the position	1	2	3	4	5
7. Ability to relate quickly to people	1	2	3	4	5
8. Information as to who will interview and who will supervise the position	1	2	3	4	5
9. If necessary, willing to relocate to accept position anywhere in California	1	2	3	4	5
10. If necessary, will take a reduction in pay to accept position	1	2	3	4	5
	Add numbers circled for TOTAL SCORE _____				

References

After deciding to apply for an administrative position, the first step in the process should be to gather or update one's letters of reference. As an assistant superintendent and superintendent reviewing candidates' files, I found many reference letters were poorly written and did not emphasize the strong points of the applicant. It is extremely important to obtain the best references possible and to be sure they are current.

Many personnel directors place little credence in letters more than two years old. Thus, even after placement in an administrative position, a biennial update of one's reference file is advisable. Most colleges and universities staff a career assistance office. A university you attended will allow you to establish a placement file from which reference letters are promptly reproduced in a professional manner and sent directly to the employing school district. The time, effort, and even the fees involved in maintaining and requesting such a file are well worth it.

Letter of Application

You take an important step toward career advancement by preparing an impressive letter of application. Sell your potential by relating your past and current experience and education to the expectations of the desired position. It is crucial to read the job announcement with great care, so as to accomplish two purposes. First, the job announcement assists you in making an informed decision about your qualifications for the position. Second, the letter of application must be tailored to the specific requirements of the vacancy.

Address your letter to a specific person. The vacancy announcement usually contains the name of the person responsible for receiving the application. Check at least three times to make sure you have spelled that person's name correctly and have used the correct title in your salutation. The title "Assistant Superintendent, Personnel" is not the same as "Director of Personnel"; an incorrect title gives an impression of carelessness or inattention to detail on the part of the applicant.

Generally, the letter of application should not exceed one page of three to four paragraphs. Each paragraph should run to four typed lines or less. The following guidelines will assist with the format of the application letter.

The first paragraph of the letter should mention the title of the position for which one is applying, firmly state that the candidate is highly qualified, and suggest the nature of the qualifications. The second paragraph should specify the applicant's credentials, education, and training that serve as primary qualifications for the position. Every requirement on the vacancy announcement should be addressed in this paragraph. For example, if the announcement requires teaching at the elementary level, mention elementary teaching in the second paragraph. The third paragraph should address other items included in the job announcement. If the announcement describes specific duties, such as budget development, or specific experience, such as working in a multicultural setting, this information should be included in paragraph three. The final paragraph should be similar to the opening paragraph in that the name of the desired position is included and a strong statement made as to the candidate's ability to do outstanding work in that position.

That the letter be superbly written, with utmost attention to style, spelling, grammar, and punctuation, cannot be stressed too strongly. Several means are available to ensure that the letter is of exceptional quality. For one thing, most word processing programs contain a spell-check, and there are several programs with editing capabilities (although, because language is so complex, editing programs are wrong about as often as they are right). In addition, comments from a friend, colleague, supervisor, or university professor who reads the letter critically will probably result in its improvement.

Finally, know your boundaries. Do not apply for positions indiscriminately. Applying for a position for which you are obviously unqualified gives the impression that you are unrealistic about your qualifications—which in turn may lead those who review your materials to wonder whether you are also out of touch with reality in other areas.

Résumé

Individuals who are just beginning to look for an administrative position may not have taken one of the first steps—preparing a résumé. Prospective candidates should have a résumé prepared that can easily be updated and tailored to a particular position. For example, a candidate with both experience as an assistant principal and background in finance might apply either for a principalship or for a position in business office. The résumé for the principalship would highlight experiences as assistant principal, while the résumé for the school business position would emphasize the financial experience. Because of a computer's flexibility in adapting the résumé to a desired job, many job-seekers find it advantageous to keep their résumé on a disk at home, rather than to send it out to a print shop. A computerized résumé is readily modified to reflect new experiences.

A résumé is an advertisement for its writer. Although the letter of application is usually the first document read by a personnel director, the résumé is generally second. Résumés fall into three categories: chronological, functional, and targeted. The chronological type is most utilized by candidates seeking administrative positions, but this choice should be based on the background and experience of the candidate and the sort of administrative job desired.

Evidence suggests that 90% of all résumés submitted are read for less than two minutes (Goodwin, 1997). Therefore, it is imperative that the utmost care be devoted to completing this document. A study of preferred résumés was conducted at the University of Wisconsin (Schramm & Dortch, 1991). One hundred forty-two company recruiters were polled to determine preferences in résumé content, format, and appearance. The findings of the study follow.

● Most recruiters prefer a standard 8 1/2" x 11" résumé. The proper length of a résumé is unclear, although a majority of recruiters favor a maximum of two pages. Between 70% and 80% of recruiters stated that poor organization and a long résumé cause them to lose interest in a candidate.

- Employment personnel are most disturbed by the following mechanical errors: poor grammar and more than one spelling or typing error. Approximately 95% of the recruiters agree that poor grammar and misspelled words limit a candidate's chance of obtaining an interview.

- Keeping the résumé neat and clean is extremely important, according to a majority of recruiters. However, recruiters did not rate high quality paper or typesetting as significant.

- The traditional, historical format is preferred by recruiters while, the more liberal, informal approach received a slightly negative rating.

- The most popular color choices for the résumé are white and ivory.

The purpose of a résumé is to convince the personnel director that the candidate has the qualifications and skills to fill the announced position in exemplary fashion. It should be formal, factual, and concise. It should contain information that makes the applicant an attractive candidate and opens the door for further consideration in the selection process.

Portfolio

In recent years the professional portfolio has become an important document in searching for and landing the job. The purpose of the portfolio, similar to that of the résumé, is to market the candidate to potential employers. It supports and extends information to be shared in the interview. Goodwin (1997) believes that the portfolio can be just the thing that sets a candidate apart from other applicants. A well-designed portfolio highlights achievements and exhibits documents to demonstrate the quality of one's experience, skills, and training in relation to the requirements for the position.

A variety of information can be included in the portfolio. It may include traditional application materials such as the résumé, transcripts of course work, education and internship certificates, a list of conferences and workshops attended, letters of recommendation, evaluations from supervisors, and special commendations. Photographs, videotapes, newspaper articles and the like may be added. Longer items, such as published or unpublished manuscripts, are appropriate in a portfolio. One might present examples of work in leadership, teaching, and community volunteer work.

Each item in the portfolio must be selected to demonstrate the candidate's skill and knowledge. The arrangement and organization of the material, as well as such details as grammar and spelling, call for careful attention. One might consider a table of contents and tab dividers to help members of the selection committee locate material quickly. If documents are included to demonstrate one's skills in writing policy and procedures, developing curriculum, motivating and evaluating certificated and classified staff, presenting staff development workshops, or the like, post-its and highlighters are tools to draw attention to important aspects of these longer documents. A post-it might explain the features of a document that make it special. Thomas (1990) gives good advice when he states that the portfolio must be graphically pleasing.

It is important to take the portfolio to the interview and keep it handy, perhaps in a briefcase, should the interviewer or interview panel asks questions about abilities that one can document from the portfolio materials. For this purpose, a portfolio might be divided into several separate folders, enabling one to bring out only those portions relevant to items raised during the interview. When facing an interview panel, one might also want to have several portions of the portfolio circulating around the table so that each interviewer has opportunity to examine at least part of the documentation.

During some interviews, the candidate may not have an opportunity to show the portfolio. In this situation, the candidate may offer the portfolio to the personnel director or the interview panel for review at a later time. In this case, be careful about leaving materials that cannot be replicated or that address confidential personnel or policy matters.

Personal Appearance

In preparing for the interview, applicants might heed the advice of Shakespeare:

> Costly thy habit as thy purse can buy,
> But not express'd in fancy; rich, not gaudy,
> For the apparel oft proclaims the man.

> (*Hamlet,* Act 1, Scene 3)

Today we want to say "man or woman"—except that it would mar the meter. In any case, many applicants for administrative positions have lost an opportunity for promotion by not following Shakespeare's advice. Candidates often appear at an interview with inappropriate dress and grooming. The competition for each administrative position is so strong that to be competent is not enough. An interviewee must also look competent. "It's not what you say; it's how good you look when you say it." This statement is superficial, yet true, according to professional image and communication consultants. "It only takes four seconds to form a first impression"—thus Jane Miller, writer and image consultant (Robinson, 1992). The personnel director and members of the interview panel form an opinion of the candidate the moment he or she walks into the room, and this opinion is based primarily on appearance and poise.

In most communities, citizens expect principals and superintendents to be role models for students. This expectation applies to dress and appearance also. One has personal preferences, of course. Moreover, attitudes about these matters vary somewhat from community to community. However, based on many years' experience in a variety of

California school districts, the authors advise prospective administrative candidates to present themselves in conservative dress and grooming.

A man makes the best impression in a navy-blue suit, single-breasted, and a white shirt with long sleeves. Cotton is a good selection of material for the shirt as it retains its neat appearance. Obviously, the suit and shirt should be carefully cleaned and pressed. Wear long sleeves for the interview; short sleeves may imply a more casual attitude than you wish to project. Men should be particularly careful about carrying money or keys in the coat or trouser pockets. During the stress of the interview, a nervous jangling of coins or keys distracts the listeners from an otherwise successful presentation. Candidates should carefully consider which tie and belt to wear for the interview. The tip of the tie should come to the top or center of the belt buckle, and the back of the tie should go through the label so the ends stay together. The belt should be new and not show any signs of weight loss or gain. Shoes should be polished and not show unusual wear. If in doubt about length of hair or wearing a beard, the usual advice is to keep the hair trimmed above the ears and shave the mustache or beard until after a contract is offered. One would be hard pressed to imagine not getting a job because one did *not* have a mustache or beard.

Female candidates should also take special care when preparing for the interview. The usual advice for female candidates is to dress conservatively according to the administrative dress of the school district. One recommendation is to observe the dress of school or district female administrators and dress for the interview in a slightly more conservative fashion. If in doubt, one is probably safe in wearing a navy, gray or dark maroon suit. The blouse should be long-sleeved and high-necked in a complementary solid color—white or cream or a pastel, not red or fuchsia. The skirt should cover the knee when one is seated. Female applicants do best in medium-heel pumps, no open toes or backs, and always hose, even in the summer. Jewelry should be simple and not dangling. It is suggested that the applicant not wear more than one ring per hand and only one bracelet. Makeup should be simple and soft and as natural-looking as possible. Hair should be styled—not teased, not bouffant, and not bleached. Nails should be manicured, with light or clear polish. If one carries a briefcase to the interview, the purse should be left in the car, as it looks ungainly to carry both. If a scarf or a necklace is worn, it should be short enough to focus attention on the face.

Men and women are reminded to wear glasses with up-to-date frames and no tinting, photo-grays, or sunglasses. Eye contact is very important in the interview, and any interference with this contact is a negative. If one is traveling some distance to the interview, it is wise to change into fresh, pressed clothes just before entering the school or district office. Time should be allowed to locate the place for the interview and arrival should be early enough to make that last final check in the mirror. This attention to dress and grooming gives the candidate that extra confidence that is so necessary in a stressful, competitive situation. Finally, walk into the interview with confidence, smile, greet the interviewers by name, shake hands firmly, and focus on getting the job. As part of the self-assessment in this category, ask yourself, "Have I made the most of my appearance? Am I considered an individual who dresses appropriately for each occasion?"

Information about the Position and Community

We have been constantly amazed over the years at how little some candidates know about a position for which they apply. I am sure that some applicants spend more time researching the merits of a particular automobile they wish to purchase than learning about the vacancy!

As mentioned previously, the Association of California School Administrators (ACSA) publishes a weekly job list. Once you know the position for which you are qualified, carefully review the announcement, then call or write the district for an application and information about the position.

Then, when you have been invited to an interview, complete as detailed a study of the district and position as time allows. Know as much about the job as possible, including the name of the supervisor and key teachers on the staff. It is particularly helpful to memorize names of persons who may serve on the interview panel. Knowing the names in advance makes it easier to associate them with faces.

Obtain a copy of the budget, annual reports, test scores, and information about staff and students. School annuals for secondary schools are often obtainable at the local public library and contribute invaluable information about the school board, superintendent, and key personnel. Information about special programs, often described in brochures or available with a phone call to district office administrators, can become an asset during the interview.

Remember to scan local newspapers for information about sports programs, special honors won by the district, and other items that might show knowledge of school and district achievements. Find out what night the board meets and check local papers for that weekday and a subsequent day or two, going back at least a year and preferably to the last board election. Identify political and community issues. This research accomplishes two purposes: it suggests questions that might be asked in the interview and engenders confidence in the interview setting. If time permits, check letters to the editor, too.

If possible, visit the community and schools several times prior to the interview. A favorite question of the interview team for principal's candidates is, "Have you visited the school?" A "no" answer can make the difference between getting the job and not getting it! Talk with community leaders, the editor of the local paper, representatives of the chamber of commerce, and business owners about the schools and community. Most important, talk with students. A stop at a local restaurant with questions about the schools can prepare you for several typical interview questions. For example, if the district has scheduled a bond election to build a new school, you can count on a question about this topic. If you become a finalist, continue your research, perhaps including a visit to a board meeting, until the second interview. Doing your homework on the school and district prepares you for questions about local problems or concerns. Usually, though, you will want to demonstrate your awareness of issues and your interest in dealing with them—but not to suggest that you have solutions in hand before you have interacted with district personnel, parents, and other stakeholders.

Networking

Let friends and colleagues know you are interested in an administrative position. They can share advance notice of positions to be announced. They may also be able to talk with you about the organizational structure and other useful information about a district or suggest contacts among their colleagues.

A high percentage of individuals who obtain an administrative position attribute their success to a mentor or supervisor who offered guidance and gave the candidate an opportunity to develop leadership skills. Often, the mentor also informed the student of job openings and telephoned a prospective employer to give a needed recommendation.

Networking should be started early, while in college. Many potential friends and future colleagues sit in your classes. Membership in clubs, sororities, and fraternities begins a network of lifelong friends and colleagues. A university professor is often in a position to know the job market and can serve as a valuable mentor. As one enters the teaching profession, additional contacts and friendships grow out of opportunities for membership and leadership in professional organizations.

The Interview

After many years of education and training, the direction of a prospective administrator's career may be decided in a brief 30- to 60-minute interview. Do you have the ability to walk with confidence into a room of strangers, and answer questions in a friendly, positive fashion? Do you have an excellent sense of humor? These characteristics can be a real plus in establishing rapport with the interview team and your prospective employer.

Several preparatory steps should precede that all-important interview. One way to gain interview experience is to sit on the other side of the table, that is, to volunteer to serve on interview panels in your own school or district. This experience shows how questions are developed and introduces the rating scales relied upon to determine the best candidates. In addition, insight is gained into the dynamics of the interview itself. Do not neglect the selection process for classified employees, as well as certificated staff. Observing interviews for secretary, custodian, or food service worker adds another dimension of understanding.

Members of selection teams review applicants' papers, thus seeing examples—good and bad—of application forms, letters of application, and résumés. As a member of the team, you can pick up ideas from good models and see pitfalls to be avoided.

Another helpful step is a mock interview. See whether friends or university classmates are willing to prepare interview questions and take the roles of the various persons likely to sit on an interview panel for the position you seek. If possible, some current administrators should be in the group. As an added feature, audiotape or videotape the session so you can review it later. The mock interview should be conducted as much like the real thing as possible, without interruptions. Ask the panel to note their suggestions during the interview; then debrief immediately afterwards. Some questions to pose to the panel include:

- Was my handshake firm (but not crushing)?

- Did I show enthusiasm?

- Did I maintain good eye contact?

- Was my body language appropriate?

- Were my grammar, sentence structure, and word choices correct and appropriate?

- Was I a good listener?

- Did I seem sincere and confident?

- Did I have an appropriate sense of humor?

- Were my answers complete, but succinct?

Visit your local bookstore or library. Books on interviewing (and about applications and résumés) are always available. Included are sample questions that may be posed and that you can use for practice. For a list of possible questions, look at Table 10. Often, the interviewee is first asked to summarize his or her background for the position. Plan a succinct statement, about three minutes long, in which you highlight the breadth and depth of your background as related to this particular position. Often an interview closes with a question or two on personal style, for instance, "What do you regard as your greatest strength? What do you regard as your greatest weakness?" The latter question is especially troublesome if not thought through in advance. Consider a weakness that can also be a strength if properly disciplined or, at least, tell how you keep your weakness in check. Remember that the panel is asking for a quality, not an event.

Be aware of the "stress interview," a technique more common in business but not unknown in education. One writer says, "A 'stress' interview is just a regular interview with the volume turned all the way up; the music's the same, just louder." The interviewer may ask "What would you say if I told you your presentation this afternoon was lousy?" or "What is the worst thing you have heard about our school district?" The atmosphere in a stress interview is mildly hostile, the questions aggressive, but "once you learn that these questions are just amplified versions of much simpler ones, you'll remain cool and calm" (Yate, 1988).

Table 10

INTERVIEW QUESTIONS

Topic	Questions
Interviewing & selecting staff	1. What are the key qualities you look for when hiring a teacher?
Employee observation & evaluation	2. What are you looking for when you visit a classroom for formal evaluation? 3. On what basis would you as a principal like to be evaluated? 4. Describe effective teaching techniques you would look for when observing a classroom. 5. Discuss three different types of classroom observation. Tell us which you consider the most effective and why. 6. What distinguishes a good teacher from a great teacher? 7. If a teacher has classroom management problems, how would you work with the teacher to improve the situation? 8. What if you suspected a teacher or staff member had a drug problem? What action would you take? 9. One of the problems facing schools today is "teacher burnout"—the 20-year veteran who has lost interest in the profession and no longer enjoys teaching. How would you renew enthusiasm for this teacher?
Conflict Management	10. How do you handle a parent complaint regarding a teacher when the teacher is at fault? 11. A parent becomes verbally abusive to another parent in your presence. What action would you take? 12. If the drama teacher selected a play that you felt was inappropriate for your school, what would you do? 13. If a spring music festival were in rehearsal and an argument occurred between the instrumental and vocal teachers about the use of the facilities, how would you resolve the disagreement?
Leadership styles, skills, & characteristics	14. What adjectives would teachers who work with you use to describe you? 15. You are meeting with the teachers of your school for the first time. What will you say to them? 16. How do you empower teachers to become effective, productive, and valuable staff members? 17. What do you see as the most critical issues facing a principal? 18. Back-To-School-Night had very poor parent attendance. The following morning your staff votes not to support this event next year. How will you handle this situation? 19. What aspects of a principal's position do you envision consuming most of your time? 20. If you had instant power and authority, what single thing would you change in education today? What results would you expect from that change?

Topic	Questions
Leadership styles, skills, & characteristics (Cont'd)	21. What is the most important role of the principal? the biggest challenge? 22. What are your major leadership strengths? 23. What are your major areas for improvement as a leader? 24. What are your hobbies and interests? 25. School management can be very stressful. How do you deal with stress? 26. What special attributes would you bring to this position? 27. Describe an outstanding school. 28. What distinguishes a good administrator from a great administrator? 29. What would a faculty meeting at your school look like?
Students	30. What steps would you take to improve student attendance? 31. What steps would you take to improve student learning? 32. What emphasis should be placed on the athletic and co-curricular programs at your school? 33. What type of students do you like to work with? 34. What type students do you teach most effectively? 35. A student tells you he or she is being abused at home. What action would you take? 36. What methods of student discipline have you found to be most effective? 37. How would you help students develop a positive attitude about school? 38. What role does the classroom teacher play in student discipline? 39. If a student reported to you that he or she had received uncomfortable sexual overtures from a staff member, what action would you take?
Collective bargaining	40. Describe your experience in collective bargaining. 41. What is the meaning of the phrase "managing the contract"?
School finance & budgeting	42. Describe your experience in managing a budget. 43. What process would you utilize to involve, students, parents, teachers, and staff in the budget development process?
Parents	44. As a principal, what are some techniques that you would use to communicate with parents and encourage their participation in school decision-making?
Community	45. Do you see a role for a principal's participation in community activities? If not, explain. If so, explain and describe that role.
Technology	46. How would you rate your knowledge of educational technology? What role should technology play in the school's instructional program?
Creativity	47. Describe any innovative programs for which you have provided leadership.
Knowledge of education	48. How do you keep abreast of developments in education? 49. Name and briefly discuss the last two books you have read. 50. Tell us about an interesting article you read recently in a professional journal. 51. If you could change three things about the way the typical elementary/ middle/high school operates, what would you change? 52. Our school will have a state program review or accreditation visit next year. Tell us what you know of the process and what steps you will take to prepare. 53. What current trends in public education please you? Displease you? Why?

Topic	Questions
Decision-making	54. As a principal, would you honor parent requests for class assignments or class change? Why or why not? 55. Some of your parents are pressuring you to schedule a sixth-grade graduation ceremony. Your school has not had this kind of exercise in the past and you don't think graduation ceremonies are appropriate for sixth- grade students. How would you handle this situation? 56. As a new principal, what will be your top three priorities during your first three months on the job?
Staff development	57. How would you structure a staff development program for your teachers? 58. How would you describe school climate? What would be the climate of your school?
Curriculum & instruction	59. How would you ensure that district-wide curriculum programs are implemented by each teacher in your school? 60. What are the latest trends in curriculum that are exciting to you? 61. What process would you use to articulate the curriculum across grades and subject areas? 62. What are your experience and knowledge regarding special education? 63. What are your experience and philosophy regarding a gifted program? 64. What are your experience and philosophy regarding bilingual education? 65. What process should a principal use to evaluate the school's instructional program? 66. Define individualized instruction. What is its place in a school instructional program? 67. Define cooperative learning. What is its place in a school instructional program? 68. Should students be involved in curriculum development? If so, how would you involve them? 69. What do you feel is the proper role of paraprofessionals in the instructional program? 70. How should student progress be assessed? 71. Are norm-referenced tests such as the SAT9 useful? If so, how would you use the test results? If not, how would you handle its administration with students and faculty?

When (notice the word is "when," not "if") you interview for a job you do not get, call the personnel officer or someone else on the team for feedback on your papers and interview. Ask what you might have done better. Ask whether you have any nervous mannerisms that distracted the listeners. If you were taped, ask for a copy.

Finally, reflect on the ethics of interview behavior. The interview is a two-way street. The panel wants to know whether you are the best candidate for the position, and you want to know whether this school or district is a place you want to work. Of course you try to put your best foot forward, and most often, the panel members want to make their organization look good, too. Of course you want the panel to notice every point at which you have the background and qualities they seek. As you prepare, you will discover that some books and articles on job-seeking tell candidates to present themselves as the type of person wanted by the organization, whether or not that person is one's real self. As a professional of integrity who wants a fulfilling position, you must decide the extent to which you will stretch yourself to fit a particular opening.

Written Exercises

More and more, an interview is preceded or followed by one or more written exercises lasting from 30 to 60 minutes. Perhaps one to three questions will be posed that might have been asked in the interview, but are to be answered on paper. These questions often include real-life problems that will be faced by the person selected for the position; sometimes they are specific to events or problems in the school or district at that particular time. As with any writing assignment, take a few moments to jot down kernels of ideas and organize them before you begin. Ask whether the writing is timed and, if so, plan your time accordingly. Read *all* the questions before you begin, because some may require more time than others. Moreover, your mind will probably begin working on the later questions even while you are writing the first ones.

The need for strong communications skills has already been mentioned in this chapter. If your writing is not as clear and effective as you would like, consider a class or a tutor to give you some pointers. There is still no better short handbook on writing than *The Elements of Style* (Strunk & White, 1972), even if the first edition was written 70 years ago.

Geography and Money

Location and income are critical considerations in obtaining that promotion. They are sacrifices that may be required if the qualified applicant really desires to advance. Many aspiring administrators, when quizzed about their inability to land a promotion, explain that they are unwilling to seek employment more than 25 miles from their current residence. Others say that they are at the top of the teachers' salary schedule and are unwilling to take a reduction in pay. The authors do not argue that all prospective administrators must be willing to accept a job anywhere in California, or out of the state. It may not be necessary to take a reduction in salary, either. But we are making a definite statement that if one is unwilling to seek employment that may require relocation, or a reduction in pay, the opportunities for promotion are greatly diminished.

The topic of administrative salaries has been a point of much discussion in the last several years. This has been particularly true in districts that are experiencing labor disputes. For example, in the Los Angeles Unified School District, spokespersons for the union often charge that the district is top-heavy with administrators and that they are overpaid. Actually, the disparity between teaching and administrative salaries is so low that many veteran teachers see little or no monetary benefit in moving into administration. In many cases, the individual who moves into administration is expected to work a longer day and year, with little additional compensation.

When deciding upon a career in administration, one must consider such financial factors as the cost of additional education and possible cost of relocation to a new community, including the purchase of a new home. Because teachers earn additional compensation for longevity, these financial considerations are particularly troublesome the longer one has taught.

For those interested in administration but concerned with the financial sacrifices that may be needed, a longer view must be taken. While the move into administration may not be financially rewarding initially, opportunities for promotion into a higher-level position improve the financial outlook. In many districts administrators also receive extra financial benefits. These may include a transportation allowance, expanded opportunities for staff development, and improved health and welfare benefits. A higher salary also has a beneficial impact upon retirement. Nevertheless, the bottom line is that an individual who seeks a career in administration solely for financial gain will probably be disappointed.

When an individual moves to take a job, his or her family is also affected, particularly if the candidate is married or a parent with children living at home. If the spouse has a professional position or a job he or she really enjoys, the sacrifice of the move to a new location must be considered. While young children may appear less affected by a change of residence, changing schools and friends is often very difficult for teenagers. Therefore, the candidate seeking a promotion in a new location must carefully consider the impact on the family.

Total your score
Are you ready for that promotion?

If you scored 90 or higher, that assistant principal, principal, or superintendent job is for you! If you scored in the 80 to 90 range, prospects are good, but your job search may take a bit longer. If you scored below 80, carefully review your preparation and training for administration to shore up areas that will make you a more viable candidate. You may also wish to give some thought to personal decisions that have reduced your opportunity for promotion.

SUMMARY

There will be opportunities for employment as a California school administrator as we move into the next millennium. The authors estimate that approximately 4,000 positions will be available each year due to increased student enrollment and the numbers of administrators who leave the profession to seek another career or to retire. A shortage of administrative candidates has been documented, especially in California (Sandham, 2001).

For candidates who desire a career in administration, one of the first tasks should be to complete an assessment of the individual's education, training, and experience against requirements for the position. The potential administrator should possess excellent communication and organizational skills and use solid decision-making processes to reach sound judgements. Other qualities of the successful administrator include task orientation and ability to give effective leadership to a group.

However, all the skills associated with effective leadership are not enough. In addition, the aspiring administrator must get the job. Many times, job acquisition skills are not synonymous with those required to do the work. Job acquisition skills include putting together an application for a position that includes outstanding references, a superbly crafted letter of application, and a résumé that convinces the personnel director and potential supervisor of the capabilities of the candidate. To be successful, the applicant should prepare for the interview by careful attention to appearance and grooming and complete a detailed study of the school district and community. Finally, the aspiring administrator may need to consider several personal decisions that will be troublesome. These decisions may include a temporary reduction in compensation and uprooting a family to move to another location for that desired position.

KEY TERMS

1. *communicare*
2. decision-making skills
3. feedback
4. Job Information Survey (JIS)
5. judgement
6. leadership
7. letter of application
8. networking
9. paraphrasing
10. perception checking
11. references
12. résumé
13. self-assessment

QUESTIONS AND ACTIVITIES

1. The first step in deciding on a career change should be completion of a self-assessment. Discuss three key elements in a self-assessment.

2. Effective communication skills are of primary importance in effective leadership. What are the essential components in effective communication? Why are they important?

3. One type of effective leadership is referred to as "charismatic." What are the characteristics of the charismatic leader? Why is he or she effective?

4. An outstanding résumé is essential in career advancement. What are the essential elements in an outstanding résumé?

5. Effective interviewing skills are essential in career advancement. List five steps in preparing for a successful interview.

6. Complete Part 1 of the Self-Assessment. Rate your experience, training, and leadership characteristics as related to a particular administrative position. Review all the items that received a rating of 3 or less and develop a self-improvement plan in these areas.

7. Complete the same task for Part 2 of the Self-Assessment. If you do not have a placement file at your university, set a timeline for establishing the file and obtaining at least three reference letters for it.

8. Volunteer to serve on an interview panel in your school and district. Make note of the questions asked of each of the candidates. Start building a file of interview questions.

9. Seek opportunities to broaden your teaching background by volunteering to teach a different grade level or subject.

10. Practice your leadership skills by running for an office in your professional organization or volunteering to serve as chair of a school or district committee.

11. Obtain copies of the Job Information Survey and write or call for information about a position that interests you.

12. Draft a letter of application and ask your supervisor, university professor, or another trusted individual to review its contents.

13. Put together a résumé and ask the same individuals mentioned in question 12 to make suggestions for its improvement.

14. Start developing (or expanding) a network of colleagues and friends who can be of assistance when you decide to apply for an administrative position.

15. If you have not completed your master's degree, consider how this task can be accomplished. If you have completed the master's degree, consider acquiring a doctorate.

Appendix A

Websites for Professional Development

Note that Web browsers no longer require the code http:// preceding the Web address (URL). However, readers with an older version of Netscape or another browser may need to add that prefix to the following. URLs do change from time to time; should that occur, a World Wide Web search engine, such as www.google.com, can find the new location.

Professional Organizations

American Association of School Administrators (AASA)   www.aasa.org

American Association of School Personnel Administrators (AASPA)   www.aaspa.org

American Education Finance Association (AEFA)   www.aefa.org

American Educational Research Association (AERA)   www.aera.net

American Federation of State, County, and Municipal Employees (AFSCME)
www.afscme.org

American Federation of Teachers (AFT)   www.aft.org

American Library Association (ALA)   www.ala.org

American Psychological Association (APA)   www.apa.org

American School Food Service Association (ASFSA)   www.asfsa.org

Association for Supervision and Curriculum Development (ASCD)   www.ascd.org

Association of California School Administrators (ACSA)   www.acsa.org

Association of School Business Officials International (ASBO)   www.asbointl.org

California Association for Supervision and Curriculum Development (CASCD)
    www.cascd.org

California Association of School Business Officials (CASBO)   www.casbo.org

California County Superintendents Educational Services Association   www.ccsesa.org

California Federation of Teachers (CFT)   www.cft.org

California Foundation for the Improvement of Employer-Employee Relations
    (CFIER)   www.CFIER.org

California School Boards Association (CSBA)   www.csba.org

California School Counselor Association (CSCA)   www.cacd.org

California School Employees Association (CSEA)   www.csea.com

California State Parent Teacher Association (PTA)   www.capta.org

California Teachers Association (CTA)   www.cta.org

Committee for Education Funding   www.cef.org

Council of Chief State School Officers (CCSSO)   www.ccsso.org

Council of Great City Schools (CGCS)   www.cgcs.org

Education Commission of the States (ECS)   www.ecs.org

National Association for Year-Round Educators (NAYRE)   www.nayre.org

National Association of Elementary School Principals (NAESP)   www.naesp.org

National Association of Secondary School Principals (NASSP)   www.nassp.org

National Association of State Boards of Education (NASBE)   www.nasbe.org

National Association of State Directors of Teacher Education
   and Certification (NASTEC)   www.nastdec.org

National Association of Student Personnel Administrators (NASPA)   www.naspa.org

National Education Association (NEA)   www.nea.org

National PTA   www.pta.org

National Policy Board for Educational Administration (NPBEA)   www.npbea.org

National School Boards Association (NSBA)   www.nsba.org

Phi Delta Kappa   www.pdkintl.org

Pi Lambda Theta   www.pilambda.org

University Council for Educational Administration (UCEA)   www.ucea.org

Western Association of Schools and Colleges (WASC)   www.wascweb.org

Government Offices & Legislation

California Commission on Teacher Credentialing (CCTC)   www.ctc.ca.gov

California current legislation   www.sen.ca.gov/www/leginfo/SearchTest.html

California Department of Education (CDE)   www.cde.ca.gov

California Department of Finance (CDF)   www.dof.ca.gov

California Education Code   www.leginfo.ca.gov/calaw.html

California Governor's Office   www.governor.ca.gov

California Legislative Analyst   www.lao.ca.gov

California Officials, Agencies, & Laws Guide   www.ca.gov/gov/official.html

California State Assembly Education Committee	www.leginfo.ca.gov
California State Board of Education	www.cde.ca.gov/board/
California State Senate Education Committee	www.leginfo.ca.gov
Los Angeles County Schools	www.lacoe.edu
National Assessment of Educational Progress (NAEP)	www.nces.ed.gov
Office of Elementary and Secondary Education	www.ed.gov/offices/OESE
Riverside County Superintendent of Schools	www.RCOE.k12.ca.us
San Bernardino County Schools	www.sbcss.K12.ca.us
San Diego County Schools	www.sdcoe.K12.ca.us
THOMAS: U. S. Legislative Information	thomas.loc.gov
U. S. Department of Education (USDOE)	www.ed.gov
U. S. House of Representatives	www.house.gov
U. S. Senate	www.senate.gov
White House	www.whitehouse.gov

Research Organizations

4Children	www.4children.org
Beginning Teacher Support and Assessment (BTSA)	www.btsa.ca.gov
California Ballot Propositions	www.uchastings.edu/library/ballotprops
California Business Roundtable	http://www.cbrt.org/education.html
California Census Data Center	www.census.ca.gov

California State Library   www.library.ca.gov

Center for Applied Research and Educational Improvements (CAREI)
                                                                            carei/coled.umn.edu

Center for Education Reform   www.edreform.com

Children Now   www.childrennow

Ed-Data: CA K-12 Schools   www.ed-data.k12.ca.us/

EdSource   www.edsource.org

Education Policy Institute   www.educationpolicy.org

Education Week   www.edweek.org

Education World   www.education-world.com

Educational Research Service (ERS)   www.ers.org

Educators Net   www.educatorsnet.com

ERIC Clearinghouse on Educational Management   eric.uoregon.edu

ERIC index to microfiche documents and journals   searcheric.org

ERIC Educational Resources Information Center   www.eric.ed.gov

Fiscal Crisis and Management Assistance Team (FCMAT)   www.kern.org/fcmat
    This resource is highlighted, as it provides links to several other sources of
    information: CASBO, legislative bills, Education Code and other California codes,
    California Department of Education, and so on.

Institute for Educational Leadership   www.iel.org

Library of Congress   www.lcweb.loc.gov

Los Angeles Times   www.latimes.com

National Assessment Governing Board   www.nagb.org

National Center for Educational Statistics (NCES)   www.nces.ed.gov

National Center for Policy Analysis (NCPA)   www.ncpa.org

Policy Analysis for California Education (PACE)
                          http://www-gse.berkeley.edu/research/PACE/pace.html

Rand Corporation   www.rand.org

Sandia National Laboratories   www.sandia.gov

School Services of California   www.sscal.com

U. S. A. Today   www.usatoday.com

U. S. Census Bureau   www.census.gov

U. S. Charter Schools   www.uscharterschools.org

WestEd   www.wested.org

Statewide Business and Community-Based Organizations

American Association of University Women (AAUW)   www.ca-aauw.org

California Business Roundtable   www.cbrt.org

California Consortium of Education Foundations   Phone (415) 326-7751

California State Chamber of Commerce   Phone (916) 444-6685

League of Women Voters of California   www.ca.lwv.org

Other Websites for Staff Development

Andy Carvin's EdWeb   edweb.gsn.org/lists.html
>   Andy Carvin's EdWeb site bills itself as a "hyperbook" that focuses on educational
>   reform and technology. It contains a list of over 100 education-related "listservs."
>   The page includes basic information on how the lists operate and how to subscribe.

CalTeach   www.calteach.com
>   This service assists teachers and administrators to locate positions in California.

EdWeb   edweb.gsn.org/lists.html
>   EdWeb also offers an online tutorial for teachers and administrators who want to
>   learn to create their own Web pages. The tutorial covers design basics and includes
>   HTML quizzes at the bottom of each lesson.

GLOSSARY

Ability to pay - A wage determination based upon the ability of the employer to meet a particular wage rate.

Absenteeism - Failure of employees to maintain a certain level of presence at the work site.

Academic freedom - The ability of professional personnel to exercise intellectual independence and to encourage it in the classroom without impediment or undue restraint.

Accreditation - Recognition given by an agency or association to an institution or place of business that meets criteria or standards established by the agency or association.

Administrative theory - A set of concepts that guides administrative behavior and influences choices from among alternative courses of action.

Adverse impact - Employment discrimination that occurs when a disproportionate number of a legislatively-protected group (e.g., women, minorities, or senior citizens) are rejected for employment, placement, or promotion.

Advisory arbitration - A process in which an impartial third party, having no stake in the outcome, hears all sides to a dispute and renders a recommendation that is not binding on either side.

Affirmative action - Programs to ensure job success for minorities, women, and the handicapped, with intent to make up for past injustices toward these groups.

Agency fee - A fee paid by all members of the bargaining unit, whether or not they wish to join or be a member of the organization. Since closed shop is illegal in California, union membership is not required, but if an agency fee is agreed to by contract, each member of the unit must pay the fee. An exception may be made on valid religious grounds.

Agency shop - A security provision in a collective bargaining contract that strengthens the union by requiring nonunion members in a bargaining unit, as a condition of employment, to pay a sum equal to the union's fees and dues.

Agreement - Mutual understanding or contract between a union and company or their representatives establishing the terms and conditions of employment.

Arbitration - Process that involves an impartial third party who collects pertinent facts from disputants and proceeds to make recommendations based on the findings. Arbitration may be advisory or binding, depending on the terms of the contract.

Arbitration, advisory - see Advisory arbitration
Arbitration, binding - see Binding arbitration

Arbitrator - A third and impartial party to whom disputing parties submit their differences.

Assessment center - An organization or program that uses simulations and activities to test individuals to determine if they have the skills and traits necessary for a certain position.

Bargaining (adversarial) - Collective bargaining focused on gaining a favorable position in contract negotiations (e.g., higher/lower salary, reduced/increased workload) with the result that board and union representatives attempt to prevail over one other.

Bargaining (collaborative) - Collective bargaining built on the premise that both sides, the school board and the union, desire to cooperative to achieve a satisfactory contract settlement. Participants must collaborate to establish agreed-upon ground rules for negotiations. This bargaining strategy focuses on problem-solving, communicating interests and priorities, and building trust. Collaborate bargaining attempts to focus on issues, rather than personalities.

Bargaining (traditional) - Collective bargaining based on the industrial model. It is characterized by official bargaining terms: formal exchanges of initial positions within a narrowly defined scope of bargaining; subsequent proposals that are exchanged until a compromise settlement is reached; face-to-face negotiations with chief negotiators; and caucuses for consultative purposes. Traditional bargaining is generally considered to be adversarial in nature.

Bargaining (win-win) - A set of principles that supports successful negotiations in which both parties win. The four principles associated with win-win bargaining include: focusing on problems, not issues; focusing on interests, not positions; seeking options to satisfy the interests of both parties; and evaluating results on objective standards.

Bargaining unit - The positions, job titles, or functions with a community of interest that defines the group of employees appropriate to join together in collective bargaining.

Beneficiary - A person named in either a life insurance policy or a retirement document to receive benefits under the plan.

Benefit - Collateral or fringe benefits are certain direct or indirect forms of compensation that do not require additional services to be performed beyond those required under the basic compensation structure.

Binding arbitration - A process in which an impartial third party, having no stake in the outcome, hears all sides to a dispute and renders a final decision that is binding upon the parties.

Bilingual/multilingual education - A series of programs for students with a primary language other than English to learn the basics of speaking, reading, writing, and mathematics in their primary language and transfer this acquired knowledge into the English language as soon as practical for the individual learner; sometimes, a program in which speakers of English and another language learn both languages in the same classroom.

Bonus - Additional compensation not part of the regular salary payment.

California Basic Skills Test - see CBEST

Career ladder - A series of related positions that move up the hierarchy of levels in an organization.

Career planning - Organizational program to assist position holders in considering their interests, capabilities, personality, and objectives in relation to career opportunities.

CBEST - The California Basic Skills Test, required of anyone who seeks certification as a teacher. The test includes reading, writing, and mathematics.

Certificated employee - An employee of a school district who retains a position that requires certification in the form of a license and/or credential issued by the state.

Certification - Recognition by an official agency that a labor organization is the designated agency for the purposes of collective bargaining.

Chemical dependency - A need for drugs (including alcohol) that may interfere with employment or performance.

Civil Rights Act (1964) - see Equal Employment Opportunity and Title VII

Classified employee - An employee of a school district who does not need state certification; generally associated with the classifications of secretary, clerk, aide, maintenance person, custodian, and similar non-instructional positions.

Closed shop - A provision in a collective bargaining agreement under which an employer may hire only union members and retain only union members in good standing. The closed shop is illegal under federal law for industries and businesses engaged in interstate commerce. The closed shop is not a permissible form of organizational security under the Rodda Act in California.

Cohort - In a demographic study, a group of individuals having a statistical factor (e.g., age or class membership) in common.

Collective bargaining (SB 160, 1975) - A process concerned with negotiation, administration, interpretation, and enforcement of written agreements covering joint understandings as to wages or salaries, rates of pay, hours of work, and other conditions of employment.

Comparable worth - A set of criteria applied consistently across an organization to determine the relative value of jobs, for example, the duties and salary of a secretary in relation to those of a custodian.

Compensation cafeteria - A set of choices in pay or benefits from which an employee may select those most beneficial for that individual.

Compensation management, also known as wage and salary administration - The development and implementation of policies to ensure that employees are paid fairly for their efforts.

Concerted activities - Actions such as slowdowns, sickouts, or strikes undertaken by employees in a group for the purpose of pressuring management.

Conciliation - The effort expended to get parties in dispute to agree.

Confidential employees - Employees who have access to and/or possess information relating to employer-employee relations within the scope of their duties, (e.g. superintendent's and assistant superintendents' secretaries).

Consumer Price Index (CPI), also know as cost-of-living index - Measure of changes in the prices of services and goods purchased by wage earners and workers.

Contract administration - Administration of the agreed-upon contract between the district and the union (e.g., hours of work or extra duty assignments); a process requiring interpretation and implementation of contract provisions and incorporating previous contract interpretations. Principals and classified supervisors play a major role in the day-to-day management of terms of the contract. Grievance machinery is employed to resolve contractual disputes.

Corrective - An approach to discipline that uses progressive counseling as a method to enable the employee to cooperate with management.

Cost-of-Living Index - see Consumer Price Index

Craft union - A labor union of workers who have been united by particular craft or skill, e.g., wood-crafters.

Credit union - A financial institution formed by employees who join together for mutual financial benefit, particularly savings and low-interest loans.

Decentralized organization - An organization in which a high degree of authority is delegated to lower levels of personnel.

Decertification - The opposite of certification; recognition by an official agency that a labor organization has ceased to serve as the designated agency for purposes of collective bargaining in consequence of an election to that effect among employees in a bargaining unit.

Defamation - The act of holding a person up for ridicule, scorn, or contempt that would injure that individual's reputation. Defamation, which includes both libel and slander, is a civil wrong.

Deferred compensation - An amount paid to an employee at a particular time after regular pay ceases; usually reserved for executives and paid upon retirement or otherwise leaving the organization .

Development - Broadening of an individuals's knowledge, understanding, and attributes along with judgement, analytical powers, ability to make decisions, and similar general skills.

Discrimination - To treat unequally or unfairly; an illegal practice that utilizes ethnicity, race, religion, national origin, or sex as a basis for hiring or firing.

Dismissal - A personnel action initiated by the district to sever an employment relationship.

Due process - A process that guarantees rights of system members and protects the union against infringement of employment rights. Due process requires that a party show "just cause" and use "rules of reasonableness."

Education Code - The body of law that regulates California education.

Educational Employment Relations Act of 1975 - see EERA

EEO - A federal requirement, established in the Civil Rights Act of 1964, that no discrimination occur against an individual because of race, color, sex, religion, or national origin.

EERA, also known as the Rodda Act or SB160. Educational Employment Relations Act of 1975, the law that mandates collective bargaining and establishes scope of representation for employees of public school districts, kindergarten through community college, in California.

EERB - see PERB

Employee Counseling - A process to help employees identify and address topics that may or may not be related to their employment, such topics spanning financial, family, crisis, career, job placement, pre-retirement, and legal concerns.

Employer-employee relations - The interaction and communication between employer and employees, especially with regard to contract management, grievance resolution, arbitration, and progressive discipline.

Equal Employment Opportunity - see EEO

Exclusive representation - The employee organization recognized or certified by the Public Employment Relations Board as the exclusive negotiating representative of certificated or classified employees in an appropriate unit of a public school employer.

Fact-finding - A process in which an impartial third party, having no stake in the outcome, and after investigating and analyzing relevant information and actions, makes recommendations for settlement of a grievance or dispute in a report to the employer and employee representative.

Fair Employment Practices - Employment law containing requirements for equal employment opportunities for minorities, women, and the handicapped.

Flexible work hours - Work schedules that allow for variations in starting and ending times and work days with individual schedules established by employees, within guidelines, to meet personal needs or desires.

Flextime - see Flexible work hours

Formative appraisal/evaluation - Ongoing employee appraisal aimed at improving the performance of position holders.

Good faith bargaining - Collective bargaining in which an employer and an employee organization discuss and exchange proposals in a sincere and honest effort to reach a contract agreement on matters within the scope of bargaining.

Grievance procedure - A procedure established by the collective bargaining agreement for resolution of disputes relative to an alleged contract violation.

Human resources - Employees in an organization; a concept giving rise to the title Director of Human Resources, rather than Director of Personnel.

Human resource training - Programs established to improve job-related training.

Impasse - A point in collective bargaining at which a party to the negotiations declares that the differences in their positions are substantial and that future meetings would be futile.

In-basket exercise - A simulation built on a mailbox scenario in which several decisions are required in a limited period of time.

Incentive payment - An amount paid to an employee over and above the regular salary in recognition of particularly effective job performance.

Induction - A systematic organizational plan to assist personnel to adjust readily and effectively to a new assignment so that they can contribute maximally to the work of the system while realizing personal and position satisfaction.

Informal organization - A power structure, apart from the official authority structure, that may involve one or more subgroups or all employees within the organization.

Initial proposal - A written offer for consideration, made by either an exclusive representative or the school district, on a matter within the scope of representation that has not previously been introduced into the collective negotiations process for the next agreement.

Injunction - A court order restraining individuals or groups from committing acts that a court determines may do irreparable harm. There are several types of injunctions: (a) a temporary restraining order, issued for a limited time prior to a hearing; (b) a preliminary injunction pending trial of a case; (c) a permanent injunction, ordered after all the issues have been heard on the merits in the actual case and as part of the remedial judgement.

Inservice education - Planned programs of learning opportunities afforded staff members for the purpose of improving performance in already-assigned positions.

Job analysis - Identification of particular characteristics of a job to ensure successful performance.

Job classification - A system to establish classes of positions based on particular skills needed to meet job tasks or specifications.

Job description - A document that lists specific tasks to be performed by an employee who holds the position, specific requirements for the position, and job titles of employees who will be supervised by and who will supervise the position.

Job enrichment - A means of making jobs more attractive by upgrading them in pay, level of responsibility, or prospects for advancement.

Just cause - A term usually used in litigation to imply the intensity of a person's commitment and how the individual may act in a given circumstance or situation.

Labor-intensive - A term describing a business or organization in which most of the resources go to labor, for example, schools.

Labor relations - see Employer-employee relations

Last, best offer - The final proposal by each party, at the end of the collective bargaining process.

Line relationship - Term describing positions along a defined line of authority, for example, the hierarchy in public education with the board of education at the top and the line of authority descending through the superintendent to the remaining management team and on to certificated and classified employees.

Maintenance-of-membership agreement - Provision in a collective bargaining agreement to the effect that workers in a union are to be members for the duration of the labor agreement or contract.

Management by objectives - see MBO

Management employee - Any employee in a position having significant responsibilities for formulating district policies or administering district programs. Management positions shall be designated by the public school employer subject to review by PERB.

Management rights clause - Section in a collective bargaining agreement reserving specific rights, or all rights not otherwise addressed, to management.

Manpower planning and balanced staffing - A process of providing the right number of people with the right qualifications at the right place, and at the right time, with a view to fulfilling organizational, as well as individual, objectives.

MBO - Management by objectives; a goal-based management process in which specific goals are established, by management or by mutual agreement with the employee, that employees attempt to reach.

Mediation - Third-party intervention during an impasse. Mediation is the first step of impasse resolution in most collective bargaining laws and involves an attempt to have both parties reach agreement or resolve the issue.

Memorandum of agreement - A short note of agreement, usually to become part of, or supplementary to, the collective bargaining contract.

Memorandum of understanding - A written agreement between the public agency and a public employee organization setting forth agreed-to terms and conditions of employment.

Mentor - An individual, often at a higher level in an organization, who helps others reach their individual goals.

Mentor program - A program established to enable outstanding, experienced teachers to serve as coaches, guides, and/or role models, especially for beginning teachers. The program is designed to enhance instructional performance. Mentor teacher programs entail special incentives for those serving as mentors.

Minority - Part of a population differing from others in some characteristic (cultural, economic, political, religious, sexual, or racial) and often subjected to differential treatment.

Motivation - Internal or external forces that influence an individual's willingness to achieve performance expectations.

Negotiations (in collective bargaining) - A process of joint decision-making between a school board and an employees' representative to establish mutually acceptable compensation and conditions of employment.

Networking - Communication among individuals for mutual benefit.

Nonexempt employees - Employees who are salaried and not eligible for union membership.

Objectives - A statement of what is to be accomplished, for what purpose, to what extent, by whom, with what resources, and within what time frame. Objectives should be measurable and linked to broad system aims and strategies.

Occupational Safety and Health Act - see OSHA

Ombudsman - A public official appointed to investigate complaints against an agency that may be infringing upon the rights of individuals.

Organization chart - A graphic representation of functions, accountability, responsibility, relationships, and levels of various positions in the organizational structure.

Organizational culture - Values, standards, and attitudes of appropriate conduct and fair treatment established and reinforced by the organization and system members.

OSHA- Occupational Safety and Health Act of 1970, governing working situations and enforced by a state agency.

PERB - Public Employee Relations Board, established by the Rodda Act to certify bargaining representatives and to review appeals related to collective bargaining, especially with respect to scope of representation and unfair labor practices; originally formed as the Educational Employment Relations Board (EERB), then reorganized as the Public Employment Relations Board, and finally given its present name.

Performance appraisal review - Employee evaluation based on actual performance compared with pre-established goals and measurement criteria.

PERS - Public Employment Retirement System, California's retirement system for classified employees.

Personnel administration - A specific field of administration wherein the primary focus is the allocation of human resources toward achievement of the school district's established goals and the allocation of rewards to school personnel.

Personnel administrator - A district-level administrator who has major responsibility for the personnel program, with title and rank sometimes Personnel Director and sometimes Assistant Superintendent, Personnel, but differing from district to district.

Personnel Commission - A three-member body appointed in accordance with Education Code provisions and responsible for administering the Merit System provisions of the code as they apply to classified employees.

Personnel function - One of the major functions of school administration, including these processes: planning, bargaining, recruitment, selection, induction, development, appraisal, compensation, justice, continuity, and information.

Personnel policies - Guidelines adopted by the board of education to give broad direction to a course of action, stating what is wanted and perhaps why and how much, but allowing discretionary action by administrators to meet day-to-day needs of the district.

Personnel screening - A step in the employment process in which applicants are eliminated who do not fulfill the requirements for employment in a particular position.

Picketing - Actions, often in conjunction with a work stoppage, by which employees protest or proclaim certain concerns by carrying placards and walking in a designated location. Picketing sometimes takes place in front of a board member's place of business, urging clients not to patronize the business.

Placement - The process of allocating newly selected employees to specific duties and responsibilities in an organization.

Policy - Broad statements of organizational intent that establish guidelines to govern the scope and boundaries of administrative decisions. There are, for example, compensation policies to govern base pay, benefits, substitutes, and employee assignments and leaves.

Privacy of Information Act (1974) - Legislation forbidding public dissemination of confidential information regarding employees.

Progressive discipline - A series of disciplinary actions starting with a verbal warning and progressing to more serious consequences for repeated infractions of the rules.

Protected class - Any group, or member of that group, protected by anti-discrimination laws.

Public Employee Relations Board - see PERB

Public Employment Retirement System - see PERS

Punitive damages - Sums of money awarded by a court to punish a party for its acts of violence, oppression, malice, fraud, or wanton and wicked conduct.

Quality circles - Meetings of a work group that are conducted regularly to identify and resolve problems in the workplace.

Quid Pro Quo - In bargaining, the practice whereby each side relinquishes something in an equal give and take; Latin for "something for something."

Ranking - Merit applied to rating the performance of employees.

Ratification - Usually applied to a vote by union employees to accept a collective bargaining agreement.

Reading Instruction Competence Assessment - see **RICA**

Recall petition - An attempt to schedule an election to replace a previously elected public official. In this process a petition is circulated, requiring a specific number of signatures. If the petition meets the required standards, a special election is scheduled in which voters have opportunity to retain the official or remove him or her from the elected position.

Recognition - An agreement by the school board to accept an organization as the exclusive bargaining agent for a designated group of employees. Within a single organization, each group may have only one exclusive bargaining agent.

Recruiting - Activities to seek and attract a large supply of candidates from whom to select employees.

Reduction in force - Temporary or permanent separation of employees from the workforce, possibly a result of recession or other financial factors necessitating reduction in personnel.

Reopeners - A contractual agreement to reopen negotiations on a limited number of items at the end of each year of a multi-year contract. Usually reopeners involve wages, pension plans, fringe benefits, or one or two other items agreeable to both parties.

Release Time - With respect to collective bargaining, time away from an employee's regular job duties when meeting and negotiating or processing a grievance. Under SB160, a reasonable number of employees shall have the right to receive reasonable periods of release time, without loss of compensation, when engaged in collective bargaining activities.

Resignation - A voluntary decision by a position holder to sever an employment relationship.

Retirement - The act of leaving district employment with continuing financial support following completion of a specified number of years of service and/or reaching a certain age.

RICA - A test required of multiple-subject credential candidates in California since 1998.

Rodda Act - see EERA

Salary - Compensation for services rendered by an employee, usually referring to fulltime employment as opposed to parttime or hourly wages.

SB160 - see EERA

Scope of representation - Topics for collective bargaining as defined in the Rodda Act and interpreted by the Public Employee Relations Board.

Screening - see Personnel screening

Selection- The choice of a person to be offered employment in the district, following a process to match the most qualified candidate with a particular job opening.

Sexual Harassment - Unwelcome sexual advances, often interpreted as a condition of employment or advancement.

Seniority - The length of service that an employee has given to a district; may refer to length of service in a specific classification.

Side letter - An addendum to the collective bargaining contract that addresses a specific situation or concern and is agreed upon by both parties.

Staff - Employees of a school or district, usually including both certificated and classified employees.

Staff development - Systematic means for continuous development of performance capabilities of personnel. The philosophical underpinning of staff development is that all employees should continue to improve job performance skills to meet changing job requirements.

Staff relationship - The role of advisor or consultant to administration, helping to facilitate decision-making without line authority in the hierarchy of the district.

Stalemate - In collective bargaining, a term used when the employee or district representative cannot agree and appear unable to make further progress.

Step analysis - An analysis of the number of staff on each step of the salary schedule to determine personnel costs for the next year. New employees, those leaving the district, and step and column increases are considered.

Stress interview - A recruitment/selection interview technique designed to identify candidates who are capable of reacting in a calm and composed manner in tense, uncomfortable, and pressure-driven situations.

Strike - A temporary work stoppage consisting of withdrawal from the workplace.

STRS - State Teachers Retirement System, California's certificated employee retirement fund.

State Teachers Retirement System - see STRS

Stull Act - The California law that requires certificated employees to develop annual goals and objectives. The law is intended to establish a uniform system of evaluation and assessment of the performance of certificated employees.

Style of Leadership - A leader's mode of leading others, often characterized as autocratic, democratic, or laissez-faire.

Summative appraisal/evaluation - A personnel appraisal given at the end of an evaluation period, usually the end of a school year. Timelines for summative evaluation are often contained in the collective bargaining agreement.

Sunset - The end or expiration of specific programs or provisions in the Education Code (e.g. bilingual education, school improvement program). Continuation of a sunsetted program requires legislative action.

Sunshine - In collective bargaining, a requirement that initial proposals by the district and the union be made available for public inspection.

Systems theory - A view of organizations as series of interrelated components that work together toward established goals.

Tenure - A system designed to provide educators with employment security during satisfactory service. Causes and procedures for dismissal of tenured employees are defined in the Education Code.

Termination - Severance of an employment relationship.

Thirty-nine month rule - A legal stipulation that—if staff positions are eliminated for economic reasons, then reinstated—the persons previously in the positions have the first right of refusal for those positions for 39 months. If an employee leaves a district for any reason and returns to the district within 39 months, he or she is entitled to his or her former placement on the salary schedule, but not to tenure.

Title VII of the Civil Rights Act (1964) - Federal legislation designed to eliminate discrimination in organizations based on race, color, religion, sex, or national origin.

Tort - An act or omission that results in injury, damage, or loss to an injured person or persons. It is a civil wrong and may be intentional or unintentional.

Training - Imparting of factual knowledge and specific job-related skills to increase an individual's aptitudes, skills, and abilities to perform specific jobs.

Turnover - Resignation from, dismissal from, or abandonment of position by employees leaving the service of an organization, often calculated as rate of those leaving in proportion to the total workforce.

Unemployment compensation - A system to provide assistance, usually paid weekly, to employees who have been terminated from employment.

Unfair labor practice - An action by an employer or union that is prohibited by federal or state labor relations statutes.

Union shop - A type of security for a union in which a newly employed individual must become a member of the union within a given number of days, typically 30.

Vocational rehabilitation - Training of the handicapped so they may perform useful work.

Wage and salary administration - see Compensation management

Wage survey - Wage study involving collection, tabulation, and analysis of data by geographic area, industry, or type of organization.

Winton Act - The 1965 California legislation requiring districts to **meet and confer** with teacher organizations on an ongoing basis. This act was superseded when collective bargaining came into existence through the Rodda Act in 1975.

Worker's compensation - Monetary benefits provided to an employee on a regular basis during part or all of a period of disability following physical injury in the performance of his or her duties.

Y-Rate - A salary freeze, typically invoked when adjustments are made for a given position, which is sustained until the salary schedule catches up to the employee's current higher salary.

Zipper clause - A statement in the collective bargaining agreement that precludes further negotiations during the life of a signed contract.

References

1992 deskbook encyclopedia of American school law. (1992). Rosemount, MN: Data Research.

Abbot, J. (1990). *New approaches to collective bargaining and workplace relations: Do they work?* National Law Institute.

AFT on the issues: Merit pay. (2001, May 8). [On-line]. Available: www.aft.org/issues/meritpay/ hurmoil.html

Alexander, I. E. (1990). *Personology: method and content of personality assessment and psychobiography.* Durham, NC: Duke University Press.

Alexander, K., & Alexander, M. (1992). *The law of schools, students, and teachers.* St. Paul, MN: West Publishing Co.

AASPA: American Association of School Personnel Administrators. (1988). *Standards for school personnel administration.* Foster City, CA: Author.

American Federation of Teachers. (2000). Average teacher salary in 1999-2000. [On-line]. Available: http://www.aft.org

Andelson, S. J. (1995). *FRISK documentation model.* Torrance, CA: Four Star Printing & Graphics.

Andreson, K. M., & Durant, O. (1991). Training managers of classified personnel. *Journal of Staff Development, 12*(1), 56-59.

Applegate, J. (1996, November 26). Disney training draws serious following *Los Angeles Times,* D9.

Ashby, L. W., McGinnis, J. E., & Pering, T. E. (1972). *Common sense in negotiations in public education.* Danville, IL: Interstate Printers and Publishers.

Austin, G. R. (1979). Exemplary schools and the search for effectiveness. *Educational Leadership, 37*(1), 10-14.

Baird, L., Meshoulam, I., & DeGive, G. (1983). Meshing human resources planning with strategic business planning: A model approach. *Personnel, 60*(5), 14-25.

Barker, J. A. (1992). *Future edge.* New York: Morrow.

Barley, S. R., (1983). Semiotics and the study of occupational and organizational cultures. *Administrative Science Quarterly, 28,* 393-413.

Barnard, C. I. (1938). *The functions of the executive.* Cambridge, MA: Harvard University Press.

Beatty, R. W., Baird, L. S., & Schneier, C. E. (1995). The performance, measurement, management, and appraisal sourcebook. Amherst, MA: Human Resource Development Press.

Bennis, W., & Nanus, B. (1985). *Leaders: The strategies for taking charge.* New York: Harper & Row.

Bernardin, H. J., & Beatty, R. W. (1984). *Performance appraisal: Assessing human behavior at work.* Boston: Kent Publishing Co.

Birdsall, P. (1998). Clue Update. [On-line]. Available: edu.sb-supt-schools,roy-c-hill,pd

Birdsall, P., Brown, D., Lalich, S., Robinson, N., Wadsworth, H., & Wasco, L. (1998). *School program update resource book 1998.* Sacramento, CA: California Institute for School Improvement.

Bishop, T. (1987). Merit pay redefined: Motivating the whole school. *Thrust for Educational Leadership, 17*(3), 12-15.

Black, H. C. (1991). *Black's law dictionary* (6th ed.). St. Paul, MN: West Publishing.

Bolton, D. L. (1973). *Selection and evaluation of teachers.* Berkeley, CA: McCutchan.

Bond, K. (1985). The teacher assessment center. *Thrust for Educational Leadership, 15*(3), 19-20.

Bradley, A. (1998). California revises training for new teachers. *Education Week,* October. [On-line]. Available: http://www.feaunited.org/news/107-4.html

Bradley, A. (1996, September 4). Class-size cuts sets off hiring spree in California. Education Week, 1, 29.

Braegar, Don. (2001, September). 1999-2000 annual report: Emergency permits and credential waivers. [On-line]. Available: www.ctc.ca.gov/reports/annual.rep.epw.1999-2000

Bragdon, H. W., & McCutchen, S. E. (1961). *History of a free people.* New York: Macmillan.

Bridges, E. M. (1992). *The incompetent teacher: Managerial responses* (Rev. ed.). Washington, DC: Falmer Press.

Bridges, E. M. & Groves, B. (1984). *The identification, remediation and dismissal of incompetent teachers.* Burlingame, CA: Association of California School Administrators, Foundation for Educational Administration.

Brookover, W. (1984). *A school learning assessment instrument.* East Lansing, MI: Michigan State University Press.

Brookover, W. B., & Lezotte, L. (1980). *Changes in school characteristics coincident with changes in student achievement.* East Lansing: Michigan State University, College of Urban Development.

Burden, P. R., & Wallace, D. (1983). *Tailoring staff development to meet teacher needs.* Paper presented at the meeting of the Association of Teacher Educators, Wichita, KS. (ERIC Document Reproduction Service No. ED 237 506)

California Dept. of Education, Educational Demographics Unit. (2000). *Public school summary statistics 1999-2000.* [On-line]. Available: http://www.cde.ca.gov/ftpbranch/sbsdir/ demographics/reports/statewide/sums97.htm

Campbell, R. (1984). *The organization and control of American schools.* Columbus, OH: Merrill.

Candoli, I. C., Hack, W. G., & Ray, J. R. (1992). *School business administration: A planning approach* (4th ed.). Boston: Allyn & Bacon.

Cangelosi, J. S. (1991). *Evaluating classroom instruction.* New York: Longman.

Carter, Chelsea J. (2001, September 11). Report shows teaching grads feel unprepared. *North County Times*, p. A7.

Center for the Future of Teeaching and Learning. (2000). The status of the teaching profession. Author. [On-line]. Available: http://www.CFTL.org

Charter schools' quality, access blasted in UCLA study. (1998). *EdCal, 28*(19), 1-2.

Chisholm, L., & Tamm, J. (1993). Does interest bargaining really work? A test using PERB data. *California Public Employee Relations, 101*, 3-7.

Clear, D. K. (1978, December). Negative statements in letters of recommendation: from defamation to defense. *NASSP Bulletin,* 34-43.

Cogan, M. (1973). *Clinical supervision.* Boston: Houghton-Mifflin.

Colvin, L. D., & Woo, E. (1998, May 19). No one knows if money is well spent. *Los Angeles Times.*

Colvin, R. (1999, January 31). Toledo mentors California in peer review of teachers. *Los Angeles Times*, p.A28.

Colvin, R. (2001, December 7). Charter schools' success elusive, study says. *Los Angeles Times*, p. A37.

Covey, S. (1989). *The seven habits of highly effective people: Powerful lessons in personal change.* New York: Simon & Schuster.

Currence, C. (1984, August 29). Shanker urges A.F.T. to move against incompetent teachers. *Education Week*, 1.

Daniszewski, John. (2001, September 2). Putin gives teachers a big boost. *Los Angeles Times*, p. A3.

Daresh, J. C. (1989). *Supervision as a proactive process*. New York: Longman.

Davies, D. R., & Armistead, C. D. (1975). *Inservice education: Current trends in school policies and programs*. Arlington, VA: National School Public Relations Association.

Deal, T. E., & Kennedy, A. A. (1992). *Corporate cultures: The rites and rituals of corporate life*. Reading, MA: Addison-Wesley.

Deming, W. E. (1986). *Out of crisis*. Cambridge, MA: Massachusetts Institute of Technology, Center for Advanced Engineering Study.

Duffy, P. S. (1975). Educational policy and the law. *Thrust, 1*(5), 27-29.

Duke, D. L., & Stiggins, R. J. (1986). *Teacher evaluation: Five keys to growth*. A joint publication of American Association of School Administrators, National Association of Elementary School Principals, National Association of Secondary School Principals, National Education Association. Washington, D.C.: National Education Association.

Dyson, R. G. (1990). *Strategic planning: Models and analytical techniques*. New York: Wiley.

Education Commission of the States. (1980). *Cuebook II: State education collective bargaining laws*. Denver, CO: Author.

Fischer, D. F., & Shipley, M. E. (1995). Improving beginning teacher success: Implications for school administration preparation programs. *The Journal of CAPEA, 7*, 35-44.

Fisher, R., & Ury, W. (1981). *Getting to yes: Negotiating agreement without giving in*. New York: Penguin Books.

Fitch, M. E., & Kopp, O. W. (1990). *Staff development for the practitioner*. Springfield, IL: Charles C. Thomas.

Follett, M. P. (1924). *Creative experience*. New York: Longman Green.

Fromach, J. W. (1992, March). Negotiating alternative fringe benefit plans. *California Association of School Business Officials Journal*, 15-17.

Frost, P. J. (1985). *Organizational culture*. Beverly Hills, CA: Sage Publishing.

Fullan, M. (1993). *Change forces*. London: Falmer Press.

Fullan, M. (1998a, November). *Successful change in action.* Paper presented at the meeting of the Association of California School Administrators, Santa Clara, CA.

Fullan, M. (1998b, November). *What's worth fighting for out there.* Paper presented at the meeting of the Association of California School Administrators, Santa Clara, CA.

Gates, J. (1985). *The traditional bargaining model: The givers and the takers.* Washington State School Directors Association.

Gellman, E. (1992) The use of portfolios in assessing teacher competence; Measurement issues. *Action in Teacher Education 14*(4), 39-44.

Glatthorn, Allan A. (1984). *Differentiated supervision.* Alexandria, VA: Association for Supervision and Curriculum Development.

Glickman, C. D. (1990). *Supervision of instruction: A developmental approach* (2nd ed.). Boston: Allyn and Bacon.

Goldaber, I. (1987). *The Goldaber win/win contract development: A thirty day process.* Miami: Center for the Practice of Conflict Management.

Goldhammer, R. (1969). *Clinical supervision: Special methods for the supervision of teachers.* New York: Holt Rinehart and Winston. A second edition was published in 1980.

Gonder, P. O. (1981). *Collective bargaining: Problems and solutions.* Arlington, VA: American Association of School Administrators.

Goodwin, J. P., & Hensley, R. P. (1997). *Professional employment portfolios.* Muncie, IN: Ball State University. [On-line] Available: www.bsu.edu/careers/portfoli.html.

Gorton, R. (1986). *School leadership and administration: Important concepts, case studies, and simulations* (3rd ed.). Dubuque, IA: Brown.

Green, J. E. (1971). *School personnel administration.* New York: Chilton Book Co.

Greenberg, S., & Bello, R. (1992). Rewrite job descriptions: Focus on functions. *HR Focus, 69*(7), 6.

Grimes, A. (2000, September 23). Internet is hotbed of online education. *North County Times*, p. D6.

Groves, M. (1996, November 24). Southwest Airlines' Kelleher still flying in the face of convention. *Los Angeles Times*, D5.

Guskey, T. R., & Sparks, D. (1991). What to consider when evaluating staff development. *Educational Leadership, 49*, 41-44.

Hamilton, H. (1988, January). The impossible: A labor contract in two days . . . or is it? *Thrust for Educational Leadership, 17*, 49-51.

Hartmeister, F. (1995). *Surviving as a teacher: The legal dimension.* Chicago, IL: Precept Press.

Helfand, D. (2000a, December 8). Teacher shortage hitting inner cities hardest, study says. *Los Angeles Times.*

Helfand, D. (2000b, December 28). Group plans to launch online K-12 curriculum. *Los Angeles Times*, p. A4.

Helm, V. M. (1994). *Multi-faceted data collection: The key to evaluating school counselors and other support professionals.* Paper presented at the meeting of the American Educational Research Association, New Orleans, LA. (ERIC Document Reproduction Service ED 376 411)

Hersey, P. W., & Beers, D. C. (1989). *Skill development for school leaders.* Reston, VA: National Association of Secondary School Principals.

Hertsgaard, M. (1998). Earth worst [Review of the book *The future in plain sight; Nine clues to the coming instability*]. *Los Angeles Times*   get date and page nos.

Herzberg, F., Mausner, B., & Snyderman, B. (1959). *The motivation to work.* New York: John Wiley.

Hick, V. B. (1994, June 13). Union story: Blue collars fading to white. *St. Louis Post-Dispatch.*

Hogan, J. C. (1985). *The schools, the courts, and the public interest* (2nd ed.). Lexington, MA: Lexington Books.

Hoy, W. K., & Miskel, C. G. (1991). *Educational administration theory.* (4th ed.). New York: McGraw-Hill.

Hughes, L. W., & Ubben, G. C. (1994). *The elementary principal's handbook* (4th ed.). Needham Heights, MA: Allyn and Bacon.

Hunter, M. (1967-71). Theory into Practice series: *Motivation theory for teachers; Reinforcement theory for teachers; Retention theory for teachers; Teach more—faster!; Teach for Transfer.* El Segundo, CA: TIP Publications.

Jensen, M. R., Robinson-Zañartu, C., & Jensen, M. L. (1992-2000). Dynamic assessment and mediated learning: Assessment and intervention for developing cognitive and knowledge structures. Cognitive Education Systems. [On-line]. Available: http://www.mindladder.com/ CES_theory01006.htm

Jones, J. J., & Stout, I. W. (1960). *School public relations: issues and cases.* New York: G. P. Putnam and Sons, 162.

Jones, J. J., & Walters, D. L. (1994). *Human resource management in education.* Lancaster, PA: Technomic.

Joyce, B., & Showers, B. (1988). Student achievement through staff development. White Plains, NY: Longman Press.

Judicial Council of California (2001). Guide to California Courts. [On-line]. Available: http://www.courtinfo.ca.gov

Just how public are school records? (1997). *EdCal, 27*(11), 1-7.

Kahl, S. R. (1980). The selection of teachers and school administrators: A synthesis of the literature. Denver, CO: Mid-Continent Regional Educational Laboratory. (ERIC Document Reproduction Service No. ED 221 917)

Kelley, C. (2000). Making merit pay work: Why school-wide bonuses and knowledge-based and skill-based pay are good ways to compensate teachers. *American School Board Journal.* [On-line]. Available: http://www.asbj.com/schoolspending/kelley.html

Kelly, M. M. (1988). The work at home movement. *The Futurist, 6*(3), 28-31.

Kemper, V. (2002, January 8). Study warns of fallout in rising health costs. *Los Angeles Times,* p. A14.

Kennedy, G., Benson, J., & McMillan, J. (1982). *Managing negotiations.* Englewood Cliffs, NJ: Prentice-Hall.

Kilmann, R. H., Saxton, M. L., & Serpa, R. (Eds.). (1985). *Gaining control of the corporate culture.* San Francisco, CA: Jossey-Bass.

Knowles, M. S. (1970). *The modern practice of adult education.* New York: Association Press.

Latino beat. (1999, February). [On-line]. Available: www.latinobeat.net.html/0224/villar.html

Levine, S. (1989). *Promoting adult growth in schools.* Boston: Allyn & Bacon.

Lieberman, M. (1979). *Public sector bargaining: A policy reappraisal.* Lexington, MA: Lexington Books.

Lindquist, V. R. (1991). *Endicott Report.* Evanston, IL: Northwestern University.

Lipham, J. M. (1981). *Effective principal, effective school.* Reston, VA: National Association of Secondary School Principals.

Long, C., & Stansbury, K. (1994). Performance assessments for beginning teachers: Options and lessons. *Phi Delta Kappan 76*(4), 318-322.

Loucks-Horsley, S., Harding, C. K., Arbuckle, M. A., Murray, L. B., Dubea, C., & Williams, M. K. (1987). *Continuing to learn: A guidebook for teacher development.* Andover, MA: Regional Laboratory for Educational Improvement on the Northeast and Islands.

Lucio, W. H., & McNeil, O. (1969). *Supervision* (2nd ed.). New York: McGraw-Hill.

Luna, R. (2001, September 29). Some school districts fail the test. *Los Angeles Times*, p. B10.

Madaus, G. F., & Pullin, D. (1987). Teacher certification tests: Do they really measure what we need to know? *Phi Delta Kappan, 69,* 31-38.

Magee, Maureen. (1999, January 16). New teachers become hot commodity in nationwide hunt. *San Diego Union Tribune*, p. N1.

Mathison, C. M. (1996). The challenges of beginning middle & secondary urban school teachers. *Issues in Teacher Education, 5*(1), 15-18.

Mayo, E. (1933). *The human problems of an industrial civilization.* New York: Macmillan.

McCarthy, M. M., & Cambron, N. H. (1981). *Public school law: Teachers' and students' rights.* Boston: Allyn and Bacon.

McCollum, J. K., & Norris, D. R. (1984). Nonunion grievance machinery in southern industry. *Personnel Administrator, 29,* 106.

McCoy, M. W., Gips, C. J., & Evans, M. W. (1983). *The American school personnel administrator: An analysis of characteristics and role.* Unpublished manuscript, American Association of School Administrators, Seven Hills, Ohio.

McCune, S. (1986). *Guide to strategic planning for educators.* Alexandria, VA: Association for Supervision and Curriculum Development. (ERIC Document Reproduction Service ED 278 089)

McCurdy, J. (1974, August 15). Teacher surplus: More graduates making it worse. *Los Angeles Times,* A15.

McGreal, T. L. (1983). *Successful teacher evaluation.* Alexandria, VA: Association for Supervision and Curriculum Development.

McGregor, D. M. (1960). *The human side of enterprise.* New York: McGraw-Hill.

McQueen, P. (2000, July 6). Teacher union eases opposition toward merit pay. *San Diego Union Tribune, 9*, 188.

Medley, D. M. (1994). Teacher evaluation. In H. E. Mitzel, J. H. Best, & W. Rabinowtiz (Eds.), *Encyclopedia of educational research* (pp. 1345-52). New York: Macmillan.

Metzger, E. L. (1988). *The changing role of the personnel administrator in the public school districts of California.* Unpublished doctoral dissertation, University of Southern California.

Millman, J. (1997). *Grading teachers, grading schools: Is student achievement a valid evaluation measure?* Thousand Oaks, CA: Corwin Press.

Mitchell, D. (1986). *Policy trust agreements, a new approach to collective bargaining.* (Policy Briefs, No. 3, pp. 1-4.) Sacramento, CA: California Department of Education, Reference Center.

Moore, D. R., & Hyde, A. (1981). *Making sense of staff development: An analysis of staff development and the costs in three urban school districts.* Chicago, IL: Designs for Change. (ERIC Document Reproduction Service No. ED 211 629).

Moore, H. E. (1966). *The administration of public school personnel.* New York: Center for Applied Research in Education.

Moore, H. E., & Hodge, J. L. (1968). The changing role of the public school personnel administrator. In *The school personnel administrator.* Tempe, AZ: Bureau of Educational Research and Services, Arizona State University.

Morrison, T. (2001). *Actionable learning: A handbook for capacity-building through case-based learning.* Asian Development Bank Institute. [On-line]. Available: http://www.adbi.org/TM/

Muller, G. D. (1978). In defense of the teacher perceiver. *Phi Delta Kappan, 59*, 684-685.

Murphy, R. (1991, April). Managers have rights, too. *Thrust for Educational Leadership.*

Naisbitt, J., & Aburdene, P. (1990). *Ten new directions for the 1990's—Megatrends 2000.* New York: William Morrow.

Nash, K. C. (1999, January 19). New teachers receive help from coaches and mentors. [On-line]. Available: http://lincoln.srvusd.k12.ca.us/pr/newsltrC4.html

National Association of Secondary School Principals. (1987). *Comprehensive assessment of school environments.* Alexandria, VA: The author.

National Center for Education Statistics. (2001). NCES statistical analysis report: Overview of public elementary and secondary school districts, 1999-2000. [On-line]. Available: http://www.nces. ed.gov/pubs2001/overview/tables06.asp

National Education Association. (1936). A handbook on teacher tenure. *Research Bulletin, 14*, 169.

National Education Association. (1991). The 1991-92 resolutions of the National Education Association. *NEA Today, 10*(1), 15-25.

National Education Research Division. (1962). *The public school personnel administrator.* (Research Monograph 1962-M1). Washington, D.C.: Author.

National School Boards Association. (1976). *The school personnel management system.* Washington, DC: Author.

National School Public Relations Association. (1979). *Managing your schools: What's ahead?* Arlington, VA: The author.

Nelson, F. H., Draws, R., & Gould, J. C. (2000). Survey and analysis of teacher salary trends 2000. American Federation of Teachers. [On-line]. Available: www.aft.org/research/2001/041601.html

Nemesh, A. (1979). The interviewing process. *Business Education Form, 33*, 19-20.

New rules for interviewing job applicants: Schools ignore them at their peril. (1977). *American School Board Journal, 164*, 28.

Nicholson, E. W., & McInerney, W. D. (1988, November). Hiring the right teacher: A method for selection. *NASSP Bulletin, 72*, 88-92.

Norton, M. S. (1989). *The school personnel administrator in Arizona.* Tempe, AZ: Arizona State University, Division of Educational Leadership and Policy Studies.

Oliphant, L. A. (1990, April). From teaching to administration—is there a career ladder? *Thrust for Educational Leadership,* 19-20.

Pascale, R. T. (1985). The paradox of corporate cultures: Reconciling ourselves to socialization. *California Management Review, 27*, 26-41.

Peters, T. (1988). *Thriving on chaos: Handbook for a management revolution.* New York: Harper.

Peters, T., & Austin, N. (1985). *A passion for excellence: The leadership differential.* New York: Random House.

Peterson, L .J., Rossmiller, R. A., & Volz, M. A. (1978). *The law and public school operation.* New York: Harper and Row.

Pfeiffer, J. W., Goodstein, L. D., & Nolan, T. M. (1986). *Applied strategic planning: A how to do it guide.* San Diego, CA: University Associates.

Plummer, J. T. (1989). Changing values. *The Futurist, 8*(9), 8-13.

Port, L. (1998). *Between a rock and a hard place.* Foster City, CA: California School Law Publishers.

Pounder, D. G. (1990). *Educational megatrends and increased female leadership in schools.* Paper presented at the annual meeting of the University Council for Educational Administration, Pittsburgh, PA.

Powell. G. (1989). Male/female work roles: What kind of future? *Personnel, 3*(6), 47-50.

Prasad, R. (1993). *The win-win model: A communication, exploration and problem solving model.* San Mateo, CA: San Mateo-Foster City School District.

Rebore, R. W. (1998). *Personnel administration in education; A management approach* (5th ed.). Needham Heights, MA: Allyn & Bacon.

Redfern, G. B. (1967). *Ways and means of PN: Professional negotiations and the school administrator.* Arlington, VA: American Association of School Administrators.

Redfern, G. B. (1968). The school personnel administrator in 1984. In *The school personnel administrator.* Tempe, AZ: Bureau of Educational Research and Services, Arizona State University.

Robinson, G. (1992, June 19). The politics of appearance. *Los Angeles Times,* E1.

Rodda, C. (2000). Searching for successes in teacher recruitment. *Leadership, 29*(3), 16-19.

Ruud, R. C., & Woodford, J. J. (1984). *Supervisor's guide to documentation and file building for employee discipline.* Crestline, CA: Advisory Publishing.

Sandham, J. L. (2001, April 4). California faces shortage of administrators, report warns. *Education Week.* [On-line]. Available: http://www.edweek.org/ew/ (search site)

Schein, E. H. (1992). *Organizational culture and leadership* (2nd ed.). San Francisco: Jossey-Bass.

Schön, D. A. (1989). Professional knowledge & reflective practice. In T. J. Sergiovanni & J. H. Moore (Eds.), *Schooling for tomorrow; Directing reforms to issues that count.* Boston: Allyn and Bacon.

Schramm, R. M., & Dortch, R. N. (1991, September). An analysis of effective résumé content, format, and appearance based on college recruiter perceptions. *The Bulletin of the Association for Business Communication, 54,* 18-23.

Seidler, E. H. (1990). Developing a policy on applicant background checks. *School Business Affairs, 56*(6), 35-37.

Senge, P. (1990). *The fifth discipline.* New York: Doubleday.

Senge, P., Kleiner, A., Roberts, C., Ross, R. B., & Smith, B. J. (1994). *The fifth discipline fieldbook; Strategies and tools for building a learning organization.* New York: Currency/Doubleday.

Sergiovanni, T. J. (1967). Factors which affect satisfaction and dissatisfaction of teachers. *Journal of Educational Administration, 5*, 66-82.

Seyfarth, J. T. (1991). *Personnel management for effective schools.* Needham Heights, MA: Allyn & Bacon.

Showers, B., Joyce, B., & Bennett, B. (1987). Synthesis of research on staff development: A framework for future study and a state-of-the-art analysis. *Educational Leadership, 45*, 77-87.

Smith, J. M. (1980). Teacher selection procedures. *The Clearing House, 53*, 314.

Smith, S. (1990). Business and labor—from adversaries to allies. *Harvard Business Review,* 129-136.

Sparks, D., & Hirsh, S. (1997). *A new vision for staff development.* Alexandria, VA: Association for Supervision and Curriculum Development; Oxford, OH: National Staff Development Council.

Sparks, G. M. (1983). Synthesis of research on staff development for effective teaching. *Educational Leadership, 41*, 65-72.

Speck, M. (1996). Best practice in professional development for sustained educational change. *ERS Spectrum, 14*(2), 33-41.

Steuteville-Brodinsky, M. et al. (1989). *Selecting, recruiting, and keeping excellent teachers* (Critical Issues Report). Arlington, VA: American Association of School Administrators.

Strunk, W., Jr., & White, E. B. (1972). *The Elements of Style* (3rd ed.). New York: Macmillan.

Swanson, H. L., & Lussier, C. M. (2001). A selective synthesis of the experimental literature on dynamic assessment. *Review of Educational Research, 71*, 321-363.

Sweeney, R., & Lindsey, R. (1992, April). Learning from conflict. *Thrust for Educational Leadership, 20*, 36-39.

Tannenbaum, R., Weschler, I. R., & Massarik. F. (1961). *Leadership and organization.* New York: McGraw-Hill.

Taylor, F. W. (1911). *The principles of scientific management.* New York: Harper and Row.

Taylor, L. C., Jr. (1981). *Factors that contribute to maturity in collective bargaining: A study of bargaining relationships in selected school districts of Los Angeles County.* Unpublished doctoral dissertation, University of Southern California.

Thomas, S. (1990). *Lasting impressions: Building a professional portfolio.* Florida: Ventana Press.

Thurston, L. M., & Roe, W. H. (1957). *State school administration.* New York: Harper & Row.

Tierney, D., Long, C., Quellmalz, E., Stansbury, K., & Estes, G. (1992). *Assessment component of the California New Teacher Project: Alternative models of new teacher assessment and support.* San Francisco: Far West Laboratory for Educational Research and Development. (ERIC Document Reproduction Service No. ED 355 194)

Townley, A. J. (1992, February/March). Landing that new job. *Thrust for Educational Leadership, 21,* 30-33.

U. S. Bureau of the Census. (1991). *Statistical abstract of the United States: 1991.* Washington, DC: Government Printing Office.

U. S. Bureau of the Census. (1998). *Statistical abstract of the United States: 1998.* Washington, DC: Government Printing Office. [On-line] Available: http://www.census.gov/prod/3/98pubs/98statab/cc98stab.htm

U. S. Chamber of Commerce. (1990). *Employee benefits.* Washington, DC: Author.

U. S. Department of Labor. (1991). *The revised handbook for analyzing jobs.* Washington, DC: Government Printing Office.

United Way Strategic Institute. (1989). *Nine forces reshaping America.* Bethesda, MD: World Future society.

Uris, A. (1978). *The executive interviewer's handbook.* Houston, TX: Gulf Publishing.

Urwick, L., & Gulick, L. (Eds). (1937). *Papers on the science of administration.* New York: Institute of Public Administration, Columbia University.

Valentine, Jerry. (1992). *Principles and practices for effective teacher evaluation.* Boston: Allyn and Bacon.

Wade, R. K. (1984/1985). What makes a difference in inservice teacher education? A meta-analysis of research. *Educational Leadership, 42,* 48-54.

Wagner, S. (1991). *From meet and confer to collaborative bargaining.* ERIC Clearinghouse on Educational Management. (ERIC Document Reproduction Service ED 370 171)

Warren, D. (1989). *American teachers: Histories of a profession at work.* New York: Macmillan.

Waters, J. L. (1976). *The changing role of California public school personnel administrators.* Unpublished doctoral dissertation, University of Southern California.

Webb, L. D., Montello, P. A., & Norton, M. S. (1994). *Human resources administration: Personnel issues and needs in education* (2nd ed.). New York: Macmillan.

Weber, M. (1947). *The theory of social and economic organization.* (T. Parsons, Ed.; A. M. Henderson & T. Parsons Trans.). New York: Free Press.

Wesley, E. B. (1957). *NEA the first hundred years.* New York: Harper and Brothers.

Wheeler, P. H. (1993). *Using portfolios to assess teacher performance.* Livermore, CA: EREAPA Associates. (ERIC Document Reproduction Service No. ED 364 967)

Wickstrom, R. A. (1971). An investigation into job satisfaction among teachers (Doctoral dissertation, University of Oregon, 1971). *Dissertation Abstracts International, 32-03A,* 1249.

Wilson, J., & Goldman, J. (2001, December 5). Defiant, striking N. J. teachers jailed. *Los Angeles Times.*

Wirt, F. M. & Kirst, M. W. (1989). *The politics of education—Schools in conflict.* Berkeley, CA: McCutchan.

Wise, A., Darling-Hammond, L., & Barnett, B. (1988, February). Selecting teachers: The best, the known and the persistent. *Educational Leadership, 45,* 82.

Wishnick, Y., & Wishnick, T. (1993). Collective bargaining and educational reform: Establishing a labor-management partnership. *Journal of Collective Bargaining, 22,* 1-11.

Wong, H., & Wong, R. (1998). The first days of school (2nd ed.). Mountain View, CA: Harry E. Wong Publications.

Yate, M. J. (1988). *Knock 'em dead with great answers to tough interview questions.* Boston, MA: Bob Adams.

Index